Security Risk Assessment

Security Risk Assessment

Managing Physical and Operational Security

John M. White
Protection Management, LLC

AMSTERDAM • BOSTON • HEIDELBERG • LONDON
NEW YORK • OXFORD • PARIS • SAN DIEGO
SAN FRANCISCO • SINGAPORE • SYDNEY • TOKYO
Butterworth-Heinemann is an imprint of Elsevier

Acquiring Editor: Brian Romer
Editorial Project Manager: Keira Bunn
Project Manager: Poulouse Joseph
Designer: Alan Studholme

Butterworth-Heinemann is an imprint of Elsevier
The Boulevard, Langford Lane, Kidlington, Oxford, OX5 1GB, UK
225 Wyman Street, Waltham, MA 02451, USA

Library of Congress Cataloging-in-Publication Data
White, John M. (Security professional)
  Security risk assessment: managing physical and operational security/John M. White.
    pages cm
  Includes index.
  ISBN 978-0-12-800221-6
  1. Crime prevention. 2. Security systems. I. Title.
  HV7431.W465 2014
  658.4'73–dc23
                           2014021032

British Library Cataloguing in Publication Data
A catalogue record for this book is available from the British Library

ISBN: 978-0-12-800221-6

For information on all Butterworth-Heinemann
publications visit our web site at http://store.elsevier.com/

This book has been manufactured using Print on Demand technology. Each copy is
produced to order and is limited to black ink. The online version of this book will
show color figures where appropriate.

Contents

Acknowledgments

I cannot express enough my appreciation and gratitude to my caring, loving, and supportive wife, Teresa. Your continual encouragement throughout my career has been helpful and sincerely appreciated. It was an enormous comfort and relief to know that you were willing to provide guidance of our household activities while I worked many long days, which often stretched into the nights and weekends. To my sons Jeromy and Joshua, my heartfelt thanks; thank you both for having patience with me over the years as I grew in my profession.

I would also like to acknowledge my peers and subordinates over years that helped form me into the person I am. From my time in the United States Navy, a law enforcement career, corporate security positions, and as an independent consultant, I have been able to professionally grow and pass on my knowledge to others and watch them evolve as well. I truly believe that everyone should share their knowledge and experiences with others as it can only help us all to achieve a more proficient profession. I want to thank my consulting peers for their assistance over the years and with this book, as well as the many security technology and security services companies that I have worked with in the past, you have all been an asset to my professional development.

In closing, I have met many honorable security professionals over the years that had a part in my professional growth, and I have sincerely appreciated your friendships and support. I have also found that each time that I step foot on a client's property I am not only bringing my knowledge and expertise to share with my clients, but I also take-away from them new ideas, solutions to past issues, and potential best practices; all of which I will continue to use to expand my knowledge base and assist my fellow security professionals to make our world a safer and more secure environment.

John M. White

About the Author

John M. White, a recognized expert in asset protection management, has over 38 years of experience including military, law enforcement, corporate security administration, and professional security consultation.

White is Board Certified in Security Management as a Certified Protection Professional (CPP), and he is a Certified Healthcare Protection Administrator (CHPA), the two highest certifications in the security profession. He is also a member of the International Association of Chiefs of Police, National Association of Chiefs of Police, the International Association for Professional Security Consultants, ASIS International, the International Association for Healthcare Security and Safety, and several other professional groups. He has also presented as a security expert at an international security conference.

White has been published in the International Association for Healthcare Safety and Security's *Journal of Healthcare Protection Management* and *Directions* quarterly newsletter on numerous occasions. He has also been published in the ASIS International's *Security Management* magazine.

Preface

Security risk assessments have been a part of security and risk management for hundreds if not thousands of years. In many ways you could trace their origins back to the beginning of time because humans have always been managing their personal security and risks to some extent. Yet the formal process of conducting security risk assessments for businesses is still developing as our world changes.

One only has to go back in history to discover when and why changes occurred. For example, although the United States Secret Service was formed in 1865, they were not assigned to protect the President of the United States until 1901, after President William McKinley was assassinated. More recent examples would be the aftermath of the September 11, 2001 attack against the United States when air travel security was dramatically changed, or how school security has transformed from open buildings to more secured campuses due to the unthinkable mass shootings. The list of causes that resulted in changes in security for individuals, institutions, and businesses are many, yet they all lead to changes being made as a result of security risk assessments and management practices.

The process of identifying risks and vulnerabilities over the years has vastly improved, and now more than ever they have become more recognized as being a standard procedure. Because of this, and the fact that our world continues to change almost daily, we as security professionals need to better understand how to assess our security risks and document our findings. The best way to learn how to perform such tasks is often by researching the subject and gaining experience in a number of ways.

Over the years there have been books written on security assessments and I personally have several of them in my professional library. However, even though this material exists, and for the most part it has been updated over the years, it is easy to see that not everyone is on the same page when it comes to developing a security assessment project plan, defining a scope, conducting the assessment, and writing a report that identifies the risks and vulnerabilities as well as the recommendations and a plan to address all identified concerns.

I have personally found that there has not been a "How To" type of book written on the subject that will include a comprehensive explanation on how to properly plan and execute a security risk assessment. Many of the previous published materials are geared towards the technology side of security, or go into great detail on what questions should be asked and answered when conducting an assessment, yet some of them can be short on details on what to do with that information once you have gathered it.

Many security directors and security consultants have also searched for information on conducting an assessment, and in some cases have just set out to try and discover the "How To" on the fly. Many others have also networked with other professionals to determine if anyone had a sample of an assessment report to review in an effort to determine what the end product will look like; probably in an attempt to understand what is in a report and how to write it.

I personally have reviewed numerous security risk assessment reports over the years and in some cases I have been surprised by the report format and content. When you take into consideration who wrote the reports some of the issues can be easily assigned to the report's author; meaning that internally written reports may not always identify all of the vulnerabilities and risks. This is easy to understand because one may not normally point out flaws in the program that they manage, and in some cases the report preparer may in fact not know how to conduct the assessment in the first place. On the other side of the equation is the professional "Security Consultant" who normally will be impartial and unbiased in their approach, yet in some cases their reports are remarkably different from their peers.

This book was written more so as a step-by-step procedure on how to plan, manage, and conduct a security risk assessment and documents your findings. Each of the major steps for conducting the assessment will be addressed in this book. However, I would encourage you all to take into consideration your risks and vulnerabilities based on your type of industry since there often can be countless differences that may not completely be covered in this material. The intent of this book was to cover the general parts of an average security risk assessment, and it is hoped that the readers can take from this material the information needed to conduct a successful assessment.

Keep in mind that reference materials only assist in the processes of preparing for and conducting an assessment, as well as the preparing of a written report. The project manager still needs to understand how to interpret the findings, make the proper recommendations for meaningful changes, and ensure that the changes implemented can be measured for effectiveness as it relates to the intended goal.

These reports may also be used in future litigation cases so it is advised to write the report using facts, and have supporting information for your conclusions and recommendations. And one final point to remember is that the formal reports can, and often do, define the preparer as credible or otherwise. You want to ensure that your report becomes a tool for change, and not ignored or left to collect dust on the shelf.

It is my sincere desire that this material will be a valuable resource for security practitioners in all fields, those who are educating themselves on security practices in the 21st century, as well as those who have oversight of security programs or services.

John M. White, CPP, CHPA

CHAPTER 1

Introduction to Security Risk Assessments

WHAT IS A SECURITY RISK ASSESSMENT?

There are many definitions given to the term *security risk assessment*. According to ASIS International's manual, *Protection of Assets: Physical Security*, a security risk assessment is "a fundamental examination that can include review of documentation, policies, facilities, technology, protection strategies, staffing, training, and other key indicators to determine the present state of the protection program (security) in an effort to identify deficiencies and even excesses, in order to make recommendations for improvement based on proven methods."[1]

In fact, the actual process of identifying security issues has been called many different things. Some of the more common names assigned to this subject have been security assessment, security survey, security audit, and risk assessment to name just a few. Generally speaking, it is a systematic on-site assessment and analysis of your current security measures, whether they are physical security measures, technology, operations, facilities, security management, policies, training, reports, or any other aspect of your security program or measures. Regardless of the title, they are all going after similar goals of identifying security weaknesses, risks, deficiencies, and even excesses, and then formulating a plan to address the findings with detailed recommendations based on industry accepted standards and best practices.

Most professionals would agree that how you go about the process of the assessment should be a uniformed approach. However, if there is one thing certain in life regarding such processes, it is that everyone who conducts such assessments does so in a variety of different ways.

Over the years, there have been numerous books that have covered different parts of a security assessment, so you would think that security practitioners would all be working from the same baseline. However, the opposite is true in many cases. Even among professional security consultants, all have different approaches and no two reports are the same.

---

[1]ASIS International 2012. Protection of Assets: Physical Security. Alexandria, VA: ASIS International.

1

Case in point—upon review of numerous security assessment reports written by independent consultants, it became clear to me that there are vast differences in style and project methodology. Some reports are nothing more than a statement of facts as determined by the author, followed by an extensive list of recommendations, most of which are not easily correlated within the report, nor are they explained in detail showing the reader what the recommendations will bring to the table if implemented. So this begs the question: if the report does not fully identify the security risk, tell the reader how to address that risk, or provide the reader with a sense of what the change will look like if implemented, what is the purpose of the assessment?

Quantitative and qualitative techniques are often used in an effort to measure and evaluate the security program's effectiveness. The person conducting the assessment also needs to consider statistics when conducting a security risk assessment because the statistics are often the starting point in establishing a baseline of sorts for the program. You cannot effectively manage a security program if you do not track security incident reports and their outcomes. If the person doing the assessment (who will be referred to as the reviewer throughout this chapter) does not have information on historical security issues (e.g., past incident reports) to determine trends, he or she will be at a disadvantage and will likely be setting the baseline from scratch.

Another part of the security assessment is the process of identifying and defining the threat, as well as identifying what the target of those threats may be. As we often find, no two industries are exactly the same, and the process of identifying and defining security risks and threats is often different depending on your organization.

Take, for example, an organization that does research and development for high-end computer components and a retailer. The security threat for the research and development organization may be in the form of stolen trade secrets, products, or even patent infringements/violations. On the other hand, the security threats associated with the retail environment will often be theft of product or cash receipts. Therefore, in the case of a retail environment, you might be looking at implementing security measures that reduce the risk of robbery, burglary, shoplifting, or even embezzlement. As for the research and development company, security's efforts may be more focused on preventing unauthorized access into research and development areas and unauthorized access to sensitive computer files. In both cases, security practitioners are often working in a proactive manner, which means they are trying to prevent an incident from occurring.

As most security practitioners know, security programs often operate in a proactive posture, whereas it is often the goal of security to prevent incidents from occurring. Law enforcement, on the other hand, is often operating in the reactive mode, meaning that they respond to calls for service as a situation is occurring or after it occurs. To conduct a security risk assessment is often being proactive, as you are looking at your program to see where you can improve based on industry standards. As part of that assessment, the security practitioner must look at past incidents, known threats, and potential targets, which in essence is being both proactive and reactive.

Today's security practitioner must be flexible and must be able to not only look to the past but also plan for the future in their daily actions. The challenges of today's security professionals are more complex than ever before. The industry in which you work has changed no matter what type of business it is. With the constant rise in workplace violence issues and threats, such as an active shooter, security professionals must adjust.

This book will only minimally touch on information technology (IT), due to the fact that most security professionals do not manage the computer systems of their companies. However, it is possible that some security practitioners are performing IT oversight to some extent, because we know there is a trend in many large corporations to bring all security systems and operations under one person, such as a chief security officer (CSO).

In most businesses, IT and security are separate, yet IT does play a role in security. IT protects the computer network systems, online presence, electronic records, and e-commerce, while the security department protects the corporate assets, which by nature of their responsibility, IT will fall under. If you are performing a security risk assessment at your organization and you are not considering your online presence or your computer network, you could be overlooking the most vulnerable portal into your organization. Although this book will address IT as it relates to the security assessment, it is not the focus and intent of this book to fully address all the security concerns associated with the corporation's computer network. There are many resources available to fully address IT security, and we would suggest that security practitioners at a minimum have a basic understanding of their network systems.

What sets the tone for most security programs can often be described as the probability of "risks." When you are assessing for risks you are evaluating for potential incidents of undesirable events. Real or perceived risks are those key factors that are the basis for the level of security measures instituted. In simple terms, if you do not believe that your company has any security risks, it is likely that you have minimal to no security measures other than a lock on the door.

Take, for example, a farmhouse in a very remote area. At this farmhouse, you are likely to find that the doors to the house and outbuildings are not locked, even when no one is on the property, and you may often find the car keys in the ignition. The owners believe that they have no real or perceived security risks, therefore they have no security. For them, this is a matter of choice.

On the other hand, when you look in the inner cities you will often find home-owners who go to great measures to secure their property. Those security measures will include deadbolt locks, bars on the windows, alarm systems, fencing, guard dogs, security cameras, and many other protection measures. They often do so because of the risks associated with their environment or geographic area. Either they have been a victim of a crime or someone they know has. It could also be that they have educated themselves in the risks around them and they are intent on protecting their assets. Again, it is a matter of choice, but the difference with them versus the rural homeowner is the real or perceived security risks.

When talking about businesses, you will likely never find a business, even in a very remote setting, that does not incorporate some type of security. However, not all businesses have a dedicated security professional responsible for the protection of the company's assets. In fact, the majority of businesses have no such person on staff. Although that may be the case, there is often a member of management that does have some oversight regarding safety and security matters.

As an example, large retail businesses often have loss prevention staff in place to reduce inventory shrinkage. For the most part, those staff members may also be responsible for many of the security protocols, policies, and technology in use. However, not all retailers have such protocols or measures in place, and what they do have barely touches on "security." In fact, if you look closely at some of the largest international retailers, you might be surprised to find that they have no security policies to speak of and their focus is only on loss prevention measures.

Some types of businesses, however, are required to have security policies and protocols in place, and healthcare is a prime example of this. Oftentimes the requirements are due to accreditation standards, yet there are also a few state laws that require security services. For example, in the state of California, healthcare facilities are required by law to conduct security risk assessments due to the high number of workplace violence incidents against healthcare staff. With that being the case, you would think that every healthcare facility had a professional security manager on staff to manage the program. However, to assume that would be incorrect. There is no requirement to have a security practitioner at the helm who takes responsibility for his or her organization's security. In many cases, smaller hospitals have no security staff at all, or they may just have one guard working the overnight shift. In these cases, they rely solely on operational protocols and policies. They will, however, have a member of the management team who is responsible for the security oversight. This person could be the director of facilities, director of information technology, the risk manager, or the safety officer. These are just a few examples of how hospitals use staff for security oversight that are from backgrounds far removed from security. Regretfully, in most cases the people that oversee the security of the organization have no security background prior to assuming this role.

SECURITY RISK ASSESSMENT INTENT

Talk to any security practitioner who has only been in the business for a short period of time and you may soon discover that they may not understand the intent of the security risk assessment. In many cases, since they do not understand what a security risk assessment is, they certainly do not understand the need for conducting one or how to conduct one.

A familiar scenario is that of a former police officer who has changed careers and is hired to run a security program for a private company. Those who have been in law enforcement understand that police officers do not normally conduct security risk assessments, as defined at the beginning of this chapter, as part of their normal law enforcement duties. I am not implying that no police officers have any experience in this, because in fact those officers that normally work in the crime prevention bureau of the police department have *some* experience with this task. Also, remember that due to the nature of the law enforcement profession, the vast majority of police officers are experienced in being reactive rather than proactive. However, a law enforcement officer who changes careers and becomes a security leader will normally grasp the concept and intent of the security risk assessment due to his or her past experiences as a police officer. Their basic knowledge base will come from a crime prevention approach from their experiences on the street, and in most cases their learning curve to understand the risks faced by their employer will not be overly steep.

Therefore, when we talk about the "intent" of the security risk assessment, we are talking about what it is we are looking for, why we are looking for it, and what do we view as being a threat or risk to our organization. Of course we also need to consider what changes should be made to our security program to mitigate any risk.

A substantial part of the security risk assessment is also to determine how effective the existing security program is at the present time. We will also look to see if the intent of the security program is being fulfilled, and of course if the intent of the program is reasonable and within industry standards or expectations.

Another driving factor for conducting a security risk assessment is often a direct result of a serious security threat or incident that has happened at your organization. Many times organizations will also conduct an assessment when a serious incident has occurred at a similar business, or even at a neighboring business.

Case in point—after each mass killing or terrorist attack within the United States, there is often an internal review conducted at many organizations, many of which may have no direct relation to the business or facility where the attack occurred. Of course those organizations that had the security incident happen at their location are often responding to, and eventually preparing for, criminal or civil actions as a direct result of the incident. The unfortunate thing is that an incident has already occurred and the organization may just now be attempting to identify its security risks. In this case, the intent for the assessment is more reactive and along the lines of damage control. In addition, if the organization completed a security risk assessment in the past, it will also likely be looking at that document as part of its review.

WHO WILL CONDUCT THE ASSESSMENT?

When the time comes to conduct an assessment, an organization may have someone on staff that is qualified to perform this task, or they may have to look for an outside resource to assist them. The most important consideration that an organization must understand is that the person they assign to conduct this assessment must have the proper background and training.

Internal Sources

When an organization is looking to find someone internally to conduct an assessment, they will often go with a security director or manager. However, as mentioned before, not all organizations have a security department in place, and therefore they may look to other departments such as risk management. Whomever is chosen or assigned the task of conducting the assessment must have experience in security operations and risk identification. They also need to conduct the review in an unbiased approach, which oftentimes has been identified as being one of the biggest obstacles to overcome when this assignment is conducted internally.

For an internal staff person to conduct a security risk assessment on their own program, which will involve identifying weaknesses, possible deficiencies, or even excesses in the program, often the assessment results can be biased. Think of it this way: you have been asked to conduct a security risk assessment that focuses on your department or operations and you know that there are internal issues that need to be addressed. However, do you really want to throw yourself under the bus and expose any weaknesses in your program? Some of you reading this may say, "yes, I would state the facts as they are." However, history tells us that most people may not be forthright in their findings. They may in fact identify internal issues, but downplay them in their final report. The reality is that self-preservation will likely come into play and may hinder the full disclosure of some information.

This is not to say that all security risk assessments conducted by internal staff members will be tainted or incomplete, because that is just not the case. If the security director has been forthcoming with information all along, he or she will likely ensure that all of the facts—the good, the bad, and the ugly—will be included in their report. The key difference is that the security director understands the importance of full disclosure as well as mitigation information. The reality is that this is a fine line to walk, but if done correctly, one does not have to fear any negative information; therefore, their reports can truly be impartial.

External Sources

There are number of different sources that an organization can look to when it comes time to find someone to do a security risk assessment. Some of those resources can be your local police department, a security guard service, a security product manufacturer, or an independent security expert.

As mentioned earlier in this chapter, crime prevention personnel from local police departments have been known to conduct security risk assessments upon request. In most cases the service may be provided at no cost to an organization. That being the case, you might wonder, why wouldn't everybody seek out this service? The reality is that police officers rely heavily on crime prevention training that they have received and often have no clear understanding of the complexities of corporate security and the ever-changing security technology on the market today. Again, I am not inferring that all police officers are not competent in conducting security risk assessments; the point is that if you elect to go this route, you must conduct your due diligence to ensure that the police officer who will be assessing your organization has the background, training, and competencies in which to do so.

Another common resource that companies will look to when it comes time to choose a source to conduct a security risk assessment are companies that provide guard services. Oftentimes these vendors will refer to themselves as "security consultants," and they may conduct the security risk assessment at a reduced cost as compared to an independent security consultant. There are many competent security contractors who will provide the service and in most cases will have trained staff who will thoroughly review your security program. However, there have been past issues associated with this type of vendor insomuch as they have been reported to steer the client into a long-term business relationship using the vendor's services and products.

The main concern businesses have expressed to me in the course of my consulting work has been that the security guard company's reviewer has made their recommendations based on what their company can do differently in providing guard or technology services to the client. That being said, I would not suggest that a guard service cannot bring value to a client if that client was to contract with them. On the contrary, if the existing security program is not functioning at the proper level that the the organization desires, and they do not wish to start over again, they may in fact wish to retain the services of the security vendor as a means to restructure their security program.

Another resource that some companies have used to perform security risk assessments is security integrators or resellers of products and or services. Some of the most common vendors that will provide security risk assessments, and who are not guard services or independent security experts, will be companies that have developed software for security assessments. There are several software programs available on the market that companies can use to conduct very basic security risk assessments. An issue I have identified with these software programs is that in my opinion they are often not comprehensive enough. Some of these programs are nothing more than questions that the reviewer answers, and depending on their answers, the program will make predetermined recommendations for change. This can be problematic because not all organizations have the same issues or will handle identified risks in the same manner. Most of the software developers state that the end user can change any question or answer. The concern with this is that if you are going to make changes, you must know what it is that you are assessing, and what the proper recommendation would be based on best practices or industry standards.

Another issue with security risk assessment software programs is that the developers may state that an assessment can be completed in just a few hours. So of course those that are looking for an easy way out may elect to go with the software program to save time. If that is the case, it is highly recommended that you research those programs thoroughly and ensure that they are written for your type of business and cover *all* aspects of the security risk assessments.

For example, in some states healthcare organizations are required to do annual security risk assessments. However, many software programs are often not comprehensive enough for the requirements of healthcare security. The main concern with the software programs that are on the market today is that those programs cover the basics of security risk assessments and often do not venture into the operational and management side of security. Security risk assessments are more complex than just asking a series of questions, because once you have the answer to those questions you must be able to determine what steps the organization takes next to mitigate any identified risks. If a software program existed that took into consideration the questions, answers, best practices, industry standards, regulatory and accreditation requirements, the client's internal needs, and for all types of businesses, you would likely find the external source discussed next using the program extensively.

Independent security consultants often state that they are independent and unbiased, which in many cases can be the determining factor for a client. If an organization wishes to conduct a security risk assessment that is truly unbiased, performed by someone not steering the client to purchase any additional services or technology, an independent security consultant is that resource.

It is customary for security consultants to review a security program and compare it to established industry standards and best practices. Additionally, since they are not looking to provide you with guard services or new technology, they will also not be trying to influence your future purchasing decisions. In addition, they should be unbiased in the sense that they will provide you with information that a staff member of your organization may not disclose. For some security directors this has caused concern as they did not appreciate the candidness of the information, yet the information was truly factual and unbiased.

Another important consideration is that not all security consultants have the same expertise. Most independent consultants specialize in certain fields of practice (e.g., healthcare, retail, or hospitality), so when it comes time to retain the services of an independent security consultant, the client needs to ensure that the consultant is knowledgeable in the client's business model and industry. The recent economic downturn resulted in an increased number of "consultants," as many security practitioners were caught up in the downsizing of many corporations. Like any other major purchasing decisions that businesses face every day, the key to retaining the services of an independent security consultant is to ensure that the firm has the knowledge and experiences to meet the needs of your organization.

Professional certification should be a minimum requirement of an outsourced contractor that will be assessing your security. Since anyone can hang out a shingle and say that they are a "security consultant," one surefire way that an organization can evaluate a security consultant is to find out if the consultant has achieved professional certification in his or her field. The most common certification for security practitioners is the Certified Protection Professional (CPP) through ASIS International. Once a security professional has met the qualifications for this program, and has successfully passed the certification exam, they are designated as board certified in security management as a CPP. This is the highest professional certification available for security practitioners and is often a requirement for security professionals in large corporations. There are other certifications through ASIS International for those who specialize in investigations or physical security. However, the CPP certification is recommended for any security consultant.

For specialized fields such as healthcare, there are other professional security certifications such as the Certified Healthcare Protection Administrator (CHPA). When an industry has a recognized professional security certification program in place, such as the CHPA, security experts that specialize in that field are recommended to have that certification as a true indicator of their expertise in that field. Since not all companies that are seeking the services of an independent consultant will always fully research the consulting firms that they are evaluating, one of the easiest ways to measure a consulting firm's level of knowledge is to verify whether or not they are professionally certified by recognized industry associations. Keep in mind that there are numerous certifications that will add initials to someone's name, yet some of those certifications require little or no testing, experience, or educational background. It is incumbent on you, the client, to check out their background and credentials.

Objectivity

It is important to keep in mind that regardless of who conducts a security risk assessment, that person needs to remain unbiased and impartial. The assessment cannot be based on personal biases or insecurity. In other words, if this assessment is being conducted by someone on staff at the organization, they need to personally detach themselves from the assessment so as not to appear to be biased. This often is the hardest thing for a staff person to do, because even though they know that what they document in the report may not be impartial, they may still include it.

As for independent contractors who are retained to conduct the assessment, they too need to remain neutral and impartial in their findings. In this case we are speaking about not trying to steer clients into further services with their companies, such as purchasing additional products and/or services. There are many contractors who will make recommendations to a client that suggest that the client further retain the vendor for a long-term relationship, so you will need to ascertain if this is an unbiased recommendation or a sales tactic.

Professional independent consultants may also make recommendations as part of the security risk assessment to increase technology or make changes in security operations, yet they should do so in a neutral manner. An example of this would be a consultant that would identify technology that is either outdated or not properly being used, and they would make suggestions for improvements but not steer that client to a specific brand or vendor. Because of this, independent security consultants are often in the best position to be impartial, unbiased, and subjective in their recommendations. They do not sell any technology products or guard services, therefore their recommendations are truly independent. Security consultants will also keep current on all security technology and services as part of their business. They may recommend technology, such as security cameras or alarms, yet you will often find that they will not recommend a certain brand. Clients can, and often do, ask the consultants for recommendations of brands, or may in fact have the consultants participate in conducting a request for proposals (RFP) in order to identify products and/or services.

HOW OFTEN DO I NEED TO COMPLETE AN ASSESSMENT?

The frequency with which to conduct a security risk assessment of your organization is dependent on many different factors. For example, as mentioned earlier in this chapter, healthcare providers in some states are required to conduct annual security risk assessments. Also, depending on whether a healthcare organization is accredited through the Joint Commission (an independent, not-for-profit organization that accredits and certifies healthcare organizations and programs), or not, there may be accreditation standards that an organization is required to meet. However, for the most part the frequency with which an organization will conduct a security risk assessment is often not driven by regulations but rather current events or internal policies.

As discussed earlier in this chapter, if a serious security incident was to occur at a school, for example, an active shooter or some other type of serious violence, schools throughout the nation tend to go through a security risk assessment based on that incident. It is not uncommon for businesses to conduct an assessment of their facilities, even when a serious security incident occurred miles away in a completely different type of organization. In other words, if an act of workplace violence occurred at a retail store in one community, it would not be uncommon for a manufacturing facility in the neighboring community to review their security program because of it. Oftentimes when this happens it is a direct result of an organization's staff not feeling safe, and this is management's response to ensure that their safety and security is being considered.

A recent example of this was after the Sandy Hook Elementary School mass killing in Newtown, Connecticut, in December 2012. After that incident occurred, many organizations reviewed their security protocols, policies, and practices because the events in Connecticut shook our nation to the core. It was much the same way after September 11, 2001, and the terrorist attacks in New York and Washington, DC. After these acts of violence occurred, and with the resulting extensive media coverage, many employees and employers questioned their safety and security.

If you have never performed an assessment, it is recommended that you conduct a security risk assessment as soon as possible as a baseline measurement of your current state of security. With the exception of industry-specific accreditation or regulatory requirements that may require annual assessments, once your initial assessment is completed, and any resulting recommendations are evaluated and implemented as needed, a follow-up review of security practices is recommended at least every three years. Of course if a security incident occurs that will likely lead to litigation, an organization may want to immediately conduct a supplemental assessment. Keep in mind that the security risk assessment reports, including all findings and recommendations, will likely be called into question during the discovery process of any litigation. It is also likely that if the litigation is a result of what is referred to as negligent security or inadequate security, the plaintiff's legal counsel may retain a security expert to review the company's security program.

Realistically speaking, most organizations do not conduct security risk assessments on a regular basis, and in many cases they have never completed one. If that has been your practice in the past, keep in mind that if you have had serious security issues within your organization, and you have never conducted a security risk assessment prior to that incident or as a result of that incident, you may be faced with litigation as a result of a foreseeability or negligence claim. Ignorance is not a defense to litigation, meaning that a defendant cannot normally claim that they did not know that there was a crime problem in their neighborhood, and therefore they took no preventive measures to reduce the risks to their facilities, staff, or customers. There are many corporations that have never conducted a security risk assessment, and when you ask them why, you might hear them state that they did not know they needed to do one, or you may even hear something along the line of "plausible deniability."

There are also times when an organization will request the services of an independent security consultant to conduct an assessment of their organization's security, yet they do not want a report in writing. When this happens, it is often clear that the organization does not want that document to exist in the event of litigation, so they will ask for a verbal report only. As you can tell, there are times when an organization fully understands the implications and the discovery process of civil or criminal proceedings, yet they still want to know what their security risks are.

HOW LONG WILL THIS PROCESS TAKE?

There are many factors that will come into play when you try to determine how long the process will take to conduct a security risk assessment. Generally speaking, the time commitment required is dependent on the size of the organization. For example, does the organization have multiple campuses and multiple buildings on each campus? Is the organization a 24/7 operation? Are there security sensitive areas within your organization (e.g., pharmaceuticals, mental health units, or firearm sales or storage)? Will there be a team conducting the assessment, or will it be just one person performing it? All these and many other questions will need to be answered to determine how long a proper security risk assessment will take. In order to properly conduct a security assessment, it is safe to say that not even the smallest of operations can conduct a full assessment in a couple of hours. As you read this book, you will have a better understanding of the complexities of conducting such an assessment, and you should be able to determine for yourself that an assessment will take time.

When considering how much time it will take to complete an assessment, you must also consider the preassessment preparation time, which is the time it takes to determine the project scope, schedule, budget, deliverables, and communication requirements, pre-site visit documentation gathering and review, and research. Additionally, there will be the actual on-site assessment, as well as the post-site visit research and report documentation phase. Keep in mind that the most often overlooked part of the assessment when determining the time commitment is the prep, research, and report time. As an example, conducting the actual assessment may take three business days (24 total hours), but the prep time may take another 12 hours, and the research and report may take an additional 24+ hours.

In general, the larger the facility, and the more complex the assessment will be, the longer it will take to complete the project and document your findings.

Now that we have defined what a security risk assessment is, as well the sources available for the project's management, and we have discussed basic information about how long a project may take and how often an assessment should be conducted, in Chapter 2 we will move into the planning phase for the project.

Preassessment Planning

SERVICES AGREEMENT

Assuming that your organization is bringing in an outside expert to conduct your security risk assessment, the service agreement (contract) will be needed to determine the basics of who, what, where, when, why, and how of your project.

The services agreement can come in a variety of different forms. For example, some projects are agreed to verbally with no written contract. Yet others will use a memorandum of understanding, a letter or e-mail confirmation, or a formal professional services agreement.

Although there is no requirement to have a written contract, it is in the best interest of all parties to have a formal document that will determine the project's scope, schedule, budget, deliverables, and several other key parts of the project. A memorandum of understanding or letter can be used as a means of establishing an agreement, however, most attorneys will tell you that it is better to have a formal written agreement that establishes the terms for the project. Therefore, as the client who is requesting the services of an outside contractor, you should be looking at protecting your interests with such a document.

The use of a formal letter or memorandum of understanding basically establishes the overall foundation of what it is that all parties are agreeing to. However, the documents are often short on details and can leave a lot of questions on the table. It was explained to me several years ago by other security consultants that they preferred to keep the written agreement process as simple as possible. In most cases they stated that they did not want to include a lot of legalese into the agreement, as it may make things too complicated for the client. Although a verbal agreement has been used in the past, and will likely be used in the future in some cases, there have been many cases where disputes have arisen during or after a project that may have been avoided with a written agreement.

Written agreements (contracts) are very common in today's society and are often in place to protect the interests of all parties involved. Look at it this way, when you go to buy a car you verbally agree to the terms and what car you are

15

buying, but in the end there will be a contract. Imagine for a minute if you will that you buy a car using a verbal agreement that establishes what the payments will be and what the schedule for the payments is, and then you fail to meet those terms. In this example, the car dealer has the option of enforcing the verbal agreement through the courts, yet what it really comes down to is the credibility of both parties and the notorious "he said, she said" situation. Because of this, with the exception of private party automobile sales, you will not find such a transaction without a formal contract. We execute contracts on almost a daily basis when we make a transaction using a credit or debit card, write a check, download an application to our smartphone, or while making most types of large financial business transactions. All agreements need to identify the terms for the services.

When it comes to a professional services agreement that establishes the terms of the security risk assessment, you should look at this agreement as a means to protect your interests. Basically, the agreement needs to elucidate different key points with regards to the project. For example, it will identify the parties involved in the project, the project schedule, management, budget, change order/amendment processes, liability limitations and indemnities, delays, confidentiality, severability, and most importantly the project scope. A formal agreement may also include information regarding the deliverables (what is it that you will receive), payment and retainer information, breach of agreement/termination, and relationship of parties to name a few. Basically, since there is no standard professional services agreement utilized by security consultants, it is imperative that the client be knowledgeable and protect their interests by doing their due diligence and review any contract in its entirety.

Segments of the Services Agreement

Now that we have identified many of the basic points that should be in any professional services agreement, let us take a closer look at some of the above-mentioned segments.

When it comes to identifying the parties involved in a project, it basically comes down to who is proposing to provide a service (vendor/consultant) and who is receiving those services (client). In most cases this would be a simple process of identifying the two parties. However, there may be cases where there are more than two parties involved, an example being a contract security company hiring an independent consultant to perform a security risk assessment for their client. Although this may seem unusual, a vendor hiring a competitor, it does happen. If this was to happen, obviously all parties would be mentioned in the agreement to some extent.

Project schedules are normally one of the last tasks to be completed prior to signing any contract. The reason being is it is hard to establish a schedule early on because in some cases it may take more than six months to finalize a project's contract. Although most contracts can be executed within 30 days of the initial contact, I have experienced projects that have taken a year to work their way through the corporation's bureaucracy. Granted, projects that take over a few months to get under contract are a rarity, but they do happen for a variety of reasons.

One of the main reasons that the contract may take an excessive period of time to be executed is often driven by budgets or legal reviews. Several past clients have also gone through the process of requesting proposals from numerous security experts as part of a formal request for proposal (RFP). Although this is common, it can also add numerous delays into the project's schedule. One of the other issues with requesting numerous proposals is the fact that no two proposals are the same. For that reason, clients have found it confusing when reviewing proposals and trying to determine if all of the submittals are addressing the client's needs. When this happens, the client normally will request additional information or clarification as needed, and this of course may also delay the process of getting the project started.

Remember this about contracts: a well-written agreement should address all areas of concern for all parties of the agreement and should establish all of your expectations up front. A formal proposal for services (e.g., security risk assessment proposal) is often used in conjunction with a contract and the two documents are often cross-referenced within each other. In other words, the proposal should refer to the contract and the contract should refer to the proposal. Do not assume that you are receiving anything that is not in writing in one or both documents. If you are a security consultant, it would be wise to have an attorney review your forms to ensure that you are protected legally, and in many cases your insurance carrier will also review your contracts. If you are a security director and you are receiving a services agreement to review and sign, you may also be required to have it reviewed by your legal team or contract compliance office depending on your organization's requirements.

Again, as stated before, no two proposals are the same, and there is no industry standard professional services agreement. It is incumbent on you to conduct a thorough examination of all forms prior to signing them. If you have questions about a form, or if it seems vague to you, ask questions. Get clarifications in writing, and if the vendor/consultant does not want to provide that information in writing, you may need to consider walking away from it.

PROJECT MANAGEMENT

When it comes time to determine who will manage the project, you will need to consider things such as qualifications, objectivity, experience, and professional backgrounds. If you as the security director plan to do this project, you really need to ask yourself if you have the background and experience to do this, can you do so objectively, and can you commit the time that it will take to plan and execute the project?

When considering retaining the services of an independent consultant, you need to look at their qualifications, experience, and professional background. You want to ensure that the consultant that you retain understands your type of business. This can be done by requesting information about past clients that they have worked with that are similar to your business, and you can also request professional references from past clients. Another way to determine who your organization will retain to provide services is to seek recommendations from your peers.

Therefore, once you have determined who will conduct the assessment, whether this is being conducted in-house or you are hiring an outside contractor, you need to establish who will be managing the process and project both internally and externally.

As we discussed in Chapter 1, the security risk assessment project may possibly be completed by someone on staff at your organization. This person could be within your security, risk management, or other related department. Of course as we have already discussed this person should have the background in security and risk identification in order to properly conduct the assessment.

Let us assume for a minute that you are going to have this project managed by someone on staff at your organization. With that being the case, this person will be the one that is responsible for establishing many of the details of the project. For example, this person is responsible for identifying the participants in the project, determining the project scope, schedule, budget, and deliverables, as well as completing the project in many cases. Provided this person has the proper background with which to complete these tasks, you must also ensure that this person has the time to complete this project.

Oftentimes when an organization elects to conduct a security risk assessment using internal resources they may not consider the fact that the project will require a full-time effort on the part of their staff. In other words, there is much more to completing a security risk assessment than just walking the campus and looking at your physical security. The project prep time needs to be considered so your organization can establish the foundation of the project so as to more or less establish the road map as to where the project is going.

Although there are plenty of qualified security professionals on staff at many organizations, they often find that their schedules can be challenging at times, and to commit enough time to properly plan and execute a security risk assessment can be a daunting task. One of the major challenges for security practitioners on staff is the fact that their work is often comprehensive and they are already managing many resources and processes on a daily basis, and to take 2–3 weeks out of their schedule to plan and execute an assessment is just not practical. With that being the case, they will often seek out the services of an independent security consultant.

Security consulting firms oftentimes are called upon to fulfill the role of the project management, the reason being that they have qualified staff that they can dedicate to the project. Seeing that most security consultants have performed security risk assessments as part of their business, they understand the process from the beginning to the end and overall can be much more efficient at conducting the assessment.

If you choose to go the route of hiring an independent consultant to complete your project, you should ensure that you establish who from that firm will be the project manager. Another consideration that needs to be taken into account is that they are qualified to perform the services that you are requesting. For example, there are many types of businesses that have unique and specialized security needs (e.g., healthcare, retail, education, etc.), and the security expert that you retain needs to have a background in that field. In other words, if you are a healthcare organization and you are hiring a consultant to manage your project, and that consultant is not experienced in healthcare, you may find that that consultant is learning as they go, and as a result may require more time for the project, which equates to more expenses for your organization.

To sum up this part of the selection process, just keep in mind that when it comes time to identifying who will manage this project, you want to ensure that they have the qualifications and background with which to complete this project to your satisfaction. Whether it is a person from within your organization, or an outside vendor, you need to consider the person's ability to be objective and unbiased. It is also in your best interest to conduct a return on investment (ROI) review of the project, because you may find that it may be more cost-effective to hire this project out versus conducting it internally.

IDENTIFY THE PARTICIPANTS

For the most part the security risk assessment cannot be completed without relying on several members of your organization. When determining who will participate in this project, you should consider all possible key players in your organization that work in conjunction with security. For example, an average security assessment team may include your legal counsel, risk management, human resources, facilities management, and corporate compliance. Of course the security department will have a major role in this project, and not only will the security management participate but it is highly recommended that a representative of the officers also be included as needed.

In some businesses you will also need to include management staff from security-sensitive areas or departments. Take for example that in healthcare you will want to include management of departments such as the pharmacy, emergency room, pediatrics and maternity, and medical records to name a few. In other businesses such as retail you may also be bringing in your loss prevention department, shipping and receiving, and finance. Although we could list a number of other types of businesses and key departments of those businesses that should also be a part of your team, we will assume that you understand that there are many variables to consider when identifying who will be participating in this project. Just keep in mind that those members of your team that are participating need to have the background and knowledge of their services that they are representing, and they must have the time to commit to this project.

When you consider everyone that will be involved in this project, you should also consider outside entities such as law enforcement, neighboring businesses, schools, neighboring residential areas, and so on. Each and every neighboring property has some effect on your overall security, and your operations will have an impact to some extent on their security.

As stated in Chapter 1, law enforcement is mostly a reactive service that responds to crimes or incidents as they are happening. However, they can offer you intelligence on crime trends and neighborhood issues that you may not be aware of. Including them as a part of your assessment is important because whether you understand it or not, they are a part of your security team.

In most cases your security department's reach ends at your campus perimeter, meaning that your staff cannot in most cases provide security to neighboring properties. In most states private security cannot handle incidents on city streets, in neighboring parks or residential areas, and so on unless they are under contract with the public agency responsible for those areas. In these areas the police will provide the security, or in the case of some private properties (e.g., apartment complexes) they may have security services provided by a contractor. That being the case, there has to be collaboration to some extent amongst all the interested parties to address the regional security issues, thus the reason to bring those other entities into the equation of your security assessment process.

As a security manager you should have already established a working relationship with all of your partners in the area around your property, and while conducting the assessment you should ensure that you have identified any security issues that they are concerned with that could or have affected your property. One way to look at this is the fact that what happens on your campus may affect the neighbors and vice versa.

Take, for example, that your campus is experiencing a rash of car burglaries during the evening hours. If that is the case, it is very possible that your neighboring businesses might be having the same issue, or they might have important intelligence to share with you. Case in point—a past retail client was experiencing a high number of car burglaries in their parking lots furthest from their building. Security was not able to determine where the suspects were entering or leaving the property and could never locate the suspect's vehicle. Once security looked outside their property and consulted with their neighbors, they found that the neighboring properties owners had noticed strange vehicles in their parking areas, and in some cases they observed people sitting in the cars for long periods of time. When all of the puzzle pieces were pieced together, it was determined that the suspects staged on the neighboring property or city streets and therefore would only briefly be on the site where the crimes were being committed. The suspects were aware of the security patrols and their routines and ensured that they were always one step ahead of security. However, once the retailer collaborated with their neighbors and the police, they were able to resolve this issue.

The importance of bringing outside entities into your assessment process is crucial. Information will flow in both directions, and you will often find out what issues the neighbors are experiencing, and maybe you will be able to assist them in their efforts to reduce security incidents as well.

When contacting the law enforcement department that services your area, you need to consider all of the agencies that may be involved. Many businesses have multiple properties in different cities and states, and if that is the case for your business, you will need to work with the law enforcement agencies for each location.

Generally speaking there are two resources that should be considered when dealing with law enforcement, and those two are the crime prevention bureau and the beat officers. The crime prevention staff will assist you with gathering crime information and stats for your area, and may be able to provide you with mitigation strategies to reduce criminal activity in your area; and the beat officer will be able to give you more precise information for your neighborhood. So now let us take a closer look at the two resources mentioned.

Crime prevention will normally be able to give you statistics for any area that you request. For example, if you were to contact them and ask them for a listing of all crimes or arrests within a one-mile radius around your property, they likely will be able to do so. Police departments gather this information and often publish annual reports for their jurisdictions, and in many cases you can find the complete reports on the department's website. The information contained within the reports is often an abridged version of the information that the police will report to the FBI for the Uniform Crime Reporting Program and can be very informative. Keep in mind that the annual reports will cover the entire jurisdiction of the law enforcement agency, and if you want property-specific information, you will have to request it from them.

The "beat cop" that patrols your neighborhood can be a very valuable source of information on trends and criminal activity such as gangs and drugs. Since the police officer is dealing with all criminal activity in the area, even for activity that has not reached the point of an arrest, their information can be very beneficial to your security department. Keep in mind that you also have information that the police officer will likely want to know, and information sharing should be a two-way street.

Oftentimes within an organization security will know of crimes that have happened and were never reported to the police. Since in most cases the victim has to make the police report and the organization is not always the victim, there may be many crimes occurring that go unreported. For example, incidents of vandalism and car burglaries occur on private property that may be reported to security, but often they are not reported to the police. For whatever reason, when security advises an employee to call the police and report the crime, the victim may not do so. That being said, the police may never hear about those crimes, and as a result of that your internal crime statistics and those provided by law enforcement will often not correspond.

There are so many issues that can arise from not reporting criminal activity to the police, yet you may not have control of the reporting process. However, if you have an ongoing relationship with the patrol officers that work in the area around your campus, you can certainly share with them any crimes that were reported to your department. When planning your assessment, set aside some time to meet with the local law enforcement representatives to discuss what you are doing, and to seek out their advice and insight as to what criminal activity is occurring in your geographical area.

PROJECT SCHEDULE

If you have never planned a security risk assessment, you will likely need to allow more time for the project than someone who has conducted several of them. Plain and simple, since there are so many variables in determining the project's schedule, it may be impossible to come up with an exact schedule. Because of this, the following information should assist you in determining a tentative schedule, and therefore you can at least have an idea of how much time this project will take. Then taking into consideration your organization and your skill level, you may be able to narrow it down even further as the planning progresses.

First, everyone has their own way of doing things and conducting an assessment is no different. The examples that I will provide for you in this section will be based on how consultants may set their schedule, but of course they are often very efficient with their time on site. Consultants have also assembled an array of research materials, forms, and questions that they will use throughout the assessment, and this of course will also result in less time needed for the project compared to someone that has never been involved with a similar project.

Next, since consultants may be coming in from another state or city to conduct the assessment, they will plan their project to take into consideration that most everything that needs to be done in your area must be completed within the one trip. What this means for the security manager on site is that they will likely be very busy and work some long days while the consultant is on site. For example, in 2012 while conducting an assessment at a very large facility with numerous satellite properties in two different cities, the organization's security director appeared overwhelmed at times with the amount of work that was completed in five days. However, I was just working at a normal pace and keeping the downtime to a minimum, and although the days were protracted, they were also very productive. The schedule could have been adjusted to last a few more days, and would have allowed for some downtime each day, but that would have just increased the project's cost and not been efficient for either party. As with many projects, time is money, and although the project's schedule may have felt overwhelming to the security director, it was a reasonable 8-hour-day schedule had everything been ready to go on day one. So let us now look at how to determine how much time is needed from a consultant's perspective.

First, let me say that there are hundreds of people that identify themselves as "security consultants," and you can bet that there are numerous ways in which they will determine a schedule. With that on the table, the following is an average way to determine the time commitment formula.

To begin a project, you will need to set aside some time to plan the project, identify the project's scope, schedule the project's meetings and inspection time, and determine how much time will be devoted to research and report preparation. The planning process for someone who has never conducted an assessment may require days, yet for an experienced professional it will likely require less than 8 hours of time.

Once you have the project scheduled, and you have set its scope, now comes the review process; basically, you will be reviewing your measurements standards/guidelines, and you will need some time for document review (policies and reports). If you are doing this in-house and you are exceptionally familiar with the information, you may not need a lot of time for this phase. For consultants the time required with be directly associated with how familiar they are with the type of industry and their past experience. This phase may take 3–6 hours of time for someone that has conducted numerous assessments.

Next comes the onsite assessment, and here is where there are just too many variables to simplify the time commitments. When planning this phase, you will have to take into consideration the size of the project, how many distinct sites there are, and how many buildings are on each site. You will need to determine how many interviews and meetings there will be, travel time between sites, and many other factors to properly plan the on-site time required.

To help explain this process, we will use an example of a 200 room hotel that has one 10-story building and within the hotel is a gift shop, restaurant, conference center that has an occupancy rating for 200 people, business center, fitness center, laundry service, loading dock, vending areas on each floor, swimming pool, and bar/lounge. In addition to the identified services and facilities, this hotel is located in the inner city in a high crime area. You have been asked to perform a security risk assessment on the entire property and all of the above-mentioned departments. So now you have to determine the time required to complete this project.

First, let us start with identifying how much time it will take to walk each floor looking at the doors, security measures, utility closets, vending areas, and a few guest rooms. If there are eight floors of guest rooms, take your number of hours per floor and multiply it by eight to determine the number of hours.

Next, determine how much time each of the service lines will require (e.g., laundry, bar, conference center, business office, and so on), and how many meetings will be required to interview management and staff. Meetings should not last more than an hour in most cases, and some of them can be group settings. For some of the services you may require additional time to address security concerns, such as in the case of the bar and business office.

Other time commitments that need to be addressed will include time with your local law enforcement, neighboring businesses, neighborhood residential associations (as applicable), and any schools that may be adjacent to your campus. Realistically speaking, the number of meetings that you schedule will be in direct correlation with the type of your business, location, criminal activity both on and off your campus, and numerous other factors.

Now that you have identified the approximate time required to prepare for the actual assessment, and the time needed to perform it, you are left with determining the time needed post assessment to conduct research and prepare the written report. A standard used by consultants is often for every 8 hours on site there is 8 hours of office work. Even though not everyone may follow that standard, it is a starting point for you to consider. The reality is that since you do not conduct assessments every month, you may require more time doing your research and report writing. The key is to determine a starting point. The office time can be very flexible as you are not normally affecting someone else's schedule because the main parts of the project have been completed.

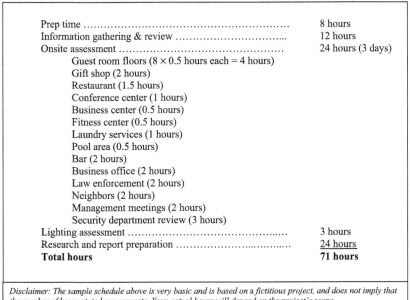

Prep time .... 8 hours
Information gathering & review .... 12 hours
Onsite assessment .... 24 hours (3 days)
      Guest room floors (8 × 0.5 hours each = 4 hours)
      Gift shop (2 hours)
      Restaurant (1.5 hours)
      Conference center (1 hours)
      Business center (0.5 hours)
      Fitness center (0.5 hours)
      Laundry services (1 hours)
      Pool area (0.5 hours)
      Bar (2 hours)
      Business office (2 hours)
      Law enforcement (2 hours)
      Neighbors (2 hours)
      Management meetings (2 hours)
      Security department review (3 hours)
Lighting assessment .... 3 hours
Research and report preparation .... 24 hours
Total hours **71 hours**

Disclaimer: The sample schedule above is very basic and is based on a fictitious project, and does not imply that the number of hours stated are accurate. Your actual hours will depend on the project's scope.

FIGURE 2.1 Sample assessment schedule.

Using the above example, we will now set a schedule that will help to determine the budget. Figure 2.1 is an example of the estimation of time based on a fictitious project as mentioned above.

Keep in mind that the above example is very basic, and in some cases may be underestimated. If you are conducting this assessment in house, you will likely require additional hours of prep and research, as well as report writing. As for consultants, they will likely add into the project a kickoff meeting and exit conference and not require as much time for prep, document review, and the actual assessment. The most important part of planning the schedule is the financial cost of what everyone's participation will entail, and that is where the budget comes into play.

BUDGETING CONSIDERATIONS

Conducting the assessment in house will mainly involve your time, and your time costs money. In order to determine the ROI of time, you have to know the true costs of the project. So when you consider conducting the assessment yourself, once you have identified the number of hours required of your time, and your staff's time, calculate those hours times the salary rate of all staff that will be working on the project (you may not have their salary information, but you can estimate what the costs might be). I have heard security managers claim that they can do the project without impacting the budget, which is not possible. Your time, and the time of everyone involved, must be factored in. Although it is true that even when you bring in a consultant your organization will still be expending internal resources for the project, there should be cost savings within your organization in all four segments of the project (prep, review, assessment, and report).

If you retain the services of an outside consultant to complete this project, your prep time will be reduced, as the consultant is absorbing those costs. In some cases the consultant may not charge for the prep time as they have previously established what is needed for this phase and they send the client a package of information requested; therefore, in the end, they may have no need to invoice for that work. In addition to that, their hours needed for the documentation review will often be less because they know exactly what they are looking for and have previously determined the measurement processes that they are using to evaluate your documents.

The main cost savings will come with the preplanning education and experience departments. By this I am referencing your experiences with planning, scheduling, and completing an assessment versus someone who has likely performed dozens of them each year. Look at it this way: if this is your first assessment, or you only conduct them once every 5–7 years, you will still need to educate yourself on the current practices and updated resources prior to getting the assessment underway. However, the consultant that does this for a living will have already accumulated an extensive knowledge base, library of materials, and should be up to date on industry standards and best practices.

Other budget considerations will include any equipment or tools needed to complete the assessment. For example, when conducting a lighting assessment, you will need a light meter and a current reference manual to guide you through the process so that you know what measurement standards you are comparing to. In addition to those items, you will need office supplies to complete your report, some form of a survey questionnaire to gather information from staff, transportation costs if you are traveling to other sites, funds to purchase crime reports that you may request from sources other than your local law enforcement agency, general reference manuals for your research and report process, and numerous other incidentals as needed. Finally, if you are intending to hire a consultant to perform the assessment, you will need to determine your budget for that expense.

Consultant's fees can be all over the board depending on a number of factors, such as the type of consultant, their expertise and background, or how long they have been in business. As far as how long they have been in business, I am referring to someone that is new to the business may work for a reduced fee to build their business and experience. They will also offer one of two ways to budget a project, hourly plus expenses or a fixed fee.

The hourly rate plus expenses type of contract is open ended, meaning you will not know the exact cost of the project until it is completed and the final invoice is sent to you. Although this type of billing method is still used by some consultants, it has been my experience that most clients prefer the fixed fee approach so they can determine their budget up front and plan accordingly.

A fixed fee contract is such that you will know exactly what the budget will be before you execute any contract. The fee will often be all inclusive, which means that all fees and expenses are included. It is up to the consultant to ensure that expenses are managed properly and the project proceeds as planned. If there are additional expenses incurred by the consultant, they will be their responsibility unless they are a part of a change order to the project. For example, let us assume that the consultant projected a travel budget of $900 when they determined their fixed fee, and at the end of the project their travel expenses actually come out to $1150 due to higher than expected airline or lodging costs. If that is the case, the consultant is responsible to cover those extra costs. However, if you were working under an hourly contract plus expenses, your organization may be on the hook for that extra $250.

Once you have established an invoicing model (e.g., fixed or hourly), you should also consider the fact that if you change any part of the project there may be additional expenditures to your projected budget. However, before any additional funds are spent, you should receive a formal "change order" or contract amendment that details any changes and their associated costs. It is up to you at that point to either accept the changes or reject them. In other words, let us say that you have a project scheduled for three different sites all within the same general area. Then you decide to add an additional property or delete one of the existing ones, therefore you are changing the project's scope and schedule. At that point, the consultant may have to adjust their travel plans, which may, for example, affect their previously made air travel reservations. If that happens and there is a fee charged by the airline to make that change, it may be a billable expense passed on to your organization even if you are working with a fixed fee. Basically, it is a change order after an agreement has been executed, and those expenses are outside of the project's scope and assumptions, and if you agree to the change, you are accepting the associated costs.

PROJECT ASSUMPTIONS

Every project will have assumptions, which are those things that everyone is assuming will happen to complete the project. For example, if I am submitting a proposal for consideration, I will assume that I will receive the information requested as part of the assessment (i.e., reports, stats, policies) and that all participants will show up for the meetings and fact-finding sessions. I will also assume that I will be granted the proper access to the facilities so that all areas can be inspected. My clients also assume that they will be getting the services as promised and my firm will follow the project's schedule. All things considered, even the best laid plans can go awry.

For example, although I will need to know what policies are in place regarding security, and how security will address incidents, there have been times when a client has not shared that information. In essence they retained my firm to assess their security program, yet they do not share the basis for their program or the known outcomes of their program. In those cases I can only review what is shared with me and duly note in the final report that we were not able to meet all of the project's goals due to the lack of information provided.

Basically, the project assumptions will come from within the project's scope and will normally restate the requirements needed to be completed in order for the project's scope to be fulfilled. So to put this in terms that relate to conducting the assessment in house, let us say you have invited several key management personnel to meet as part of your project, yet 50% of your participants do not show up for your meetings or are not available when you are doing the assessment within their department. As a result, your project will likely require additional time to reschedule the meetings and inspections, and to actually do them, all of which will affect to your project's schedule, budget, and scope.

DELIVERABLES

To define *deliverables* for the purpose of this book and your project, we are talking about the final report and any recommendations for improvement and mitigation. Once the project has been completed (e.g., planning, review, inspections, interviews) it all comes down to the formal report of findings. The report will be your tool that identifies any security risks or vulnerabilities, and will include recommended steps to correct any deficiencies.

The report has to be completed in a manner that is unbiased, and it should not contain personal opinions. Much like any other official document it should contain only the facts and recommendations based on industry standards and best practices. Although this is not supposed to get personal, reports have been written that will from all appearances, get very much so.

Over the years, I have read reports submitted by other "security consultants" and have been taken aback by some of the comments included within them. I have had new clients tell me that their security director tendered their resignations upon reading the reports that other consultants submitted on a previous assessment, as they felt that their integrity and professionalism were destroyed by the report's contents. Although several of the findings of the reports were accurate when it came to things like the security technology and staffing, none of the important findings were acted on because the report was discredited by the organization's administration due to the personal attacks aimed at the security director.

I have also heard of consultants submitting final reports that were not well received yet they were very detailed and accurate. The actual problem was that the organization's security management did not agree with the findings, and because of that the client decided to conduct another RFP for a completely new assessment. Although that is an option that any business can take, before you go in that direction you need to determine if it is a quality issue or if you just do not agree with the findings. Keep in mind also that a new assessment will certainly require additional time and money to complete.

The moral of the story is this—if you are writing this report as an internal consultant (e.g., security director), you must be able to write it in an unbiased manner and do so without prejudice. If you have been having ongoing dialogue with your supervisor all along, there will likely be nothing in this report that will threaten your job security or credibility. The same holds true if you have retained a consultant to conduct the assessment and write a report; the report should not be a threat to your job security—more so, it should be a reinforcement of what you have been telling your administration all along.

If you are someone that was retained to come into the organization to conduct the assessment, your report needs to be factual and informative. This is not the place to tear the client apart using your vast knowledge and experience; it is the time and place to educate the administration about not only what they need to consider fixing but what they are also doing correctly. It is all about giving them the knowledge and tools with which to mitigate the identified deficiencies and improve their program.

CHAPTER 3

Project Management

SECURITY MANAGEMENT VERSUS SECURITY CONSULTANT

As discussed in Chapter 2, early on in the planning process for your security assessment, you will need to identify the project's management internally. In most cases, your internal resource will come from within your security department if you have one in place. However, the majority of businesses do not have a security department; rather they have someone that is responsible for the overall security of the organization. In these cases, you can either assign someone else within the organization to be the project manager or hire out the service to a security consulting firm. Either way you must consider things such as qualifications, objectivity, experience, and professional backgrounds of whoever is going to manage this project.

In those cases where you have a security department, the organization needs to determine whether or not the person that manages the department is up to the task of conducting the assessment. Unfortunately, it may not always be the case that you have someone on staff who has the background and skills needed to perform such an important assignment. Having been in such a position early on in my security career, if I had been asked to conduct a security risk assessment on my employer's campus, I would have had to locate a book to find out not only what an assessment was but also how to conduct it. And although my career prior to security management was in law enforcement, it still did not qualify me to conduct a proper assessment. There is more to a security risk assessment than most people understand, and therefore the person who manages the process and outcomes must be competent and knowledgeable.

There are risks with having an inexperienced person conduct an assessment. First, as was discussed in Chapter 1, the security risk assessment report is a document that may be pivotal if there is a legal case against the organization. That being the case, you want to ensure that the report is properly written and addresses all of the risks and vulnerabilities, as well as mitigation strategies that are proven effective. Keep in mind that whatever is written in the report can either help or harm your organization and has to be based on factual information that can be verified.

If the person that authors the report is not current on the industry standards or best practices, how can they measure their program's effectiveness or intent?

Another concern is the fact that the inexperienced manager may not be aware of legal/regulatory requirements, security incident trending, and proper training standards, not to mention best practices. The most important step to planning the security assessment is determining who will administer it so it is in your organization's best interest to ensure that the person assigned is competent.

If your organization does not have a proprietary security department (in-house employees assigned to provide security services), you may have a contract security company providing your security staffing and/or security management. If that is the case, you can consider having that company conduct the assessment. Although this has been done in some organizations, there have also been cases where an independent security consultant in retained to perform the security assessment, as well as evaluate the contracted security services being provided. In these cases, the organization may want to ensure impartiality and may feel that the contract security company might not provide full disclosure on any internal issues within the security department or its security guard service contractor.

The importance of a properly conducted security risk assessment cannot be overstated. Several years ago, I was asked to review six previously written assessment reports for different campuses spread across a large geographical area. The governing body of all of the campuses had previously requested that their organization's security departments, which were in many cases sworn peace officers, conduct the security risk assessments at each site. It was shared with me that the organization was involved with numerous critical internal issues and that there were several pending litigation cases as a result of negligent security claims. My services were retained to review the internal assessment reports and give an opinion on the thoroughness and facts within the reports. However, in the end all I could state with a high degree of certainty was that they did not have security risk assessment reports. Each of the six reports failed to document even the most basic industry standards, let alone the critical failures that resulted in their losses and pending litigation. In all cases, they never addressed the majority of the security measures that were in place, nor did they appear to even know what it was that they were supposed to be evaluating. Those reports had to be the worst-case scenario for a "security risk assessment," and in the end, they had to start over again.

INTERNAL PERSONNEL

Let us say that you are the security manager and your supervisor has requested that you conduct an assessment of your employer's business, and now the time has come where you really need to determine if you know what to do. This is where a few security practitioners will believe that either they can or cannot complete the assignment. The reality is that anyone can conduct the assessment provided that they have enough knowledge and experience to do so. But if you have never conducted an assessment, and you have not conducted sufficient research prior to getting started, you may want to consider bringing in an expert. The most common reason why projects do not achieve their intended results is the fact that some security practitioners do not have the training and resources from the beginning. Therefore, they cannot effectively manage the process from conception to completion.

One of the most requested tools that someone will seek out when it comes time to do their first assessment is a copy of an actual report so that they know what ones looks like. It is a lot like reverse engineering, they figure that if they can see what the final product is supposed to look like, they can basically look for the same or similar issues within their company and make the same or similar recommendations. But remember, no two projects are exactly alike, so if you are copying someone else's report, you may be missing some very critical parts of a proper assessment. The reality also is that you would be hard pressed to find someone willing to give up their report so that you can use it as a template.

For the most part, it is not that no one will give you the format that they use, it is more about the reports being very confidential due to security-sensitive information and possible liability exposure. It is like I tell my clients each time I provide them with their report—it is in their best interest to keep copies of the document to a minimum and only those that have a need to read the entire report should read it. You have to keep in mind that the information within the report (e.g., security risks, vulnerabilities, and possible liability issues) should be considered confidential at all times. In reality, the contents of your actual report can be very sensitive in nature and should be treated as such.

I am often asked for copies of the report, or at least my recommendations, by employees when I am conducting the site inspection. It seems that the organization's staff is very much aware of the value of the report's content, or in the case of labor unions, they may want the report for negotiations or leverage. If you are doing the assessment in house, you may be asked the same thing, and maybe by other members of management as well. In order to prepare for answering such requests, it would be judicious to have that conversation upfront with your supervisor and possibly your legal office before you start the project. Know in advance how many copies will be made and who will receive them.

If you have never conducted an assessment, it would be a good starting point to do your research on what you are about to embark on, and ensure that you fully understand the sensitivity and importance of the assessment. Resource materials such as this book will give you the ins and outs of how to conduct the assessment and write the report. However, what it cannot do is ensure that you are impartial and forthright with your findings and recommendations. That is where your integrity and competence will come into play, as well as your professionalism.

One of the best practices that may help you throughout the process is developing a team approach to the assessment. Remember, you cannot conduct a proper assessment without the assistance of others, so determine who will be on your team and what their roles will be. For internal managers, you may want to look at your risk management, facilities, human resources, legal, compliance, and other pertinent departments. You may be performing the majority of the work, but you will need a support system in place as you go.

SECURITY CONSULTANTS

As previously stated, if you are retaining the services of a "security consultant" to perform the assessment, you must conduct your due diligence to ensure that this professional is competent, experienced, knowledgeable about your industry, and, most importantly, is independent.

When trying to determine their competence, you can look to their references as one measurement, but also look to see if they have professional certifications.

Client references are much like personal references that we have all provided on job applications, meaning that no one will list someone who will not give a good reference. In some cases, the business references provided to you may be from clients from many years ago. So in most cases you will have no way of determining whether or not the reference was a recent client or one from 20 years ago without asking the reference when you call them. The point is that you need to spend the time to call any references and ask them the questions that you have to ensure that the reference is credible.

As we briefly discussed in Chapter 1, when it comes to professional certification, the most recognized professional certification within the security profession is the Certified Protection Professional (CPP) through ASIS International. In order to reach this level, a security practitioner must have verifiable evidence of knowledge and management skills in eight key domains of security: security principles and practices, business principles and practices, investigations, personnel security, physical security, information security, crisis management, and legal aspects. An applicant for this certification must have at least nine years of security experience, with at least three years of that experience as the responsible charge for that program. Once a person qualifies to sit for the exam, and passes it, he or she is ASIS board certified in security management.

Although the CPP is the certification most often held by security consultants, there are numerous other certifications depending on the type of industry that a professional specializes in. For example, ASIS International also has the

Professional Certified Investigator (PCI) and the Physical Security Professional (PSP) certifications. In addition to those, you may also find security consultants with certifications such as Certified Fraud Examiners (CFE), Certified Security Consultants (CSC), Certified Protection Officers (CPO), and Certified Healthcare Protection Administrators (CHPA). The different possibilities for initials that someone may have after their name are many, and it is always good practice to conduct your research on what the initials represent and how they relate to your needs. In most cases, certification indicates that a professional has mastered that field and has competencies that are verifiable and measureable to a defensible compilation of industry standards. However, there are a few certifications that do not require any examination or qualifications assessment and only require a person to submit an application and fee to obtain it. These "certifications" offer no value to anyone, including the "consultant." Certifications must require recertification, which will necessitate ongoing continuing education and training. This ensures that the certified practitioner stays up to date in their profession through continuing education and training.

Another means by which to determine their qualifications is to evaluate their experience. In order to do so you will want to determine how long they have been in business and how many times they have performed a security risk assessment as an independent security consultant. The Great Recession resulted in a lot of new "security consultants" hanging out their shingles due to downsizing and layoffs, and although there were likely many competent professionals that entered the consulting business in the last five years, there were also many inexperienced security people that believed that they could become "security consultants."

Experience comes with time, and you certainly do not want a security consultant to learn how to conduct a security assessment at your facility and at your expense. Most security consultants have company Web sites for anyone to research their company, and like any other Web site, you can often tell by the quality or content of the site if a firm appears professional or not. The key is to independently verify what you see online.

Specialized Knowledge

When you call a consultant, you should be prepared with some questions to ask them. You can start by explaining what you are looking for and then ask questions to determine whether or not they have the knowledge base that you are seeking. For example, I have received a few calls over the years for highly specialized security services that were outside of my expertise. One such client was in the planning process of designing and building a sensitive compartmented information facility (SCIF). Although the client was interested in retaining my firm for their project, I recommended another firm that had more relevant experience in such facilities. What it came down to was that I felt it was in the client's best interest to retain a firm with specialized experience in the planning, design, and project management for the SCIF. That may seem counterproductive to some people, but as a professional one must know when to step aside. I know of several other consultants who have done the same, but in most cases it is up to the client to screen potential security consultants for their experience. If when you are interviewing a security consultant you get the sense that they do not have the proper experience, trust your instincts.

When it comes to "knowledgeable" about your industry, it does not mean that the consultant has worked in a field like tire manufacturing if your company manufactures tires. In many cases security standards and operational goals are similar across the board, but there are some industries that have specific security standards. When that is the case, the consultant you are retaining must be knowledgeable in those standards.

Let us take, for example, that you have a medical office complex for which you want a security risk assessment conducted. With this type of facility and operation, you will want a security consultant who has experience in not only conducting assessments but also in healthcare, which can include the Joint Commission, Center for Medicare & Medicaid Services (CMS), and the Health Insurance Portability and Accountability Act (HIPAA). The basics of security management can be addressed by most independent security consultants, but when you are dealing with a specialized field, you need to ensure that any security consultant you retain has the experience and knowledge base to properly evaluate all of your operations and security risks.

Independent Consultants

In reference to an "independent security consultant," I am speaking of those consultants that are truly independent insomuch as they are not trying to sell you services such as cameras, alarms systems, or guard services. Most of the top security equipment manufacturers have "security consultants" on staff and their job is primarily to assess your needs and sell you their products. I have worked side by side with many of these people over the years, and they truly know their products. What they do not know is how a security program is properly managed and implemented.

When seeking an independent security consulting firm, look for firms that are nonproduct affiliated. Basically, they should not profit from purchases made by their clients based on recommendations made by the consultant. This is not to say that all security consultants that work for a security services firm will not provide you with professional services, because that is not the case. Keep in mind though that you will likely see references in their final reports that recommend services or products that they sell. Although an independent security consultant will also make recommendations based on your needs, they should not be brand or service specific.

References are yet another tool that you can use to conduct your due diligence process. Professional consultants should without reservation provide you with a minimum of three past clients' contact information upon request. If they cannot provide you with the client information, this may be an indication that they are new to the business and have not established any clients. Once you have obtained that information, it only takes a few minutes of your time to call those references and ask them some basic questions to assist you in determining if you want to retain their services. Some of the often-asked questions are:

- What services did you hire them to complete?
- Did the consultant meet the project's scope and schedule?
- Were you completely satisfied with their work? If not, why not?
- Did the final report address the findings and offer mitigation strategies?
- Would you recommend the consultant's company?

There are several other ways to conduct your due diligence when selecting a security consultant. For example, most professional consultants have been quoted in news stories or trade publications. In some cases they will have those articles or interviews posted on their company Web site for you to review. If there is no information on their Web site, you may elect to conduct an Internet search of the consultant's name and/or company name to see what is revealed in the search results. You can also seek out referrals from your peers to see who they have used in the past and who they would recommend. If they recommend someone to you, ask them if they have used their services in the past or just know of them—there is a difference, and you need to ask probing questions to get the information you are seeking.

In the end, what it comes down to is whoever conducts your security risk assessment must be competent, knowledgeable, professional, and experienced. Whether that person is on staff or an external security consultant, it is your job to determine whether or not they are up to conducting the project for your organization. Keep in mind that the goal of the services that the person will provide is to identify and make recommendations to reduce your security risks and vulnerabilities, so it is imperative to have a professional managing the project from the start to finish. Although it does happen, this should not be the time or place to work within an unrealistic budget or schedule. Whether you conduct this assessment internally or hire an outside security consultant, these projects will cost your organization both time and money.

Now that you have identified who will manage the project, it is time for that person to develop the project's scope—in essence what will they be assessing, where the project will be conducted, and numerous other important factors such as budgets, schedules, and intent.

CHAPTER 4

Defining the Project Scope

THE PROJECT SCOPE

When it comes time to plan the security risk assessment you will need to decide what the scope of the project will be. In other words, what will the extent and reach of the project entail? Will it be specific to one issue or take into consideration all parts of security for all of the organization's properties? What is it that you will be looking at, evaluating, measuring, analyzing, questioning, and/or verifying? Will it include a review of the department management? What parts of your department or the organization will be involved in the assessment? Will this include just one department, one building, the entire campus, or multiple campuses? Who is going to do what? What will they will be doing? Where will it be done? When will it be done? How will it be done? And finally, why is it being done? In this part of the preassessment planning, the project principals need to ensure that the intent of the project's goals will be identified and in writing so that everyone agrees on the scale and extent of the project. As the security manager or the staff person responsible for planning the security risk assessment, you must determine all of the above and then some.

For someone who has never performed a security risk assessment before, this can be a daunting task. The reality is that defining the scope is not that difficult. However, the difficulty usually results from not being informed or understanding what it is you are trying to accomplish. Many times when I ask a client what they want included in the project's scope there is an awkward period of silence on the phone. When that happens, it has been my experience that the client will state that they have not defined the scope or the intent of the project and they are open for suggestions. Because this happens more often than not, it has been my practice to ask a series of questions of the client to help me define what it is that they are looking for, and thus the process of defining the project scope begins.

There are several questions to be asked and answered when determining the scope of the project, such as where the project will be located. Several years ago, a client asked me to conduct a security assessment at a medical center. The security director stated that the project would only include the main medical

39

center campus, and he provided the street address for the medical center. As part of my due diligence, I asked if any other buildings other than the main hospital would be included, and I was told that there were no other buildings. Of course I also asked the security director questions along the lines of what parts of his security program he wanted reviewed and many other questions, and after I got the answers to those questions, I set about to put together a proposal for his review and approval. My firm was successful with our proposal and we mutually scheduled the site visit. However, much to my surprise, once I was on the property I discovered that there was a problem with the true scope of the project.

The project was scheduled to last three days and reportedly included only the main campus at a specific street address, but it turned out to be a much larger project than anticipated. The issue came down to the fact that the security director was stating what he believed to be the hospital campus, and I was assuming a totally different definition of that campus based on my questions during our initial contact. The reality was that not only did he intend for the main campus to be a part of the project, he also intended approximately 20 other buildings to be included; these buildings were not attached to the main hospital but were spread throughout the neighborhood and community. Needless to say, adjustments had to be made, and done so expeditiously, so as to redefine the project. The end result was that all properties were fully assessed and done so without having to start over, yet the days were much longer than anticipated to accommodate the added sites. The end result was a win–win for both the client and my firm, yet it was not a practice that anybody would want to see repeated.

The above example demonstrates how important it is to clearly define the project scope, and that neither the client nor the consultant should make any assumptions that cannot be fully disclosed within a proposal. If you as a security manager are planning a project, you too need to ensure that you have fully determined the scope of the project so that you can set a schedule and assemble your team. The security risk assessment is never conducted in a vacuum, meaning that you will be meeting with others as part of this assessment, so you will need to coordinate work schedules for your interviews and site visits. Therefore, to truly understand the scope of the project about how much time the project will take, the preplanning coordination is paramount to a successful outcome. The extra time spent defining your project's scope can save you and your team hours of work later if you have underestimated your scope.

When you set out to define your project scope, you also need to consider where the project will be conducted, including all buildings, grounds, and parking areas. Because of the issue that I mentioned above that occurred several years ago, I now ask for all street addresses, building names, and parking lot names or numbers. I also request the approximate square footage of each building, and the number of floors in each building. The square footage and the number of floors help me determine how much time will be needed to conduct the assessment at that building. If you personally will be conducting the security assessment, you can basically use the same information to try and determine how much time you will require for this project. Unless you have completed several of these assessments in the past, it will not be an easy undertaking to determine the time commitment required, but it does give you a basis from which to start.

Other things to consider when determining the project scope are will you be assessing security technology such as a card access system, video surveillance, locking key systems, alarm systems, as well as patrol operations, incident reports, security policies, staffing levels, security training, and other services or documents? Exterior lighting levels and campus landscaping will often be included in the security risk assessment. If your organization is mandated by law to have security measures or programs in place, you will want to include those in your project scope as well. Some types of businesses (e.g., healthcare or education) may have specific accreditation standards or requirements related to their security program that will also need to be evaluated.

To sum up the determination process of the project's scope for the security risk assessment, think about what will be included such as the locations/sites and any special requirements that must be addressed. If your company is retaining the services of a security consultant, the consultant will often provide you with a detailed project scope statement as per your requirements based on what you tell them during your initial conversation. Remember this, if you are retaining the services of an outside consultant to perform your security risk assessment, and when you receive the formal proposal you determine that the project scope does not include some of your requirements and it needs to be adjusted, all you need to do is let the consultant know what changes you want. In most cases there may not be a change to the overall schedule or budget of your project provided that you are not making substantial changes such as adding additional buildings or locations. If you are doing this project yourself, although you may make changes as you go, you certainly need to consider the other members of your team during the conception of this project and not make any changes that will adversely affect them after the project has commenced, or you may be having meetings by yourself.

It has been my experience that oftentimes when organizations request a written proposal for a security assessment, they do not know what they want. They know they need this thing called a security survey, security assessment, or risk assessment, but they do not fully understand what is included. One reason why this may happen is that the person requesting the proposal is not a security practitioner, but rather he or she is often an administrator of the organization. With that in mind, I find that I have to educate requestors as I lead them through a series of questions in order to define their project scope.

Several times in the past when a company was requesting responses to a formal request for proposal (RFP) they would ask that the firms submitting proposals define the project's scope. In many of those cases this happened because they were not sure of what they wanted and they wanted to see what the experts would suggest. In those cases the experts would either have to assume that the client was looking for what an "average" assessment entailed, or they would need to ask the client additional questions to narrow or clearly define the scope. Defining the project's scope in the RFP certainly makes it much easier to respond with an accurate submittal. However, the vast majority of requests are not formal RFPs, meaning they are verbal requests, and there is no preestablished project scope defined.

When it comes time to identify what will be assessed, unless you have a narrowly focused project scope that is only looking to address a predetermined concern, you will often review many or all of the following:

An evaluation of existing management, practices, operations, and technology, and making recommendations for best practices or industry standards in the following areas:

- Evaluate all security technology (e.g., card access, video surveillance, alarms, security systems)
- Evaluate security key control systems
- Evaluate the security incident reporting processes
- Assess violent crimes in each location's service area
- Review current security policies
- Review security accreditation standards or regulatory requirements
- Evaluate the security training program and offer expertise regarding specialized security training programs for the security department and organization
- Evaluate security patrols/operations/scheduling
- Evaluate construction site security risk and mitigation practices
- Provide security staffing models and recommendations
- Assess exterior lighting levels, parking lots/structure areas, and campus landscaping to determine potential security concerns/issues
- Make recommendations with priorities, based on national best practices, of ways to prevent crimes from occurring on the company properties
- Review workplace violence prevention strategies
- Review past security incidents through a thorough evaluation of client's risk data and incident reporting system, identify and rank trends, and give recommendations for the ongoing mitigation strategies

- Analyze current methodology and recommend tactics to improve security collaboration with local municipal agencies and private businesses
- Assess security staffing ratios in comparison to the industry standards and/or recommendations
- Examine current customer service approach and make recommendations based on best practices for the security industry
- Review security policies to ensure proper operation and common approach is present and consistent with industry standards
- Evaluate current Crime Prevention Through Environmental Design (CPTED) practices and make recommendations based on industry standards

As stated many times already, each project is unique and your scope may include some or all of the items listed above, and you may include more site-specific requirements as well.

As you can see, the information above determines what it is that you will be doing to complete this project, as well as establishes the steps that you will take to reach your goals. However, keep in mind that depending on your type of business, you may have numerous industry-specific additions to the scope of the project. For example, in healthcare you may be adding information regarding the Joint Commission, and schools may be adding information regarding the Clery Act, and so on. The items listed above will normally cover all types of industries in general, but they are really only the starting point. One also must consider federal, state, or local laws as they pertain to security, as well as any accreditation standards.

MEASUREMENT STANDARDS

If you are conducting this assessment yourself, you will want to identify what it is that you are planning to evaluate and what resources you will use to measure the effectiveness of the security operations. In other words, you must know where you are headed with this project and how you plan to get there, and how you will measure both your goals and outcomes.

Oftentimes the measurement tools may be industry recognized and accepted standards/guidelines (e.g., ASIS International, International Association of Healthcare Security & Safety (IAHSS) standards, or the Department of Homeland Security). There are many different resources available depending on the type of industry in which your business operates. By knowing the resources and by using them to determine how your program aligns in concert with them, you are effectively putting your program alongside a proven and accepted practice to determine if you meet, exceed, or are deficient to the standards/guidelines. However, keep in mind that the standards/guidelines in most cases are not requirements. Therefore, your program may in fact not be equal to them, and it still may not be a serious issue.

So let us say that your security program is *not* a mirror image of an industry standard for your type of business. Does this mean that your organization is at risk for a legal or compliance cause of concern? Not always. Take, for example, those in the healthcare field; the IAHSS has several very well-defined guidelines published for their membership, and they will often share them with those not in the association. According to the IAHSS Web site (www.iahss.org), "IAHSS guidelines are intended to assist healthcare administrators in fulfilling their obligation to provide a safe, secure and welcoming environment; while carrying out the mission of their healthcare organization. IAHSS guidelines support the need to comply with all national, state/provincial, county and local requirements and are intended to be in harmony with all regulatory, accreditation, and other healthcare professional association requirements and guidelines. The Industry Guidelines are operationally focused and less prescriptive."

The last sentence above clearly states that they are focused on operational needs and not requirements or how you should run your program. Even for those hospitals that are accredited through the Joint Commission or Det Norske Veritas (DNV), their security operations are measured against standards that do not require you to manage security in a certain manner, only that you take certain things into consideration and can address their standards in the manner as best defined by your organization. For the most part, guidelines and standards are proven methods of operation that have been vetted and accepted by industry experts. So if you are evaluating your program, why not use a proven and effective measurement standard?

One of the benefits of using proven methods that your peers have accepted is that when the day comes when your security program is under review as a part of legal case, you will know that the attorneys and experts retained to examine your program may often be using the same standards in their review. If you are not using industry standards/guidelines, and your program falls short of what most other security programs are doing, you may be facing an uphill battle throughout the litigation case.

Another effective resource that is often used when conducting a security risk assessment is security-related "best practices." A best practice is a practice or procedure that has time after time shown exceptional results as compared to standard practices commonly used, and once they have achieved and maintained their desired results over a defined period of time, they are often considered benchmarks from that point forward. Additionally, a best practice can continue to improve over time as new advancements are tested and evaluated and shared throughout the industry. It is much like the invention of the wheel so many years ago, and the adage that is still used today by many—why reinvent the wheel? When someone else has developed a best practice for security operations and it becomes an industry-accepted benchmark, it is often emulated by others and adjusted to fit their specific needs, and thus it improves over time.

The challenge with best practices is often the process of getting the word out that they exist. Some professional associations publish best practices, but mainly it comes down to networking with peers to find out what benchmarks or best practices they use. It is believed that if there were to be a central repository of best practices available to security practitioners, it may in fact increase the professionalism of our vocation. The reality is that there are security practitioners out there today that are dealing with issues that more than likely have already been addressed by others, and in many cases there may be a best practice established that has been vetted by others. If only that information was available to all security practitioners, the learning curve may be changed so that an organization could quickly adjust to any security deficiencies.

As part of the process of conducting a security risk assessment, I often come across security programs that have developed best practices as a result of past incidents. The organizations have put a lot of work into their after-action plan and in the process have developed what can only be described as a best practice. In most cases, they will allow the sharing of their best practice with other organizations and other security professionals, and in some cases accreditation bodies.

However, a few times in the past I have found that there can be a strong sense of "proprietary information" with regards to the practice, and it is not allowed to leave the organization. A practice that has been identified as "proprietary" by some organizations and is not shared can be a result of what has been described as "copyrighted material," or maybe their legal counsel does not wish to have it disclosed for a number of reasons. It has even been observed that a security professional that developed a practice did not realize what they had, and were not confident in how it would be accepted by their peers. Oftentimes it comes down to working closely with the security professionals of that organization to explain to them how their excellent work can benefit others and the profession in general.

Overall, when you are evaluating your security program, or that of a client, you will need to know what the industry standards and best practices are, whether they are published or not, and measure the security program using the practices as benchmarks. If you have no best practices to draw from, and you are not current on industry standards for your type of business, what will you organization use as a measurement standard?

LOCATIONS INCLUDED

When it comes to defining the project scope, you must know where you are going to be conducting the assessment. In other words, identify the specific addresses or locations.

As mentioned earlier in this chapter, I experienced a past client that had a definition of their campus that was very different from how I defined it. What was believed by me to be one large campus of buildings that were all attached and on one large site was actually dozens of buildings spread throughout the community. The mistake was all on my end for not getting clarification up front, and I have since changed my business practices to ensure that everyone is on the same page from day one.

Over the years since then I have developed a process of information gathering that is, surprisingly enough, not used by all security consultants. That process basically asks for all street addresses for every building or parking area that will be assessed as part of the project. Case in point—during an RFP in August 2013 a large university was requesting proposals for a security risk assessment and they identified their main campus as being the project's location. I had been on that campus several times in the past for another project, and I knew how large the facility was. However, in my planning for this RFP I had to consider the fact that there might be new buildings since I was there last, or some buildings may have been renovated. Therefore, I went online to research the site, and it became clear what the campus looked like and how much work was involved—or so I thought.

Over the next few days, I researched the university and waited to see if any additional information was coming during the normal question-and-answer period of the RFP. After a few days of no additional information, and in light of my past mistake, I inquired if there were any additional properties not on the main campus that would be included in the project. It was not too much of a surprise that the university acknowledged that there were several other locations throughout the community and in an adjoining city that would be included in the project. What was surprising was that no one else asked.

The risks of not knowing your project's scope as far as what properties will be included in the project are many. If you are conducting this project as a consultant, your risk is underestimating your budget, schedule, and resources needed. If that is the case, you will arrive onsite and then have to go through that awkward conversation that a mistake was made and now there needs to be a change order. Or the consultant may have to compress everything into the time allotted.

Consultants normally have the scheduling process down to a science and will often know how many hours it will take for each phase of the assessment. So if they are going to squeeze in the extra sites, the question is, how are they going to do that? Will they be staying additional hours or days, or will they compress the already fixed schedule? In addition to that, if they stay extra hours or days, will they be invoicing your organization for that extra time? Since my practice is to clearly define the project's scope upfront, with all sites identified in advance, this does not normally present an issue later down the road unless the scope changes at the request of the client. In those cases where their new request only requires a couple of extra hours (1–2), I am likely to give that time during the evening and not bill the client. When the scope changes substantially, we will obviously have a conversation and work out a mutually acceptable solution.

If you are retaining an outside vendor to conduct your assessment, you must ensure that your project scope is well defined by mutual consent. Street addresses are your best bet, and in the case of parking lots, they are often numbered or identified in some manner, so identify them in whatever way both parties fully and clearly understand their locations. Another way to identify locations on large campuses may be building names, and if you are going this route, it is advised to provide a campus map with all buildings listed on it to all of the project's participants.

If you are conducting this assessment in-house, you still must determine what locations will be a part of your project. In many cases, you will need to confer with others within your organization to determine the scope because they may have different needs. For example, administrators may have certain aspects of the security program that they want to review. Key departments such as security sensitive areas may also have some important concerns that they want to address that may not be on your radar screen. For example, if your property has a pharmacy on it, there may be FDA or DEA regulations that the pharmacy needs to follow and measure that your security department may not normally handle. The same holds true for research-and-development departments or those departments that deal with government contracts. If you set your project scope without knowing exactly where your assessment will be conducted, or what will be included, your project's schedule and budget may likely become overwhelmed in a hurry.

So far, we have defined what the security risk assessment is, conducted our preassessment planning, and learned about the different choices for project management, and we just finished defining the project's scope. Now it is time to get things underway and start gathering the information that we will be evaluating during the actual assessment.

CHAPTER 5

Information Gathering

As you begin the process of your security risk assessment, one of the first things that you will need to do is gather the information necessary to measure and evaluate your security program. If you are utilizing the services of an independent security consultant, you will likely be asked by that person for numerous reports, policies, and trending information that you have been monitoring. So let us look at this part in two phases: first, where you are conducting the assessment yourself; and second, where a consultant is performing the assessment on your behalf.

INTERNAL SOURCES

Whatever route you go with, when it comes time to get your assessment underway, you will need to review your existing security policies to ensure that they are up to date and still relevant. As a standard practice, policies should be reviewed at least every 3 years for any changes. By doing so, you are reviewing them to ensure that any operational changes that have been made over time have been incorporated within the policies, and whether or not there are sections that need to be added or removed. As you know, policies can and often will be used for operational effectiveness, disciplinary actions, and of course they will also come become an important resource if there is a litigation case.

Over the years while conducting security risk assessments for clients, I have found several policies that were out of date, and that the security department staff were performing their duties contrary to the written policies. Although catching those changes during an assessment is more of a check-and-balance process, if there is a civil litigation case brought against an organization, the policies in place at the time of the event will be used. There have been past cases where an organization found an error with a policy postincident and then revised the policy to reflect their then-current operations. However, keep in mind that the attorneys, and their security experts, reviewing the case will be asking for policies in effect at the time, as well as any revisions made since the incident.

49

As mentioned in Chapter 2, when it comes to policy reviews, you will likely know your existing policies extremely well, and you may even have written them. Although that may be the case, you should still review what is recorded within your policy to ensure that there have been no operational changes made since the last policy review. As for what policies you should consider for your review, it really comes down to any policy that is related to any part of your security program. Following is a list of policies that should be considered, but keep in mind that your actual list may include additional items.

- Citizen's arrest
- Workplace violence
- Use of force
- Weapons in the workplace (including anything that officers carry)
- Aggressive incidents
- Access control
- Gangs (any policies related to gang members onsite)
- Security codes (code silver, pink, purple…or equivalent)
- Civil disturbance
- Security escorts
- Security sensitive areas
- Lost & found
- Key control
- Company safe
- Petty cash—(organization-wide)
- Visitor access management
- Security alarms (panic, burglary, hold-up, personal protection)
- Patrol procedures
- Shift duties for officers
- Investigations
- Incident reports
- Trespass
- Strike plan for security operations or response
- Staff identification
- Visitor identification
- Security department policy manual (department specific)
- Training program—FTO program

In those businesses that have specialized programs (e.g., healthcare), you may have additional policies that address that type of business. As an example, following are some of those policies that you might be reviewing:

- Forensic patients (policy and form used for forensic staff orientation)
- Restraints (both clinical and custodial)
- Security risk patients (mental health, gangs, police holds, CPS, forensic)

- No info patients
- VIP patients
- Pharmacy security
- Emergency department vehicular access
- Mental health holds/patient watches/standbys or related
- Patient valuables
- Morgue security
- Patient identification
- Birthing center infant security

Another source of relevant information that should be reviewed will include all past security reports for at least the last three years. In most cases security departments will maintain the reports for at least that long, and in some cases they might be required by law, accreditation standards, or internal policies to maintain them for a much greater period of time.

When reviewing the past incident reports, you should be able to ascertain whether or not your program has improved over a period of time. By that I am talking about measuring your program against the number and types of security incidents that have occurred. In essence, if you have been making adjustments over time to your program, and those adjustments are often the result of past incidents, you should find that with those adjustments the numbers of security incidents have actually declined. If not, you may need to consider a different approach.

To take it a step further and explain what this would look like to you, let us assume that you have had several previous incidents of unauthorized access into a security-sensitive area. As a result of those incidents, you changed your policy with regard to operations such as increasing security rounds, changing door lock/unlock times, and so on. If your changes were effective, you should have realized a decrease in the number of incidents regarding unauthorized access. However, if the numbers have not changed at all since those changes were instituted, or maybe they went up, then you will find that you have to revisit the policy and possibly make additional changes to mitigate the problem. Your goal should be to reduce your security incidents through effective management and operational policies and procedures. Remember, you want your incident numbers to trend downward over time, and during your assessment you are measuring and evaluating all trends.

Just how important is it to monitor security incident trends for your organization? It can mean all the difference in the world when it comes to staffing, patrols, technology, and management. As an example, during a recent security risk assessment I asked the security manager to identify the most common security incident within his organization and what he had done to address that issue. Much to my surprise, he could not name any security concerns.

Taking it a step further, he was asked how many workplace violence incidents occurred within the last 3 years, and if the number of incidents had increased or declined over the last 12 months. There was that deer-in-headlights look on his face, and he was not able to identify any trends in security incidents over any period of time. His inability to answer the questions was not due to the fact that there were no incidents, because to the contrary he mentioned numerous past incidents of violence. His lack of tracking and trending of those past incidents was the main concern. The question is, how would you know what the effectiveness of your program was if you were not able to trend the security incidents or measure the outcomes of mitigation strategies?

Not even the best security programs can prevent all security incidents, but in order to know how to properly manage your security program, you must know what your threats are and where they will likely occur. Taking information from security incident reports and tracking that information looking for trends and other identifiable information, you can make adjustments to your program to reduce the likelihood for future incidents. In the case above, if you are not tracking incidents, and not looking for trends, you are certainly in a reactive posture and do not appear to be making any needed adjustments to preclude incidents.

Look at it this way, if your organization has been experiencing a number of car burglaries, there are several ways to look at the incidents and respond appropriately. One of the ways to evaluate the problem is to look at the times of day and day of week that they are occurring. You can also look at the locations where they occur and what items have been stolen. With the information gathered you may make adjustments to the security patrols and staffing levels to address the times, days, and locations of where the incidents are occurring. With regard to the items being stolen, you may identify a trend that indicates that certain types of cars are more likely to be burglarized, or that the suspects are going after certain items (e.g., GPS devices, cell phones). Once you have established what the trends are, you can make effective operational adjustments.

If you are not currently running monthly or quarterly reports on your security incidents, you must consider doing so. Tracking can be done the old school way with pin maps, but better yet there are several incident report software products on the market that will produce reports with a few clicks of a mouse. Of course the software programs offer you the best collection point of information and can offer you more flexibility with maintaining long-term statistics. Whichever way your program tracks the security incidents reported to your department, be sure that the information is available to the officers.

Security officers are working the front line for your security program, and because of that they need to have up-to-date information on what security incidents are occurring. In many cases what often happens is that the information is tracked, and hopefully trended by management, but the officers have not seen that information. I have spoken with many officers who stated they knew of past incidents but had never seen any information on trends, so the reality was that they did not have a complete picture. If that was the case, how can we expect them to be effective in performing their duties, which is normally being proactive and preventing incidents from occurring? Those programs that track trends and share that information with the security officers often find that they have a much better mitigation strategy in place and security officers are more effective overall. Basically, management is providing them with as much information as possible, and therefore the officers have more tools at their disposal to address security concerns before they become incidents.

Another source to pull information from may be your risk management or legal departments. Human resources may also have information available to you regarding workplace violence issues. Although I would hope that security is always in the loop with regard to workplace violence and theft issues, this is not always the case. My experiences have shown that about one-third of security programs are not consistently involved with all internal issues. I have not tracked all the possible reasons for this, but in many cases there seems to be a culture of other departments handling security-related issues and not sharing those results with the security department.

During past projects, I have found that the departments that are not likely to share information will be Human Resources, Risk Management, and Administration. The reasons that I have heard include it is a confidential personnel matter, or administration felt this matter needed to be handled at a much higher level. So in essence the investigative arm of the organization (i.e., Security) is not at the table during crucial security-related matters. They want security to manage the risks, but they do not collaborate with security on all the risks that are present. With this in mind, I would suggest that when you are pulling together your information and data for your security risk assessment, you have a conversation with these departments and any other ones that you might feel necessary, and get them on board with your needs and requests.

EXTERNAL SOURCES

Security Consultants

Although everyone performs the assessment in relatively the same manner, their information gathering may be either less or more in depth in nature depending on their approach, or depending on what they have been asked to review.

The big difference between you reviewing your own program or having a security consultant review it is the fact that the consultant is providing you with an unbiased review and is able to bring an outsider's perspective of your security program. For those that have ever wondered if their policies were effective, or wondered if their security program was at or above average, an independent review can be very beneficial.

Since most professional consultants have years of experience to draw from, and have reviewed numerous other security programs, they can bring a wealth of information to the table for you and your organization. They often will have extensive knowledge of current best practices and may also be an asset when it comes to reducing your risk exposure based on their past or current litigation work. However, keep in mind that the consultant must have the background to evaluate your program if it is a specialized field. This is why you need to ask the questions of their expertise in advance.

Oftentimes when I begin a security assessment project I will ask the client for documents and reports based on their business type and needs. Although there is no one comprehensive list that I use, because I tailor to the needs of each client, following is a general list of many of the items that I will request in advance of my site visit. These items, and other ones that I may request, will be used to measure the security program's intent versus the actual operations. In other words, with the information requested as well as the policies, you should have an effective means with which to determine whether or not your program is compliant with your policies as well as if it is properly managing security mitigation efforts and outcomes.

- Property maps for all sites as part of this project
- Incident report totals (last 3 years)
- Police crime reports for an area of one-mile radius of the campus
- Total number and types of arrests made on campus (last 3 years)
- Any quality improvement programs/initiatives related to security
- Annual reports for assaults/batteries on staff (last 3 years)
- Workplace violence assessments (last 3 years)
- Documented training for security staff
- List of training provided to *all* staff related to security (last 12 months)
- Any labor/union issues/concerns related to security
- Monthly alarm test reports (last 3 years)
- Hazard vulnerability analysis (last 3 years)
- Security department business plan (if applicable)
- List of regulatory organization's standards that security addresses, is required to comply with, or measures as they relate to security
- Security management program
- Security statement of authority
- Security sensitive areas—list of areas designated and annual training for those areas (last 3 years)
- Security program reviews (last 3 years)

- Fiscal year security budget with year to date (YTD) totals
- Project descriptions and plans for any pending or in progress security upgrades

If the security department staffing and management are being reviewed as part of the assessment, there are other things that you may want to review. It will not always be necessary to request the items listed that follow, but in those cases where an independent review is being conducted by an outside consultant, these items may be requested in advance of the site visit:

- Security management's résumé or curriculum vitae
- Copy of all position specific competency evaluation tools
- List of training each officer received in the last 3 years
- Annual training program information (types of training, hours)
- Job descriptions for each position in security
- Security staffing schedule for current month

In those cases where your security operations are required to follow accreditation guidelines or standards, or when they might be required to be in compliance with state laws, information regarding those prerequisites will also frequently be requested. Case in point—in some states security officers are required to be licensed and/or the department's training program may be regulated by the state. In those cases you will often find that security consultants will request documentation related to the standards and statutes. Since there are so many different regulations and standards related to security, suffice it to say that if your security program falls under any special regulations, you should be reviewing all applicable information to determine compliance.

Security consultants often will seek out information from other entities prior to the site visit or in conjunction with it. They may contact the local law enforcement agency in your area, or other resources. In doing so, they may be seeking information to complement or validate any information that you provide, or they may be seeking out additional information to evaluate once on site. These resources are often considered external sources.

Police and Online

Police statistics are often looked at for a security assessment, but as mentioned earlier, you must keep in mind that the information provided may not be consistent with your internal records. If you have not already done so, you may want to go to your local law enforcement's Web site and determine if they post their crimes stats online. For example, the Los Angeles Police Department (LAPD) has a link on their main Web site page that will direct you to crime mapping and COMPSTAT. If you follow the link (www.crimemapping.com), you will see what a service like this has to offer. Although this web link is on the LAPD Web site, the company that manages the Web site is used in many different states. Your local law enforcement agency may or may not use the same service, but either way you can enter your street address in the search bar and determine if crimes stats are on file for your location.

Other external sources are available to you as well, and in some cases they will charge you a fee to get your crime information. One such source is a company called Cap Index (www.capindex.com). This service will provide you with a crime index score based on local, regional, and national crime information. Their service provides you with forecasting data to help you plan for your security mitigation efforts as well as crime prevention strategies. Many businesses use this service on an ongoing basis. They also review information from this service when they are planning a new location or as part of an expansion project.

The thing to remember about online services, especially those that charge for their services, is that for the most part they are getting their information from data provided by local law enforcement agencies or that has been sent to the federal government. If you want to do the work of gathering your information on your own from your local law enforcement agency, you certainly can do that. However, in order to get regional and national data to compare to, you will need to use the services of a company that compiles that information, as it would just be too expense and labor intensive to try and gather that information on your own. For example, one of the online services charges approximately $300 for a detailed report and ranking score for a property. There is no doubt that you would spend a lot more than that in time and fees to generate that same information if you did the work yourself. Ensure that your return on investment makes sense before you set out to go it alone.

Third-party Resources

Additional online resources that you might find helpful in your security risk assessment project planning may include a number of the sites listed below. You will need to decide which sites, if any, are applicable, and research them to determine whether or not they have information that you might need (listed in alphabetical order).

- ASIS International (www.asisonline.org)
- Bureau of Justice Statistics (www.bjs.gov)
- Bureau of Labor Statistics (www.bls.gov)
- Centers for Disease Control and Prevention (www.cdc.gov)
- City-Data (www.city-data.com)
- Centers for Medicaid and Medicare Services (www.cms.gov)
- Crime Reports (www.crimereports.com)
- Crime Statistics (www.fedstats.gov)
- CSO Online (www.csoonline.com)

- Disaster Recovery Journal (www.drj.com)
- Energy Information Administration (www.eia.doe.gov)
- Environmental Protection Agency (www.epa.gov)
- Federal Bureau of Investigation (www.fbi.gov)
- Federal Communication Commission (www.fcc.gov)
- Federal Emergency Management Agency (www.fema.gov)
- Federal Energy Regulatory Commission (www.ferc.gov)
- Federal Trade Commission (www.ftc.gov)
- Government Accountability Office (www.gao.gov)
- Healthcare Information and Management Systems Society (www.himss.org)
- HIPAA—Health Insurance Portability and Accountability Act of 1996 (www.hhs.gov/ocr/privacy)
- International Association for Healthcare Security & Safety (www.iahss.org)
- Identity Theft Assistance Center (www.identitytheftassistance.org)
- Identity Theft Statistics (www.creditinfocenter.com/identity/id-theft-stats)
- Insurance Information Institute (www.iii.org)
- National Committee on Vital and Health Statistics (http://www.ncvhs.hhs.gov)
- National Council for Prescription Drug Programs (www.ncpdp.org)
- National Counterterrorism Center (www.nctc.gov)
- National Cyber Security Alliance (www.staysafeonline.org)
- National Fire Protection Association (www.nfpa.org)
- National Incident Management Systems (www.fema.gov)
- National Institute of Justice (www.nij.gov)
- National Institute of Standards and Technology (www.nist.gov)
- National Nuclear Security Administration (www.nnsa.doe.gov)
- OPE Campus Security Statistics (www.ope.ed.gov)
- USA.com (www.usa.com)
- U.S. Dept. of Health and Human Services (www.hhs.gov/ocr/hipaa)
- U.S. Geological Survey (www.usgs.gov)
- U.S. Postal Inspection Service (www.uspis.gov)
- Uniform Crime Report (www.fbi.gov/about-us/cjis/ucr/ucr)
- U.S. Department of Justice (www.doj.gov)
- U.S. Department of Labor (www.osha.gov)
- U.S. Department of the Treasury (www.treasury.gov)
- U.S. Nuclear Regulatory Commission (www.nrc.gov)
- U.S. Federal Transit Administration (www.transit-safety.volpe.dot.gov/data/samis.aspx)

Court Records

Depending on the extent and reach of your security assessment, online court records may also be a resource that you refer to as part of your planning or research phase. In most cases you can access these files at no cost at the courthouse in your area. For those cases where you are gathering information for a site that you do not presently work at, in the case of security consultants, you may need to pay for this online research depending on the government agency that retains the information.

For the standard security risk assessment you will likely not need to access these types of records. However, if you are including workplace violence historical data at the request of the administration, and there has been a past incident that you are reviewing, you may certainly need to know what is in the court records. Remember that court records are public records, so they may not include all of the information that an internal entity of the organization may have. So when it comes time to write the security risk assessment report, it is best to keep this in mind so you do not disclose any confidential information in your report that may become public, without first consulting with your administrative contact.

STAFF SURVEY

A survey of the organization's staff is an effective way to acquire information that would take forever to congregate if you had to interview a decent sampling of staff. These types of surveys can be completed on paper or online. To plan this type of research and information gathering, remember to keep your questions short and to the point. In other words, ensure that the survey does not require a lot of time to complete, or you may find that people will not complete it.

If you are going to use a paper form to conduct the survey, keep it to one page. For online surveys, the easiest way to measure your survey size is by the number of questions. In both cases keep your questions to no more than 10, and ensure that they are true/false or multiple choice. You can include a comment section in the event that the person wants to elaborate on their answers. Ensure that your questions are clear and direct and that you are using simple language (e.g., no jargon) that survey participants will understand. The types of questions you use will determine what kind of information is collected. In essence, do not lead your respondents to answering questions a particular way based on the words used or question's configuration.

The main concern with the paper form survey is the fact that they may not get returned even if the person completes it. You will also have to consider the fact that some handwriting is not easy to read, and that you will still need to tabulate the results into a spreadsheet or other tool in order to develop relevant data (i.e., charts and graphs). This type of survey can be very labor intensive, and again staff may either not complete it or forget to return it to you when it is completed.

Online surveys are often the preferred tool to use for surveys, as they offer a quick means to complete the survey, and when they are completed they will often automatically be returned to you without the employee taking any action other than clicking their mouse. Another great feature using the online survey is that you can often set it up to generate reports that can include the charts and graphs needed for your final assessment report.

There are some other issues regarding staff surveys that I want to caution you about. First, in many large corporations there may be an issue with security staff not being able to send e-mails to *all* company staff. What I have found is that this is fast becoming the rule, where it was the exception just a few short years ago. What this means to you is that you may not be able to send out a survey, either paper or online link, without first obtaining authorization within your organization. As a security consultant who uses online surveys in most cases, this has caused numerous issues with getting the surveys in the employees' hands or in their e-mail inbox. You may be able to get around this restriction by speaking with your administrators or IT department.

The other issue that you may experience is when your legal or compliance department does not want the survey conducted. When this happens it may have to do with discovery of issues later down the road in the event that the organization has a pending legal case. For those security practitioners conducting the security risk assessment internally, this may not ever come up. However, for security consultants this problem has been an issue. The only way to really explain it is that there may be an undisclosed confidentiality or labor issue, or they do not want the survey results documented.

If you plan on conducting a staff survey to get their feedback into your security program, you can make the survey in-house with the assistance of the IT department. They can often take your questions and place the survey on a webpage located on your organization's intranet so that it remains secure and controlled internally. I have used this method in the past with great results, and in most cases there is no expense other than time needed to complete this survey. If you use an outside source to generate, send, tabulate, and prepare the final data, you may be looking at a one-time expense for this service.

When preparing your questions for surveys, keep them to one sentence if at all possible. Multiple choice questions are often better than true/false questions, as they require more thought to answer. This is not the time or place to seek out warm and fuzzy responses with your questions, because you really want to find out the staff's true perception of the security, good or bad, and use that information to either validate or improve your program's effectiveness. This is one of those areas where impartiality is important, and you must write the questions in an unbiased manner.

Following are sample workplace violence questions that you can ask that will not steer a person to respond in any certain way. Remember, you are seeking their honest input, and you do not want to infer that there is a security problem.

- Have you been a victim of workplace violence? (define *workplace violence* as per your policy)
- If you have experienced workplace violence while at work, did you formally report the occurrence(s) to management?
- Do you feel that workplace violence has increased, remained the same, or decreased over the past year?
- Overall, do you feel safe at work, including inside and outside of the building?

Once you have generated the survey, sent it out to staff, and received their replies, it is then time to put that information to use in determining the staff's security concerns. Do not take personal any comments that they make, and watch for those results that are all positive or all negative. There are resources online that can help you develop your questions, or you can choose from pre-certified questions, so that you can ensure that you are getting proper results.

PROJECT INTERVIEWS

Staff and management interviews are essential when conducting the security risk assessment. As mentioned in Chapter 4, you cannot conduct this assessment in a vacuum, and you really need to speak to people throughout the process.

In preparing for your assessment, you will need to identify who will be interviewed, and plan on conducting random interviews as you walk the property. You will also need to have your questions ready to go, and it is this information gathering phase that is the best time to prepare those questions.

Since time is usually not endless, you should not plan on asking dozens of questions in your interviews. In fact, you will likely spend more time listening to the responses to your initial questions and conducting follow-up questions. Although I will always have a series of questions ready to ask, the reality is that my preplanned questions are a very small portion of any interview. In most cases I am interested in getting the conversation going and then allowing it to proceed without interruption if possible. There have been some cases where I asked only a few initial questions and the main part of the interview was listening and asking follow-up questions to their comments.

For example, during one security assessment at a large hospital, I was meeting with the emergency department management and physicians. I started the interview by stating my intent and purpose for the meeting. At that point there was an explosion of emotions from the hospital staff, and some very insightful information was shared. Unfortunately, the security director who was present in the room took a lot of heat during this meeting; he remained quiet and let me manage the entire process. The comments made by the management and physicians were relevant, although very emotionally charged, and my response was to steer their energy to an outcome-based process and away from personal attacks. For me the process was much like filtering out the irrelevant information and trying to determine what the real issues were.

There are always those people within the organization that complain a lot about security, and often when I am onsite I hear all about them. My approach is that I want to talk to them even though the management representatives may prefer that I do not. My feeling is that I need to know what the critics of security have to say so that I can address their concerns. Granted, I have to first determine whether or not their complaints or concerns are valid and not based on past run-ins with security staff. For those security practitioners that conduct their own security risk assessments, they may often just ignore these types of complainers and not give them the time of day. I am not saying that anyone can change someone's perception of security if they have a serious lack of confidence in the security program. However, I have been very successful in changing perceptions of this type of person provided I give them time to air their grievances and offer them constructive feedback and choices.

In one organization where I was conducting an assessment I was told about a security officer who complains about everything, and he was known to be very resistant to change. Even though he did not come to work until the night shift, I stuck around on my own time to talk to him because I really wanted to understand what made a person like this so bitter.

At first our meeting started out where he was sitting down with his arms and legs crossed; these were nonverbal clues that he was not interested in participating in the process. I am not the type to give up very easily, so I kept at it until I could find some common ground that we both could relate to. Once we were there, and we shared a few laughs, he opened up and discussed his concerns. In the end he seemed almost relieved to have gotten all of that baggage off of his back, and throughout the rest of the assessment he was a great resource for me. It is my belief that had the organization's management taken the time to do the same thing that I did, they may have been able to resolve this employee's bitterness and mistrust at a much earlier time.

Remember this, although you will plan whom you want to interview, you must also plan to conduct random interviews as well. There is not an assessment where I do not ask several staff people at random points throughout the process a few questions. The numbers of these interviews are strictly based on the project timeline, what departments I am in, and what issues are being raised.

If I had to quantify the number of random interviews, it would be in the neighborhood of 10–15%. I have to keep in mind that staff have a job to do, so in some cases I may only get to ask a person one or two questions before they have to return to their duties.

With the information gathering process completed, we will now move into conducting the actual assessment. Keep in mind that the previous information is a guide, and you may actually do things differently based on your business type and preferences. As you move into conducting the security risk assessment, you may need to make additional changes. As I have already said numerous times, there is no standard way that all security practitioners conduct these assessments, as everyone seems to have a different style and approach. The common goal is to identify the risks and vulnerabilities and develop a strategy to minimize or eliminate those issues.

CHAPTER 6

Physical Security Assessment

At this point, you have completed your preassessment planning and have either made the decision to conduct the assessment internally or retain the services of an independent security consultant for this project. As part of this preplanning, you have also completed your documentation review, defined your project's scope, and identified the participants. In essence, you have laid your foundation for the project and it is now time to get the physical assessment, the boots-on-the-ground phase, underway.

If you have planned everything well, you should have a firm schedule to work from, and all participants will be ready for their participation as the time comes. Keep in mind that the best-laid plans can get derailed due to an emergency, so be ready to make adjustments as you proceed. Remember also that many people have adjusted their schedules to participate in this assessment as per your request, so it is in everyone's best interest to keep the project going barring any critical emergency. We all know that things happen, so consider having a plan in place in which you can delegate someone else to handle anything that comes up so that you and your team can stay on task for the duration of this phase of the assessment.

If you have retained a security consultant to perform this assessment, there will likely be plenty of time for you as the security director to step away and handle any crisis while the assessment continues. I am not sure if there has ever been a security risk assessment that I was conducting where the security representatives did not have to excuse themselves to deal with an important issue. In those cases, I was able to adjust my routine to keep things moving without any interruptions. In fact, several times in each assessment I will let the security director know that if they need to take care of something it is okay, because the reality is that they do not need to be present for every minute of the assessment. However, keep in mind that if you are conducting this security risk assessment internally and you step away, your project will likely come to a halt and this may be an issue for you and your team.

63

KICKOFF MEETING

In most cases, a security risk assessment will commence with a meeting of some type. Many times this meeting is referred to as the "kickoff" meeting, as it signals the start. The attendees of this meeting should be the key people of the project, and the meeting itself sets the tone and final schedule of the assessment.

The people normally at this meeting can include numerous different representatives from throughout the organization, such as:

- Security management
- An administrative representative
- Risk management
- A safety officer
- Department heads from security-sensitive areas
- A law enforcement representative
- In specialized industries, you may also include representatives from your strategic partners.

The key point to remember about who will attend is that you need to decide who has an important role in this assessment process, and ensure that they are at the table for the initial meeting. More importantly, you do not want this meeting to fill an auditorium either, so your discretion is important.

Ideally speaking a kickoff meeting would be less than 15 people and should not take more than 1 hour to complete. Your goal with this meeting is to bring the key players together to reaffirm the project's intent and scope, and to address any last-minute issues before the team commences the physical assessment. If you have retained a security consultant to perform the security assessment, they will often manage this meeting for you.

Once you have reaffirmed the project's scope and intent, there may be new issues that are identified during this meeting. This is very common as someone in attendance may ask that you also look at a previously unidentified security concern, or they may ask why you have not mentioned a security issue that had been identified in the past yet not mentioned in the scope. You will need to be ready for such topics and discussions, and you must also be ready to speak to them at that meeting to some degree. This is not to say that you will change your project's scope at that moment when something else is thrown onto the table, because what comes to light in the meeting may in fact be something that is already within your scope, just not individually identified. The best way to handle any new issues that come up at this meeting, or to address anything else that is not planned, is to ensure that you and everyone else is clear on what the issue is and agree to address it during the assessment if possible and time allows.

If you have planned your project well, there should be few if any surprises at this meeting, and those that do arise should be respectfully noted. It has been my experience that when you open this meeting you need to state the purpose and intent of the security risk assessment and your words must instill confidence. If you allow this meeting to get sidetracked, you may find that your entire project's scope will change, as will your schedule.

In kickoff meetings that I have held, I normally take 15–30 min to explain the project's scope, intent, and schedule, and then I will open the floor to questions and discussions. If those in the room have that 8 a.m. blank look on their faces, I will ask questions of them that get the conversation going. It is often the case that once the conversation is underway you will have to carefully watch the clock because time will fly by and you may exceed 1 hour without realizing it.

At these or any other meetings, you need to take good notes. No one can mentally recall everything that is said in a meeting, so either take the notes yourself or ask that someone else in the room do it for you. If you ask that someone else take notes, be sure to let them know how you want the notes recorded. For example, you would likely want the comments noted as close to word for word as possible, the names and titles of those making the comments, and any other pertinent information.

In some cases, people have digitally recorded these types of meetings. If you were to do this, ensure that everyone knows it is being recorded. There is often information shared in these meetings that may be sensitive in nature, and you may be required to offer full disclosure that a recording is being made. Keep in mind that state laws vary, and there may be restrictions on recording conversations.

There are times when numerous meetings are held throughout a security risk assessment project. In some cases, I have had clients ask for daily briefings, at the beginning or end of each day, where any issues identified that day or the previous day will be addressed. Oftentimes the meetings may be as simple as the project managers getting together for a few minutes before they start the day, or for a few minutes at the end of the day. These types of meetings are normally informal in nature. If these extra meetings are a part of your project, you will need to schedule them and plan for a meeting location.

INTERVIEWS

The most important thing that you can do when you are interviewing anyone as part of this security risk assessment is to listen to their comments and concerns. This means that you have to take the time to hear what they are saying without interruptions. We all know the importance of listening, yet it is very common for people to interrupt someone else in a conversation.

When you are sitting down with someone, or a small group of people, it is your job to get the conversation going and keep it going, but also to keep it on track. Before the meeting, you should have a list of questions that are related to the department or service that you are meeting about. The best scenario is to conduct the greetings so everyone at the table knows each other, and then ask questions to get people to start talking. This process may be difficult for some people, and that is where the list of questions will come in handy.

Questions should be open ended so that you will get participants to give more than a yes or no answer. In some cases, you may just get blank stares from those at the table, which means that you will have to work a little harder. Once you get the conversation going, do not interrupt it unless you need to redirect participants to get back on subject. At that point, you should be taking notes and identifying comments that you want additional information on for clarification, but you should not stop the conversation just yet. I have found that the best way to get the information that you are looking for is to listen for it in what the participants are saying. If you stop them several times so that you can clarify a point, they may lose their thought process and forget to mention some critical information.

If you are the project manager, you may find that the people that you are speaking with may not be fully open and honest with their comments. This may be because they do not want to complain to you or about your department. That is an inherent risk of conducting an assessment in-house, but you can work around it with probing questions. Keep in mind that you may be uncomfortable with their comments, because they may be critical of your program, but you really need to listen to what they have to say. No matter how much you may want to correct their thinking, it is best to let them state their opinions without interruption. Of course, you will want to take notes for follow-up, and make sure that when it comes times to ask them follow-up questions, you do not come across as defensive. This is not the time or place to explain your program or management style; more so, it is the fact-finding phase and you must be willing to hear the facts according to them.

If someone tells you that everything is great and they have no security concerns, I would recommend that you do not give up so easily. During a typical security assessment, I hear that several times, yet I never accept that response without several attempts to verify that they truly feel that way. In other words, there are some people that sincerely make this comment, but it has been my experience that the majority of staff has something to say and you have to work to get them to speak up.

Throughout the entire interview process, whether it is a one-on-one or group meeting, it is important that you listen for the true meaning of the comments made and get clarification before the meeting is over. There will be times when you can sense that there is an important issue that needs to be addressed but the person making the comment will not share more details in a group setting. When you find yourself in such a situation, take note of the person's name and title and arrange for a private time to discuss their concerns.

One final example on conducting interviews is asking random staff for a few minutes of their time to talk about security. Of course, you should let management know you will be doing this. My normal practice is to let management know at the kickoff meeting that I will be doing this and that I will keep the random interviews to one or two questions. This type of interview, like most others, can be a challenge if you are conducting the security assessment in-house. The key to them is be open minded and nondefensive, and most of all a good listener.

Independent security consultants will often find it much easier to get staff to talk openly and candidly. They are not on staff at the organization, so there is no preestablished loyalty. At the beginning of most conversations, I always tell those that are present that what they say is confidential. I am interested in what they have to say, and I will not use their names with their comments in most cases. Consultants have an important role in gathering the information and documenting it when applicable. One benefit of an independent security consultant conducting the assessment is the fact that they are not a part of the security department; therefore, staff are more likely to speak candidly to them versus someone from within the organization. This is important when you have someone that is very critical of the security department or management because a security consultant can often determine the true issues and take all of the emotions out of the equation.

CONDUCTING THE ASSESSMENT

As part of the security risk assessment, you will likely be covering a lot of ground inside and outside of all buildings, and may be even some site visits off the main campus. The order in which you conduct the physical assessment is not important in most cases other than the fact that, for example, you cannot conduct an exterior lighting assessment during the daylight hours. I have found that planning the walking assessment very much depends on the type and size of the facilities. Weather may also have an impact on your schedule when it comes to the exterior assessment, yet that is an easy adjustment to make if needed. You need to determine what process works best for you and your timeline, and proceed when you are ready.

The following picture (Figure 6.1) is of a form that I have used in the past to document important parts of the actual site inspection. Although this is one of many pages that I have designed and used, it is shown as an example of the things you will look for during your assessment.

DEPARTMENT	BUILDING NAME:				
DATE		TIME	WEATHER		LIGHTING DAYLIGHT/DARK
CONTACT NAME:			CONTACT	CELL:	OFFICE:
DEPARTMENT:			PHONE		

LIGHTING:

EXTERIOR LIGHTING:	MOTION PHOTOCELL SWITCH	FIXTURES AT ENTRANCE/EXIT: YES / NO	
LIGHTING CONDITION:		FIXTURES IN REACH:	Y / N
ALL LIGHTS WORKING: Y / N	NO. NON-OP:	LOCATION:	
ENTRANCE / EXIT LIGHT WATTAGE (IF KNOWN): FRONT	SIDE	REAR	
LIGHTING NOTES:			

WINDOWS:

ALARMED: Y / N	TYPE:	NOTES:	
SECURE:	LEVEL: G 2 3 4 5	NOTES:	
SINGLE PANE: Y / N	DUAL PANE: Y / N	GENERAL CONDITION:	
SCREENS: TORE MISSING N/A	SCREENS NOTES:		
GLASS: BROKEN MISSING	GLASS NOTES:		
WINDOWS COVERED BY LANDSCAPING MATERIALS: Y / N	NOTES:		

EXTERIOR DOORS:

EXTERIOR DOORS: HOLLOWCORE SOLID WOOD STEEL	WINDOWS IN DOORS: Y / N		
EXTERIOR DOOR LOCKS: DEADBOLTS (S OR D)	GLASS RISK: Y / N	LOCKING KNOBS Y / N	TAMPERING Y / N
DELAYED EGRESS: Y / N	HOW MANY DOORS:	CARD ACCESS OVERRIDE: Y / N	REMOTE RELEASE: Y / N
DO LOCKS GET CHANGED WHEN KEY IS REPORTED LOST OR STOLEN? Y / N			

EMPLOYEE WORK SPACE

LOUNGE? Y / N	ALARMS: Y / N	SECURE ROOM? Y / N	WPV HISTORY? Y / N
LOCKERROOM Y / N	CO-ED Y / N	SHRED BOX/BIN? Y / N	NOTES:
EVACUATION PLAN? Y / N	CCTV Y / N	NOTES:	

LOCKS / KEYS

ARE ALL KEYS ACCOUNTED FOR? Y / N	CHANGE LOCKS WHEN LOST/STOLEN Y / N	TYPE OF KEYS
ACCESS CONTROL IS USE? Y / N	DEADBOLTS (SINGLE/DOUBLE) UNIT DOORS: Y / N	
LOCKS/KEYS NOTES:		

PARKING

OFF-STREET PARKING: Y / N	LIGHTED: Y / N	FENCED: Y / N
STREET PARKING: Y / N	BIKE RACK: Y / N	
PARKING NOTES:		

VISITOR CONTROLS:

CHECK-IN REQUIRED: Y / N	ID REQUIRED: Y / N	LIMITED VISITORS: Y / N
ESCORTED: Y / N	REGISTRATION: Y / N	PHOTOS: Y / N

GENERAL NOTES:

FIGURE 6.1 Sample information gathering form for security risk assessments.

BUILDING EXTERIOR

For the exterior of a property, it is best to break it down into sections. By that, I mean if you are conducting an assessment on a campus that covers the equivalent of six city blocks, you may want to break down that area into a more manageable size. I have found that separating the exterior into sections (e.g., parking, common areas, building exteriors) makes it easier to track your progress and be more efficient with your time and efforts. You can chose to start at the campus perimeter and work your way inward as well, but again it is whatever works best for you.

Over the years, I have found that large campuses need to be divided up into smaller parcels so that I can plan my time better. If there are multiple buildings on a campus, I will schedule them individually so that I again know how much time is needed. I may or may not share my schedule's finer details with my clients because such details are not relevant in most cases. As an example, my project schedule may show 4 hours of time scheduled for the exterior survey, but not exactly how I am going to use that time.

Walking the exterior of a building can go rather quickly depending, of course, on the size of the building. Normally, I find it is best to start and end at the main entrance of the building. With that in mind, let us get started with the exterior assessment.

Starting at the main entrance you will be looking for all security related issues and concerns. For example, you will look at doors, locks (windows and doors), mechanical equipment, landscaping, access control issues, traffic patterns (pedestrian and vehicular), and any signs of criminal activity or policy violations.

Exterior Doors

When looking at the exterior doors, you want be certain that they are closing on their own, and if they are supposed to be locked, that they are in fact locked. While conducting a security assessment last year, I found that 20% of the exterior doors to a large high-rise building were not secured even though their policy required that they were to be locked and checked several times during each shift. Some of the doors had been unlocked for so long that the locks were rusted open, which of course was an embarrassment to the security management who thought their staff was making rounds.

Other concerns with exterior doors could include the type of doors, for example, hollow-core versus solid, and are the door hinges exposed so that anyone could remove the hinge pins and take the door off? Looking for signs of tampering is also important, such as pry marks around the door lock. You should be pulling on each door handle to ensure that the door is secured and also that the hardware will not come off in your hands, because that does happen! Look around the door for security risks because you may find a hidden key close by, or there may be a brick or rock in the vicinity. Now you may be asking what a brick or rock has to do with the security assessment? Finding such items near a door is almost always a sign that someone is propping that door open at times, which may be defeating your security measures.

At each door, look around 360° to see what other security risks you may find. Are there hiding spots where staff may be concealing company supplies to pick up later after their shift? If the door has a keypad on it, is the access code written anywhere around the door, such as on the doorframe? Each exterior door should get the same scrutiny as you walk the campus.

Windows

Windows are also a potential security risk for a business, because in many cases windows are accessible at ground level. The fact of the matter is that windows can often be your most vulnerable portal because most of them do not have alarms on them, and they are often found to be unlocked.

Many buildings have windows that can be opened for ventilation if needed and therein lies the problem. If staff open a window for ventilation during the day, they may close it before they leave, but often they forget to lock it. Most security rounds are not made within locked offices and work spaces, but even if they were, most security officers do not check windows to ensure that they are locked. When you are walking the exterior of the building, you should check to see if you can open a window from the outside. In those cases where a window is not at ground level, but within reach, you will want to check the windows when you are conducting the interior assessment.

Other issues to watch concerning windows are the signs of tampering or pry marks. If you find screens that have been cut, you need to get those repaired as soon as possible. Privacy issues may also be a concern with windows. For example, when conducting an exterior assessment at a medical center back in 2005, I was able to see patient names and medical conditions on a marker board that was visible to the public sidewalk outside of the medical unit. This of course is a HIPAA (The Health Insurance Portability and Accountability Act of 1996) violation and was addressed immediately by the medical center.

Landscaping

All along the exterior of most buildings you will almost always find plants and trees that may be a security risk. Trees may present an issue of a path to the building's roof or higher floors. Bushes and shrubbery may offer areas of concealment. The review of landscaping is an important aspect of the security risk assessment, and often the easiest fix to make for the least amount of money. Although landscaping in many cases adds to the campus appeal, it can also make the campus feel unsafe if not properly placed and maintained.

Landscaping needs to be well trimmed and maintained throughout the year. If you cannot see behind a bush, it is probably time to trim it. The easiest way to look at this is that if you cannot see someone standing or kneeling behind the bush, you need to take corrective action. Pay special attention to landscaping around walkways, windows, and entrances/exits, as you will want to reduce the hiding places in areas where pedestrians walk.

Fencing

Not all building or properties will have fencing, but if your campus does have it you need to look for any security issues related to the fence and gates.

Start by determining the intent of the fencing. Is it really needed, and, if so, is it effective? Over time, fencing has been installed and removed as a result of different needs and circumstances. In many cases it is installed as a result of past security incidents or the threat of such. The original intentions may have been good, but over time those reasons may no longer be a concern, or in some cases the existing fencing may no longer offer enough security.

Take, for example, an apartment building that installed a fence 10 years ago because of a crime problem in the neighborhood. However, over the last few years, the area has been cleaned up with new construction and effective police patrols, and the entire dynamics of the area have changed for the better. Yet the apartment building still has that fence, and at this point it looks out of place and gives the impression that the complex might be unsafe.

Fencing is not common in most business districts unless those districts are in a high crime area. The intent is often to control access into and out of a site, yet oftentimes you will find fencing only on a few sides of the property, not all the way around it. The fact of the matter is that fencing is used more in residential areas than in business properties.

Parking areas may have fencing around them if they are for employees only and you are trying to restrict access to the lot. It has been my experience that this is more common in the inner-city areas than in the suburbs or small communities. When speaking with property owners about their reasons for fencing, they often state that they want to keep certain people or vehicles out of the lots. However, I often find that the entire lot is not fenced, the gates are either not working or left in the open position, or there is a way to get around the gates. One such client had several surface lots and almost all of them had fencing on three sides, yet the back side was not fenced. They also had pedestrian gates going into the lots, yet the gates were often propped open or not locked. Therefore, their intent was to keep certain people out, yet there was no way to achieve this intent to any degree of certainty. One of the questions that they had for me was whether or not they should fence in some newer parking lots. My response was simply, why? You will spend well over $100,000, and you will still not be securing the parking lots.

Fencing can be a deterrent, and is often used as a crime prevention through environmental design (CPTED) feature, but you need to carefully review your intent and security needs before you go to the expense of fencing in an area.

Criminal Activity

As you are conducting both the interior and exterior security assessments, you need to be looking for signs of criminal activity. On the outside that may be signs of gang activity such as tagging or graffiti. Other signs to look for are abandoned cars that may actually be stolen cars. Often during exterior assessment I will find signs of drug activity, namely hypodermic needles, small pieces of tin foil that may have burn marks on them, or even signs of a mobile meth lab. You may be walking over some very important warning signs and at first glance may think it is nothing more than litter.

About 10 years ago while walking a parking structure at a medical center in the Midwest, I came across items that to most people would be just trash. However, in an area of about 150 square feet I located all of the ingredients needed to make meth. It was obvious that someone had been cooking meth in a mobile meth lab and threw their trash out before they left. Since parking structures are often very busy places with cars coming and going at all hours, we were not able to identify what car left the trash behind, even after reviewing the security video of that area.

Another client property was adjacent to an older apartment building, and according to the client's security there were a lot of drug users living in the apartments. We surveyed the client's property and located numerous syringes behind the shrubs between the buildings. When security was asked what they are doing to address this problem, they only commented that there is nothing they can do. Really? Can't they increase their security presence? Can they work with law enforcement or the apartment building's management? Can they remove the shrubs or at least trim them back? Sure, there are plenty of things that you can do if this is happening on your property. The worst thing you can do is accept it as a way of life and do nothing.

When conducting the security risk assessment, you need to look for the obvious and not so obvious, and then determine a plan of action to mitigate any identified issues.

Parking Areas

Parking areas are often the areas where most crimes will occur outside a building. Whether the property is a school campus, retail store, medical center, or industrial area, there is an inherent risk with parking areas due to the fact that there are people in them, oftentimes alone, and there are vehicles that will often contain valuables.

Burglaries of cars are probably the most common crime in parking areas, followed by other crimes like car theft, vandalism, and assaults on people. When you look at parking lots around malls and retail stores, you are also likely to find serious crimes such as robbery, sexual assaults, and purse snatchings. Each and every potential crime that could occur in your area needs to be evaluated for the risk.

The geographical area where the property is located also presents some unique challenges. For example, in some areas of the southwest United States, when it gets very hot outside you will often find car windows partially open. In the Midwest, it is not uncommon to see keys in the ignitions of numerous cars in parking lots. In fact, at one property I visited for an assessment I found that about 10% of the cars had the keys in the ignition and the cars were unlocked. To put this into perspective, the 10% represented over 75 vehicles.

Lighting Assessment

Exterior lighting is an important part of your security system and is one of the most important crime prevention tools that you can employ. Take, for example, using security officers for your crime prevention strategy outdoors. Let us say that you staff one security officer to patrol your building's exterior at night because you feel that the presence of the officer will be more preferable to staff than any other measure. Although staff may in fact want an officer outside, the reality is that this officer cannot be in all places at the same time, nor can they watch everything going on around them. Officers also need breaks and can become distracted when speaking with someone or driving.

Lighting, on the other hand, is always present, if used properly, and has been proven to discourage and prevent crimes from occurring. As security professionals, we know that lighting can be a deterrent to criminal activity, yet we do not always know what the proper levels should be or how to measure those levels or verify the effectiveness of it. We may also be getting pushback from others over the costs of new lighting or speaking to the return on investment of adding lights. That is why it is important to understand lighting and for you to be able to demonstrate with a degree of credibility the value that lighting will bring based on industry standards, recommendations, and best practices. Simply speaking, if you were to walk into your supervisor's office and ask for $100,000 for new lighting, you have to be prepared to qualify your request with facts.

The security industry as well as the lighting industry have both provided us with factual information for us to use as a baseline. I will address those recommendations later in this chapter, but for now I will discuss the perception of lighting.

Over the years, I have tested many theories of the perception of lighting. For example, when asked what the lighting levels should be, or if the lighting is adequate on a certain property, I will often ask what they think about their lighting. During the resulting conversation, it becomes clear that they believe that their lighting is not adequate and often state that staff complain about the poor exterior lighting. However, there have also been numerous times when I have heard from the client that their lighting levels are acceptable, yet during a preassessment campus tour the night before the assessment I have found that over 35% of the exterior lights are not working or were covered with vegetation.

I have also been to sites where the company staff are predominately males and they feel that the lighting levels are great! But then when you visit a college campus or a medical center, where females often outnumber male employees, you will often find that the females will perceive lighting levels as substandard, even if the light levels meet the industry standards. My point is that everyone has a different perspective on lighting levels, and that perception can vary due to life experiences, gender, age, and numerous other factors. With that in mind, how do we determine the proper lighting levels?

From my experience, I would suggest a hybrid approach when determining what works best for your property. In essence, you will still use the industry standards and recommendations, as well as any zoning requirements for your location, but you should also use a measurement standard based on perception.

Years ago when I was conducting a light assessment as part of an annual security risk assessment at a university, we established a small working group to conduct the light assessment. Within the group was the vice president of student services, a facilities representative, security management, and three students (one male and two females). Although we used a light meter to measure the lighting levels, our primary tool was the students' perception. In almost all cases, all of the males present thought the light levels were average-excellent, but we found that the females rated most levels as poor-average. What we found was that no matter what your light meter readings are, and how you personally feel about the light levels, staff or students may not feel safe and may insist on better lighting. Therefore, if your measurements indicate that your lighting meets standards, does that mean that you should not request improved lighting? No, it just means that you will need to make your case based on more than just the light meter readings.

When it comes time to conduct your light assessment, I always recommend that clients form a small group just like the example above. Although I always conduct my lighting assessments alone, I will always ask staff or customers that I meet during the light assessment for their opinions.

I will include in my report the findings and recommendations, and suggest that the client review my findings based on the industry recommendations as well as the results from their own team. In reality, I give them the standards and light levels, and they use those as their baseline tool only. Part of my recommendations is often to utilize the services of a lighting engineer if there is a substantial difference in the scientific measurements findings versus their team's perception. In other words, if the light measurements obtained from the meter meet the industry standards, and their team believes that those lighting levels are really substandard, it may be time to bring in a lighting engineer to review all of the information and determine the best way to resolve any differences.

In many cases an organization may not need to add any additional lighting to increase their light levels. Numerous times I have found that the issue is actually lights that are underperforming due to age of the bulb or other reasons such as the light lens (cover) will often yellow over time or can become dirty due to bugs and dirt (see Figure 6.2).

On most sites, I have found that numerous lights are not working, the timer has not been adjusted due to seasonal time changes, and lights are obstructed by trees and bushes. On one campus I found that their parking lot lights were barely casting a shadow at night, and the cause was that the bulbs were so old that they were just slowly dying. Like most everything in our world, there is a shelf life on light bulbs, and you should have a preventative maintenance plan to address the lighting. My recommendation is to conduct at least two lighting assessments per year, with the primary focus being during the winter because of the shorter daylight hours. However, either security or maintenance should check the lights regularly to locate any lights that have burned out and make repairs promptly.

FIGURE 6.2 Discolored light cover.

The locations of lights are also important. Basically, you need to ensure that the lighting is in the areas where it is needed. When conducting the assessment, look to see if there are walkways or parking areas that may need improved lighting. Look for dark areas, and determine if those areas need lighting. When trying to decide if they need light, think about whether or not people walk through those areas to get from one building to another, or to get to the parking areas, dumpsters, smoke areas, and so on.

When you find an area that you believe needs additional lighting, document that area and your reasons for increasing lighting. If you are taking photographs for your report, if possible, do so without using flash because you will want to show what the area truly looks like, and your camera flash will only add artificial light to the picture.

If you are going to use a light meter, be certain that you understand how to use it, and also make sure that you use the same measurement throughout your assessment. There are two measurements often used with light meters, LUX (the unit of illuminance and luminous emittance) and foot candles. In the lighting industry, foot candles are a universal unit of measurement used to calculate acceptable lighting levels of interiors of buildings or outdoor spaces.

Finally, when conducting the light assessment, be sure to conduct your research on the best way to take measurements with a light meter. Although the recommended light levels are listed below, the proper use of a meter depends on several factors, such as the style/brand of meter and what light levels you are evaluating. Because there are so many different factors to consider, I would suggest that you speak with a lighting engineer to determine what meter will work best for you, and hopefully they can also train you in the proper use of it. Other sources of information on the use of the meters can be located in several published books and manuals available online.

Table 6.1 represents the lighting recommendations as published in *Protection of Assets: Physical Security* by ASIS International.

Finally, remember that proper lighting can improve the appearance of an area and have positive psychological effects on people in those areas and give them a better sense of security.

BUILDING INTERIOR

When conducting the security risk assessment on the building's interior, you will need to take into consideration the size, type, and use of the buildings when you are planning and executing your assessment.

For example, if you are conducting a security assessment within a big-box retail store, you are generally speaking of a large open space with additional

Table 6.1 Guidelines for Minimum Lighting Levels

Application	Minimum Lighting Levels–IES Standards (fc)	Comments/Other
Perimeter fence	0.50	NRC 0.20 fc
Outer perimeter	0.50–2.00	NRC 0.20 fc; DoAFM 0.15 fc
Open areas	2.00	
Open parking lots	0.20–0.90	IES high vehicle activity 2.00 fc
Covered parking structure	5.00	
Pedestrian walkway	0.20	IES 7.50 fc at ATMs
Pedestrian entrances	5.00	DoAFM 2.00 fc
Vehicle entrance	10.00	DoAFM 1.00 fc
Building facades	0.50–2.00	
Gatehouse	30.00	
Loading dock exterior	0.20–5.00	
Loading bay	15.00	
Office—general	30.00–50.00	
Office—task	50.00–70.00	
Interior public areas	10.00–20.00	
Retail store	50.00	
Bank—lobby	20.00	
Bank—teller	50.00	
Bank—ATM	15.00	IES 30 fc on preparation counter

IES, Illuminating Engineers Society of North America; NRC, Nuclear Regulatory Commission; DoAFM, Department of Army Field Manual; fc, foot candles.
Table used with permission of ASIS International.

shipping and receiving areas, product storage areas, office space, and maybe a few staff spaces such as locker rooms and break rooms. Also, within many large retail stores there may be separate retail services such as restaurants, hair salons, banks, and numerous other such spaces. When planning your assessment, you will need to determine what spaces are included and excluded. In most cases, the smaller retail spaces are tenants, and they may be responsible for their own security under their contracts, so if you were to also be asked to conduct an assessment within those spaces, you may need to have a separate agreement.

When it comes to other types of businesses, for example, healthcare, you will need to take into consideration the different departments and services that you will be assessing. Notably, there are some high risk areas within medical centers that will require more of your time. A manufacturing facility may also have high security areas such as their research-and-development department, and your schedule and plan must also consider this. Look at it this way, you need to know all that is being assessed and how much time it will take, and then once you get into these areas, you have to know what it is you are looking for with regard to security risks.

It has been my approach to separate internal areas into manageable segments, just as I do on the exterior. Namely, I will preidentify internal departments that will need additional time and I schedule them separately. For the rest of the building's interior, I may start on the top floor and work my way down, skipping the departments that will require extra time, and then I will come back and assess those departments individually. This approach has worked very well over the years for a number of reasons.

First, I find that in many buildings where there are multiple floors, the floors are often set up the same. For example, in a high-rise hospital or hotel, all floors above the second or third floor may be identical, so conducting a security risk assessment tour on those floors can go fairly quickly. If there is a department or area on one of the upper floors, such as a bar and restaurant on the top floor, I would assess that floor separately within the overall project. Basically, the approach is to use the project's time efficiently and yet cover all areas using the time needed as required. This reduces the chance that the project schedule will get off course.

When walking each floor or department, you will be looking for security risks or vulnerabilities. Again, it is best to have a plan for an interior security risk assessment so that you are not just wandering aimlessly throughout the building.

Start by looking at the entrance to the work space—is the security level of the entrance appropriate? During a medical center security risk assessment in the past, I entered the pharmacy from the staff entrance and found the entrance to have a very high level of security technology. For those that do not know about the security of pharmacies within medical centers, this department often has some of the highest security levels for a hospital. However, even though the staff entrance was very secure, I found that the department's main entrance door was wedged open and there were no security measures in place. Also, in the department I located the keys to the narcotics storage room in the door's lock and staff were not present. Again, this was a very substantial security risk. It was only after I mentioned the main entrance and the narcotics room security issues a few times that security took steps to mitigate the risks. My point is that you need to be looking for security risks and vulnerabilities, and address them immediately based on their risk level.

Also at the entrance you may have a counter where staff greet others and assist them as needed. Look at this counter and determine if the counter height is sufficient. If this space has security risks, such as the potential for verbal or physical confrontations with customers or staff, is the counter height so low that someone can reach or jump over it? I have spoken to many staff members working behind counters such as this, and there are almost always comments made like

"I do not feel safe." When I ask the employees why, they tell me of times where people have reached across the counter and assaulted them or damaged equipment. At one business that I was assessing, the staff told me that several times people have jumped the counter and chased the staff. If these issues are possible at your organization's facilities, you need to both evaluate the potential risks and identify corrective actions to reduce or eliminate the risks.

When it comes to doors and locks, you will need to determine if the doors need to be locked at all times or just at certain times. You may find that management of a certain department will not want the door locked during business hours, yet they or their staff may complain that unauthorized people enter their work spaces. Often this is more of a staff convenience issue of not wanting the door secure, yet the fact that the door is not locked causes the security risks that they are complaining about. This is where you need to have conversations to determine if there is a better way to manage this.

Internal Traffic Flow

Regarding internal traffic flow, there are several factors to consider, but basically the point is to look at how staff and customers flow throughout your facilities and determine if the flow patterns are properly managing your security risks or adding to them.

One of the easiest ways to explain this is to use an example that everyone has likely experienced more than one time. What I am referring to is when you go to the doctor or hospital for medical treatment. You are always met at the door to the treatment areas when your name is called and you are escorted to a particular room or treatment area. Once you have been seen and treated by medical staff, you are almost always allowed to find your own way out. To put it in simple terms, they control your entry and do very little to control your exit. In one emergency room, I heard numerous complaints about patients and family members entering offices and closed-off areas of the department, yet when staff explained their flow patterns and processes, it became clear that they controlled inbound flow but patients were on their own to find their way out.

If your business has a similar setup, you should take another look at the risks associated with such a protocol. You may not be a medical office, but if you control access to departments such as Human Resources, yet you do not manage their exit, you have the same issue. Only your organization can determine the proper traffic flow and intent, as well as how you will manage both, but you as a security professional need to be able to determine the security risks associated with the organization's plan and address them both during your assessment and ongoing. The most common pushback you will likely experience will be the staff convenience concern—that is where management or staff will not want to spend the extra time to walk someone out. You, however, can determine the risks and make a qualified recommendation based on past incidents, staff complaints, industry standards, and best practices.

Stairwells and Elevators

Stairwells are required by building and fire codes, yet in today's world, they can be the least used means of traversing from one floor to another. In some facilities, staff are encouraged, or may be even required, to use the stairs versus elevators. However, in most high-rise buildings, the preferred method to get from one level to the next is the elevator, even by security officers.

More and more you will find that stairs may be controlled by security so that once you enter the stairwell the only exit option you might have is the ground floor. This is to keep unauthorized people from entering work spaces on floors that they have no business being on. In some cases, you will find card readers on each level of the stairwells so that if you have authorization to enter that floor you can do so.

Elevators, on the other hand, are widely used, and this can be due to time management practices or just the convenience factor. Since elevators are in all high-rise buildings, you may often find that your staff would prefer this method of travel versus climbing the stairs. So what risks or vulnerabilities are associated with both means of travel? Simply put, stairs are your biggest security risk due to many different reasons. First, though, let us look at the elevators and what security risks are associated with them.

Elevators in most buildings are not controlled, meaning that once you are on the elevator you can likely get to any floor. There is a trend where access control may be installed into elevators during new construction so that a business can control floor access rights all the time, or just after hours. Although many high-rise buildings would prefer to have this option in place now for existing buildings, the costs to retrofit an elevator can be in the $10,000–$50,000 range per car. The issue is that you cannot just go into an elevator car and shaft and install the controls, as elevator companies will not normally allow such measures. They will, however, work with you to install the equipment in most cases, but the costs will be high. This is the reason why during new construction or elevator upgrades or replacements you are more likely to see changes made.

Since most businesses cannot afford to upgrade their elevators, they are more likely to manage flow to floors by using staff to control traffic flow once you step off the elevators. Or, they may use facility design features such as elevator lobbies that are secure, so that once you step off the elevator you will find that all office and works space doors are secured and require some type of staff intervention to allow you into a space. Regardless of the means with which your organization controls access to work spaces, you need to review such practices and determine if there are any identified security risks.

A few possible risks may be the fact that the doors in the elevator lobbies are not secured, or maybe they are propped open (that convenience factor again). Another risk may be that those doors can be remotely unlocked by staff without knowing who is outside the door. After-hours access to floors may be the main security risk if it is not properly controlled.

The after-hours concern is centered on staff or customers that may have authorization to be on one floor after normal business hours, yet when they are leaving the building there may not be a way to control what other floors they can gain access to. This is often found in buildings that have multiple tenants, such as a high-rise with a restaurant on the top floor and several other business offices on lower floors. If you do not control the elevator's controls, you have to consider controlling each floor's after-hours access rights. Stairwells, on the other hand, often have the same issues, yet will often present more security risks and have a much higher risk factor.

Stairwells have been known to be at risk for such things as sexual assaults, falls, and homeless people living in them, as well as many other risks. Because stairs are not used nearly as often as elevators, there is a possibility that a crime or accident can occur in a stairwell and go unnoticed for hours or even days. Case in point—the recent case (September 2013) in San Francisco where a patient eloped from her hospital room. Security was called to search for the patient, which is very common in hospitals, and after what was reported as an extensive search, they were not able to locate the patient. However, 17 days later, the patient was found deceased in a stairwell. Although the facts of this case are still be determined at the time of this writing, it appears that the patient entered the stairs the day she left her room and never made it out of the stairwell. The main point is that stairwells need to be checked often by security officers as part of their rounds. If someone slips and falls in the stairwell, they could go unnoticed for an extended period of time, mainly due to the infrequency with which stairs are used in today's world. It should be part of security's routine to walk each stairwell during their shift.

When conducting the assessment, be sure that you walk into each stairwell and look for security risks on every floor. Since elevators often have a much lower rate of security incidents, I make it a practice to only use stairs to get from one level to another during an assessment. Because of this, I have located numerous security vulnerabilities within stairwells, including unsecured access to mechanical rooms and equipment, roofs, and information technology (IT) closets. I have also located fire hazards, water leaks, homeless bedding, as well as stolen items that had been stashed within stairwells to be picked up at a later time. One of the most overlooked areas in stairwells is the underside of the stairs at the ground or basement level (see Figure 6.3). This is the location where the stairs end at the lowest level, and in most cases this area is not

FIGURE 6.3 Stairwell vulnerability identified where someone can conceal themselves or stolen items.

enclosed with some type of fencing or walls. That being the case, this is where you are likely to find a homeless person's property, or stolen items.

Other areas to check while conducting the interior tour are your mechanical, storage, technology, and janitorial closets and spaces. I am always amazed with how many of these areas are not secured and are found to have several security risks. You will almost always find some type of sign on the door indicating restricted access, yet the doors are often not locked.

The security risks with these areas are many, as it only takes one unauthorized person to enter a telephone or IT room to tamper with the equipment to bring a company to its knees. Critical infrastructure such as your computer networks and telephone systems need to be secured at all times, yet during numerous assessments I have found that these spaces are unprotected. When talking to security and IT staff, I am told that they both thought the other department was monitoring the security of space, but as we know, it is often the security department that has the responsibility to maintain the security measures.

Security Sensitive Areas

Most businesses have some form of a security-sensitive area. For example, it may be the office of a retail store where cash receipts are stored or the space used to store inventory that has not been placed on the sales floor. Manufacturing facilities may have areas that are considered to be security-sensitive areas, such as research and development or product storage.

In some industries, there may be multiple security-sensitive areas. Healthcare facilities are often highly regulated and must follow federal or state laws, or accreditation standards, and because of that they may have several designated security-sensitive areas (e.g., Emergency Room, Maternity, Pediatrics, Medical Records). Whatever your business model is, and whatever you designate as a security-sensitive area, you must pay special attention to these areas as part of the security risk assessment.

When you are assessing the areas that you or your management team have identified as security sensitive, you need to look for all possible security risks associated with them. You will likely have the standard access control, key control, lighting, alarms, and so on, but you should also know what your peers are doing for similar areas and conduct your due diligence to ascertain if there are any best practices available that may address the security measures. The main point is that when you are conducting the assessment of these areas, you may need extra time, and you may also need to focus on specific security measures. Remember too that these areas will be accessed by others, some of whom may not have the proper clearance to be in those areas but are there with an escort, and you need to ensure that the security measures are appropriate and are being met.

Internal Department Controls

An important thing to keep in mind is that inside a work space there may be internal security controls in place, and you will need to assess them as well.

Internal controls may be security cameras, alarms, locks on doors and windows, or restricted access to supply closets and files. This is another one of those parts of the assessment that will be dependent on what type of business you are protecting, and where you have to have the knowledge base to draw from when you are in those areas.

If you are new to the organization, and you have not yet had the time to have one-on-one meetings with all management staff, now is the time to have that meeting and determine what security measures they have in place and where they feel their risks are. That being the case, you should ensure that some extra time is allotted for those meetings because you will need it.

One of the easiest ways to get the information that you need to fully understand the security issues of a department is to ask probing questions. I cannot begin to tell you how many times I have heard that a department had no security issues, yet with persistent probing questions, numerous concerns were identified.

Another way to assess the security of an area is to look in all spaces and behind every closed door. In the past as I was looking behind locked doors, I located access portals to the roof. When I climbed the ladder, I found a roof hatch that was not secured and had no alarm contacts on it. After climbing the ladder and going out on the roof, I found numerous means by which someone could get access to the roof from the grounds, and if they did so they could enter the building undetected.

There were many other times when checking behind closed doors that I was able to locate sensitive files that were required to be secured or access to high security areas. The main point here is that you must be willing to thoroughly search a building and/or department to ascertain any security risks even if someone tells you that there are no concerns with department. In most cases, the people telling you this information have no security background and may not know that risks are present.

The main points covered in this chapter are the general steps of a security risk assessment. Keep in mind, though, that there are numerous, different aspects of an assessment depending on the type of business and what that business is trying to protect. Before you embark on conducting the assessment, you should be familiar with all of your security measures and technology in use, and have a respectable understanding of the security risks that your program is dealing with. If not, you will likely not fully understand the program's intent, and therefore you will not understand what it is that you are evaluating and measuring for program effectiveness.

In the following chapters, we will discuss additional parts of the actual security risk assessment, and go into more detail about some of the most common findings for each part.

CHAPTER 7

Security Department Operations

The actual assessment of the security department is one of those parts of a security assessment that may or may not be included within a project's scope. Again, it really depends on whether or not the assessment is being conducted in-house or by an independent security consultant in most cases. However, I have seen internal assessment projects where there was a fairly candid appraisal of the security department operations and in no means painted a sterilized image that there were no issues. When discussing this with security management after the fact it was determined that the underlying issues were well known, and that management had all along kept their administration informed as to what the issues were and what steps were being taken to mitigate those issues. In essence, the security management had nothing to hide and therefore could be openly critical of internal operational issues.

Taking an independent look at your own department can give you a comprehensive awareness of the current state of operations, yet it is often easier to do then it is to document those findings because you may feel that documenting negative findings will reflect poorly on your management skills. As mentioned in an earlier chapter, it is always better to identify your findings before someone else does, as it gives you a better opportunity to resolve concerns and develop yourself and your department into a more professional operation.

So what is meant by conducting an assessment of your security operations? Basically, it amounts to a complete and comprehensive review of every aspect of the program. You will need to look at your budget, expenses, staffing levels, scheduling, training, equipment, leadership structure, patrol operations, your management plan, policies, post orders, and numerous other components of the program. Nothing is really off the table depending on the intent of the project's scope.

MANAGEMENT REVIEW

Over the years many clients have requested, as part of a security risk assessment, to also review the security management's qualifications, leadership abilities and style, and give an opinion on their overall management. Sometimes there have been previously identified concerns of a manager showing favoritism to some staff over others, or in a few cases the management was antagonistic toward security staff and as a result there was a serious morale problem where staff had made complaints that the workplace was "hostile." When these types of issues are prompting the assessment of the department the normal practice may be to bring in an outside security expert that can provide an unbiased assessment as to the department's operational effectiveness and internal challenges. Keep in mind that this type of assignment is dependent on the internal issues, and not all requests to review a department have the more severe underlying issues as mentioned above.

In the majority of cases when an organization's administration requests that the security management be reviewed, they are more interested in whether or not the department is being managed in the most efficient manner as possible, and this service is often just a sub-part of the overall security risk assessment. In other words, administration may just be looking to see if the operations are following industry standards or best practices. To narrow this down even further, these types of reviews are often performed in security departments that have recently hired new leadership and when the new manager does not have an extensive background in security management or risk/vulnerability assessments.

Some of my more recent reviews along this line were due to management being in an interim position and the organization wanted to get a better idea of where the department was in comparison to other similar departments. Their concerns were that the previous management had left their employment under questionable circumstances, and security's overall perception was remarkably tarnished due to past incidents within the security operations. Those employers desired to review the security department before they searched for a new manager, as they wanted to see if the department had any other internal issues that may undermine any new manager's efforts. In simple terms, they wanted to determine if there were any other underlying issues that may hinder a new manager's ability to move forward, and they wanted to see if anyone on staff such as an officer or lead officer had the abilities to manage the department.

SECURITY CULTURE

As you have likely realized by now, security management is not for everyone. Depending on the type of operation (e.g., industry type), and the security risks and vulnerabilities associated with your business type, there are a variety of management styles that encompass the security profession. In some cases the manager over security may have no security background at all and in fact may only have the responsibility over security due to the fact that they drew the short straw. On the other hand, in many companies the security manager may have an extensive background in corporate security management. The reality is that no two programs are exactly alike due to the manager's background, their management style, and the corporate culture.

A major part of the security risk assessment will depend on the corporate security culture; how important security is throughout the organization. Some companies may place very little value in security, and therefore the manager may have a minimal background in security. Years ago I observed a culture change occur where on one day security was a major part of an organization's overall culture, and the next day it was no longer important due to a new CEO or governing board. So when you are conducting a security risk assessment that will undoubtedly result in a number of recommendations, you need to understand the corporate culture's as it relates to security and how that might affect your findings.

If you are the security manager and you are conducting the assessment of your department, you should be very familiar with the company's philosophy and how security fits into it. That being said, even if your present culture is not conducive to making the needed changes to your program you should still proceed with identifying and documenting your finding.

I had the pleasure to know a security director many years ago who assumed that it was a waste of time to document his findings if they would result in increasing the budget, or having to seek capital funds. He was in many ways just going through the motions daily and not trying to make any changes, because he felt that he would be wasting his time and energy. However, one morning he arrived to work and checked his email only to discover that the person that he felt was standing in the way of progress no longer worked for the company. He was summoned to the CEO's office for a briefing and asked if there was anything that security had been trying to accomplish over the last several years but had been held back. Although he had several changes that he wanted to make over the years, he could not recall any of them at the time. So in reality he lost his opportunity to shine at that moment, and it was all because of his management style, not being proactive. Remember, things can change at any time, and if your style is to be unprepared you too may miss the opportunity to further your agenda when the moment is right.

MANAGEMENT SPAN OF CONTROL

One of the goals of the security risk assessment is to identify operational issues that may adversely impact the security department's ability to perform. What is often found in many organizations is the fact that span of control is such that the number of officers versus the number of management personnel are not properly set. The span of control often refers to the number of direct subordinates that a supervisor has. Generally speaking the proper span of control that has been widely accepted over the years is somewhere between three and 10 employees for every supervisor. That is not to say that there may not be upwards of 12–14 employees per supervisor in some organizations. Just remember that the more officers reporting to one supervisor can result in communication issues and missed opportunities.

It has been my experience to find that the span of control ratio is on average 1:10. The highest ratio I have ever come across was 1:75, and as you might imagine there were some issues with reporting and communications and there were many concerns associated with morale. Table 7.1 shows the ideal, average, and less than desirable ratios. There are ways to get around this issue, and you may have adopted some of these ways as part of your operations.

Table 7.1 Sample Span of Control

	Span of Control
Ideal	1:5
Average	1:10
Less desirable	1:15 or greater

First number represents the supervisor, and the second number represents the number of direct report staff for that supervisor.

One way to get around this is to institute lead security officer positions. Often there are budgeting reasons why a security manager cannot hire additional supervisors, yet if you are not allowed to make supervisor positions you could possibly seek approval for lead security officers. Lead officers are often paid a small percentage above the highest level of the officer pay scale (e.g., 5%), and they can take on a lot of responsibilities and improve communications. In most companies lead officers cannot discipline staff or make any hiring or firing decisions, but they can be a great resource for a manager that has a large number of direct reports. Often times it is also much easier to get a lead position approved than that of a supervisor. (See Figure 7.1 for a sample security staffing chart.) Your goal is to ensure that all officers have an easy to navigate route to address their concerns, and whatever way you get there is not as important as just getting there.

During several assessments over the years I have found that it was firmly stated upfront that there would be no chance that the number of staff would be increased as a result of the assessment findings. Almost as if I was being told, *do not bother even making that recommendation because it would go nowhere.* However, the person that is conducting the assessment has an obligation to be impartial

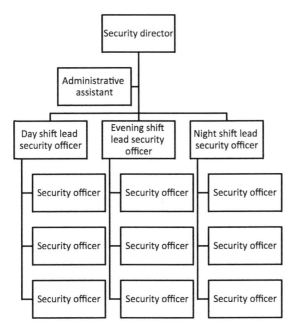

FIGURE 7.1 Sample staffing chart.

and factual with their findings, and should not omit an important part of the findings. Look at it this way, if you fail to make recommendations you are in effect implying that the current state of the program is acceptable yet in your professional opinion you may disagree. In the end you can list your findings and make the recommendations based on your professional opinions and do so in a manner that does not come across as noncompliant.

Many security departments follow the ranks and structures of law enforcement or the military. It is not uncommon to find corporals/leads, sergeants, lieutenants, captains, and chiefs in many larger security departments. Of course including all of these ranks will often only be found in very large departments, but in most security departments that have over 15 officers you will likely find at least one supervisory level other than the manager/director.

So when you are looking at your management structure look at the span on control, and insure that you have a process in place to allow for after-hours issues that the officers will be confronted with so that they know who can make a decision at that time. Otherwise you may be getting several calls at night or on your days off, or worse yet the officers will not do anything and thus your department's effectiveness could diminish over time.

It is always a good practice to insure that an employee has only one supervisor that they report to. When a member of staff has more than one supervisor that they report to they may find contradictory directives and uncertainty in their work assignments, which may result in less than desirable performance issues.

SECURITY MANAGEMENT PLAN

A management plan for the security department is often like a business plan that identifies the way your department is intended to be operated both day-to-day and over the long term. It will often illustrate the means used to design, execute, evaluate ongoing and manage the security risks for the organization's environment. Furthermore, the program is often intended to identify both general and high security risks, as well as state an organization's mitigation strategies to develop effective response procedures, and how they are intended to minimize the risk of personal injury or property loss.

A management plan often will include the typical intent, structures, and evaluating methods for the security operations, which may include the overall philosophical and intellectual structure in which these systems will function and be measured. The plan will identify the high-risk and security sensitive areas of the organization and will establish the authority of the security management to take action when a condition exists that could result in personal injury to individuals or damage to equipment or buildings. In theory the management philosophy and corporate culture of your organization defines how it views security management and how your organization intends for it to function within this plan.

In some industries you will always find a formal security management plan (e.g., healthcare) as it is often a requirement of an accreditation body. Still other types of industries may have a similar plan that may have another name but serves the same intent. If your security program has no such plan how does your department identify your program's intent, risks and mitigation strategies?

These types of plans, as well as all other operational policies and procedures should be reviewed and revised as needed as part of your security risk assessment. If you have retained the services of a security consultant to review your program they should be asking for this information as part of their project's scope. The reviewer needs some form of a baseline standard for which the organization has established as their intent for the security program, otherwise how can you ascertain if the program is effective or not.

STATUTORY AND REGULATORY REQUIREMENTS

Within the United States there are statutory requirements for security officers that may mandate licensing and backgrounds checks which will include fingerprinting. However, there are still a few states where there are no licensing requirements at all, and a person can still be hired without any training and be placed on a post the same day. Prior to September 11, 2001, the laws regarding security guards/officers were in many cases lax, yet since then many more states have adopted more stringent standards and laws regarding the security industry. However, some of the states require that only contract security officers (those that work for a security company) be licensed and proprietary officers (those that work for your company and are paid by your company) may not require a state license. The key is to know what laws apply to your operations and if you are compliant and meeting the statutory requirements.

The first step in evaluating your program is to know the laws that apply to your industry and each location in which you provide services. As an example, if your company has several locations throughout the country, you may find that officers working in one state are required to have a license, yet officers in other states may not. To a much lesser degree you may find that municipal or county ordinances may also have regulations that affect your security department.

As with most other processes to determine information needed to properly assess your requirements you can often go online and research the laws. In those states that require licensing they will have that information online as a matter of convenience. However, it may not be easy to find because the state department that oversees security licensing is not uniform across the country. For example, in California the department that regulates security is the Department of Consumer Affairs, yet in many other states security compliance falls under the Department of Public Safety.

To confuse the matter even more, the laws in which security are required to comply with can be in several different resources. Using California as an example again, security may find that the laws with which they must comply may be located within the Penal Code, Health & Welfare Code, or Business & Profession Code. Other states have similar structuring of regulations but again it comes down to knowing all of the requirements that govern your security operations.

Networking with your peers is a great way to learn the laws and requirements that are applicable to your operations, yet it is advisable to seek out more than one source in some cases. Several years back I was speaking with a security manager and I inquired as to how he was addressing the state law regarding workplace violence. There was that awkward period of silence followed by his response, what law?

In addition to security personnel being required to be licensed, some states require that the security department itself be licensed. This can often be a means in which to identify the security departments within the jurisdiction, and such registration and licensing can be the precursor to compliance audits at some future date and time. These random audits of security departments are often to verify compliance with licensing, training, and registration requirements.

SECURITY STAFF SCHEDULING

With regards to your staffing levels, are they consistent with your department's goals and identified risks? In other words, if you have identified that an area of your facility is at a higher risk for a security incident during the day hours when most people are onsite, is your staffing such that there are sufficient security officers to on duty during that time to minimize your risks? That seems like common sense, but the reality is that in some departments they staff for after-hours only and rely on other personnel to address the peak times.

Case in point, many small colleges or hospitals may have no security officers working during the day time hours, and will likely staff security officers during the evenings or overnight hours only. In reality during business hours they rely on managers or ancillary departments to handle security concerns. Staffing in this manner may actually increase your risks due to the fact that untrained personnel are performing security functions, and they likely have received no security training in managing risks or security threats.

In most cases where security is staffed only during non-business hours, it is a result of the company's culture and budget restrictions. There is often another risk associated with this staffing model that many companies have not considered, and that is the safety and security of the officer working alone at night.

More often than not there is only one security officer working the overnight shift at many businesses. This presents risks that are not identified until something goes wrong, and there is either a lapse in security or the officer suffers an injury or illness on the job. If your staffing plan is to have one officer working at night, do you have in place a plan or protocol to insure that they have arrived to work, and that they are checking in with someone during their shift? Unfortunately I have seen both issues become reality in the past.

In one case the security officer never arrived for work and several of the campus buildings were unsecured for the night. In this case it was customary of company staff to leave work without locking doors because they knew that security would be making rounds shortly and they would insure that the doors and windows were closed and secured. However, since no security officer reported for duty, the risks for this business were extremely high for at least 12 hours. Could your business survive such a lapse in security?

The other case involved a lone security officer working a large 75 acre campus that had 12 multi-story buildings. The officer worked an 8 hour shift and was required to make rounds several times during his shift. However, during one of his shifts he suffered a head injury that caused him to lose consciousness. Upon investigation they were not able to determine whether or not the officer was assaulted, but they did realize that there was no protocol in place to insure the safety and security of the lone officer. From there they established a plan that addressed that risk without hiring additional staff.

Both of the examples above can happen and likely will happen to some extent within those organizations that have not considered such risks. Your security staffing levels and scheduling will play an important role in your risk mitigation strategies.

Scheduling of officers is often driven by the duties in which they are required to perform, and where they will perform them. The more responsibilities that the security officers have per shift, the more likely you will see more than one officer working at a time.

In some cases I have seen over 10 security officers working on a shift, yet the officers were not being used for security services. In one case the officers were performing duties not associated with typical security operations; rather they were being used as receptionist, couriers, and cashiers. The risk that this staffing model presented was the fact that the organization had previously identified several security risks that were not being addressed because they did not have enough security officers. However, in reality they had more than enough officers working, but they were not utilizing the officers for security purposes.

So how can you determine if you have the right number of security officers working? Well that is one of those questions that have been tossed around for many years within the security profession, and to this date there is no one industry accepted standard that provides for a clear answer to that question. There are formulas that some experts will recommend, such as a staffing ratio that is tied to the number of square feet that is being patrolled. There are also several other types of formulas that basically give you a number as a baseline as well. But in the end you will not likely succeed in walking into your supervisor's office and saying I need additional staff according to this formula. It just does not happen that way, because we will always be asked to justify the additional staff based on more detailed information.

When it comes down to determining the number of security officers that you need, you first must identify what it is you want to protect; at what time of day and days of the week you want this protection; and what fixed posts versus patrol routes you want covered. So let's assume that you as a manager have determined that you need 24/7 coverage due to your business type and the risks that you have previously identified. Your business has three buildings and several parking lots, so you have determined that you want an officer checking the buildings perimeter and parking areas 24/7. Your plan is to also have a security officer working the security control desk 24/7, and you will staff one officer inside each building during business hours, which are nine to five Monday–Friday. Since the officers will need breaks at some point during their shifts you have determined that you want a supervisor on each shift that will provide the breaks and handle supervisory duties as needed. Now with this information we will now determine the number of officers needed for this staffing level.

First, since some positions are 24/7 we will determine how many full time equivalent (FTE) officers are needed for those positions using the formula below:

8 hour shift $\times$ 3 shifts (24 hour period) $\times$ 365 days in the year
= 8,760 hours $\div$ 2,080 (hours worked per year for a full time employee [40 hour/week $\times$ 52 weeks]) = 4.21 FTE's.

Using this formula you will need the equivalent of 8.42 officers and 4.21 supervisors for coverage of the outside officer, desk officer, and shift supervisors to fill the schedule and duties that you have determined need coverage.

Since the inside officers are only working an 8 hour shift 5 days a week, you will use a different formula:

8 hour shift $\times$ 3 officers (re: 3 buildings) $\times$ 5 days/week $\times$ 52 weeks/year
= 6,240 hours of coverage $\div$ 2,080 (hours worked per year for a full time employee [40 hour/week $\times$ 52 weeks]) = 3 FTE's.

As you will see the results for this formula indicates that you will need the equivalent of three officers for coverage of the three buildings interior. However, there are still other factors to consider.

Another step in determining the number of staff you will need is the fact that officers and supervisors will on occasion call off or take vacation days. There is also the issue of vacancies due to terminations or resignations so you will need to cover those hours as well. In both cases you can cover the hours with existing staff on an overtime basis, or you can insure that you have part-time officers or on-call officers available when needed.

The final factor that some security managers have to consider is where the security department is required to perform duties other than security. An example of this is where security officers perform courier duties, shuttle service, cashier duties, and so on. These types of non-security related services are common in some industries, and yet they will often detract from the intent of the security program to protect the organization's assets.

One of the most common ways to find efficiencies in a security program is to ascertain what services the department is providing that are not a traditional service for security. In the worst case scenarios I have found security officers washing company cars, changing light bulbs, repairing electronic appliances, and picking up and delivering lunch for other company staff. None of these tasks are historically associated with security yet some organizations use security officers, who are in many cases their only means of protecting company assets, to perform meaningless tasks that derogate from security's mission and often lead to the devaluing of the security program.

If a security program is performing such services there are ways to effect changes. As part of the assessment you will need to document the lost value of your security program and demonstrate how you determined that value. In a sense you are reverse engineering the return on investment (ROI) for the security program. You will also need to address the increased value to the organization's asset protection program as a result of your recommendations to redirect these non-security tasks to another department. The oversight that most security practitioners make is they will recommend changes, yet they fail to document in detail the key points on how they propose to achieve their goal. Throughout my career in corporate management I asked others to show me the value of the changes they wanted to make and explain what the intended outcome will be and from there we can determine the proper course of action.

Overall, when you are assessing your security staffing and scheduling look for opportunities to become more efficient, and insure that your coverage addresses the intent and identified risks or vulnerabilities, as well as any security concerns related to peak demands.

SECURITY PATROL OPERATIONS

In most cases security officers make predetermined and/or random patrols in order to check the status of an organization's security and safety. There are some cases where officers are assigned fixed posts which may require them to remain in a static position for their entire shift. Whatever process your department utilizes, you need to evaluate your operations to determine whether or not your current practices are efficient and in line with your department's goals and objectives.

Since patrol routes, posts, and duties vary due to a number of factors, you will likely not have an industry standard that you must follow, rather you will have determined your program's intent based on your business type, facilities, staffing levels, use of technology and numerous other factors. Patrol operations are often set by security management based on priorities established within the security management plan or department business plan if applicable, or may be administrative directives. The types of assets as well as business types will also factor into the equation when establishing patrol operations.

As you can see, and likely have already discovered, there are numerous variables when it comes to determining what security rounds/patrols are going to made, and how often or when they will be conducted. What it comes down to is your indentifying your vulnerabilities and risks, and determining how you will address those concerns as part of your operations.

Your security risk assessment will likely lay the foundation for your operations if properly conducted. As part of the assessment you need to evaluate what patrols or fixed posts you are currently staffing for, and determine if those posts or patrols are effective based on industry standards or best practices. One way to measure their effectiveness is to review your security incidents to ascertain if the patrols are having any effect on them. In other words, if you have established a security patrol in the parking garages due to a high number of car burglaries and yet the number of incidents continues to climb, you might ask yourself if the area is just too large for one officer, or if the officer's patrol routes are counterproductive.

Fixed posts often offer the least amount of ROI for security staffing because you are positioning an officer in one place for an extended amount of time. The position may be of high strategic value based on your type of business, however the difference is that the roving security officer can check on numerous positions throughout the organization during a shift and often does on a random schedule, yet a fixed post will always be there which is very predictable. The number of officers assigned to a fixed post, one in which they are not allowed to leave, should be kept at a minimum whenever possible.

When you are evaluating fixed posts you will need to look at what policies and procedures are in place for that position. An example of this would include whether or not that post can be vacant if the officer is required to respond to an emergency, is the position staffed when the officer goes on break or during shift changes, and so on. When conducting past security risk assessments I have found that an organization's policies were that the fixed security post is required to be staffed at all times, yet security officers will often leave their posts unattended. According to the security officers they knew they were supposed to stay at their post, but there was an emergency and they made the decision to respond, even though it was against policy. The reality is that this happens more often than you could imagine, and if you are convinced that it could not happen at your organization you may want to investigate that. The fact of the matter is that it is fairly common and because of that you need to have a plan in place to address it.

An example of a plan would be to insure that your post assignments and policies address the protocol if the officers have to leave their posts for any reason. Within your post orders you will likely need to identify when an officer can leave, and what steps they should take to secure their posts prior to leaving or insuring a relief officer is present. So in essence address the who, what, where, when, why and how an officer can leave a fixed post.

In many cases officers can become indifferent or bored on fixed posts, and can easily become distracted. On the other hand, officers making patrols by walking or riding a bike are more likely to remain focused and alert and can cover more areas.

When evaluating your patrol assignments and their coverage you should look at the intent of the patrols and determine if they are addressing your security risks. Since you have already reviewed the past security incidents and trends as part of your assessment, you can now measure your security officer assignments to determine if they are designed to be proactive and preventive in nature, and have they had a positive effect on reducing the number of security incidents compared to past statistics. Plainly speaking, are your patrols effective? If not, why not?

As with any assignment you have to determine if the security officers are fulfilling their assigned duties. If you are receiving complaints that doors are being found unsecured often, or that doors are not being unlocked as scheduled, this may be the result of officers not making their rounds. There are some factors where officers may be late getting to a designated area due to an emergency or urgent matter. The point is there will always be the possibility of an officer late to lock or unlock a door or check an area, but it is the repetition of such that may be cause for concern. Keep in mind that the patrols, duties, intent, protocols and several other factors associated with patrol operations are often addressed in details in the security department policy manual.

SECURITY POLICIES

Why are policies written? Why are there so many of them? In many cases policies are a result of an identified problem that has presented itself, and a company wants to ensure that that concern does not occur again. A simple example would be the attendance policy that most organizations have in place. Although we may not know the origins of the first policy on attendance, as you might imagine, somewhere in history a company was dealing with attendance issues and made the decision to write a policy that basically says show up at work or be disciplined.

In many cases policies give staff a clear direction. They address the purpose, intent, procedures, and often the terms of discipline in the event that the policy is not followed. In some cases I have heard managers state that they do not like policies because they offer little or no flexibility in the manner in which employees can handle a situation. Although that may work in some settings, without a clear direction on expectations of staff you cannot know with any degree of certainty how they will perform, or if they will perform.

We will leave the true purpose and intent of policies to be discussed by legal, risk management, and human resource professionals, and focus more on how the policies or lack thereof can increase your security risks.

In the event that your organization is facing legal actions as a result of security negligence there may come a time during the discovery process where your policies will be requested and reviewed. When this happens you will want to know that the policies are current, relevant, comparable to industry standards, and they are being followed. In reality there will likely be several other factors that the lawyers and expert will be looking at, but for the purposes of this chapter we will only address the five listed above.

A policy is often an expression of the corporate culture, rules, and expectations of staff, yet in many cases those documents can be vague. Even the words used within a policy are often "misunderstood" as the intent is not what you perceive it to be; at least that is what I have been told in the past. One such example is where a policy stated that at no time will an employee place an item in a particular location, yet when an employee did so and there was a serious incident management argued that staff has "discretion" to not follow the policy. Really? The policy was very clear, yet the intent was apparently left open to interpretation. Keep in mind that a judge or jury will determine the intent if it gets that far through the legal system.

When you are reviewing your policies as part of the security risk assessment, insure that they are all inclusive if that is what the intent is. In other words, if you have a policy that states clearly that a certain action is not allowed, yet you intend for security staff to perform that action, state that in the policy. Another factor to look at is have the contents of the policy become a mute point, in other words if a policy states that the all staff must park in Lot A, and that lot no longer exists, it is time to update the policy.

As a general rule policies should be reviewed at a minimum every three years. It is a good practice to have the original policy date, as well as any revised or reviewed dates on each policy. When you revise a policy it is recommended that you retain a copy of the old policy in the event that you need it at a later date. If an incident happened on July 1, 2013, the chances that a civil suit being filed right away are slim. So if you change your policy after the date of the incident, both the new version and the previous version that was in effect on the date of the incident will often be requested for review and relevancy.

SECURITY RECORDKEEPING

As a standard practice, security records should be maintained for 5–7 years. In some cases there may be a requirement or standard that sets the number of years at 10 or more. If you are not sure on how long your records should be saved you should speak to your legal counsel or risk management, or research any applicable laws, accreditation standards, or industry specific security associations for best practices or guidelines.

The types of records that many security departments maintain will include security incident reports, officer logs, staffing schedules, monthly/quarterly/ annual reports, complaints, officer shift reports, sign in logs, lost and found records, and any other reports or forms used by your department. Previous versions of policies or post orders should also be maintained.

Many security departments have been transitioning over to electronic records which make the issue of storage space requirements a thing of the past. For those of you that still use paper forms you may find that the amount of documents in storage often require more than a few file cabinets. If that is the case, and your records are stored off-site you need to insure that the storage facility is secure. Regardless of the means in which you file your records, you need to be able to access that information when you are researching your past incidents, as well as compliance to any standards or regulatory requirements as part of the assessment.

As stated in Chapter 5 a review of past incidents and statistics are often an important part of a security risk assessment. If that information is not available, how can you effectively measure your program's progress, success or outcomes? Security documentation is not something that is collected and stored without analyzing the information. It is important that a security program has in place a process where they review all incidents, as well as other security documentation, and follow-up on such information in an effort to mitigate any security risks or vulnerabilities that may be addressed within the reports or documents. If you are not conducting any follow-up of identified security risks or vulnerabilities then what is your expected outcome of collecting the data?

SECURITY INCIDENT REPORT FOLLOW-UP

The writing of security incident reports is standard practice regardless of whether or not you have a security department. In companies that have no formal security department they still will require that staff and/or management complete a report whenever there is a security incident. The compilation of such information is important to the overall security management plan, and also will often assist other departments such as risk management, compliance, and legal services. Without a plan in place that insures that all incidents are documented, you cannot effectively manage your security risks because you may not know what risks are present. It is also important that the process of documenting incidents is not confusing or cumbersome, because if it is not easy to document an incident you may find that staff may in fact be in opposition to writing the report in the first place.

With the ever-changing technology in use in today's society the process and means in which to write reports has become easier, and can often be completed from any location and stored in one location online. In years past security incident reports were always documented on paper forms, and then that information had to be entered into databases for storage and statistical generation. Over the last several years it has become more common to input the incident information directly into a computer based software program that will automatically merge that information into databases that can easily pull together security incident statistics when needed.

The tools for writing reports often may include network computers, electronic tablets or smart phones. In some cases the information is entered directly into the software program, and in other cases someone may need to download that information manually. Either way, technology is making the input, processing, storage, and data retrieval much easier and more cost-effective. Of course there will always be the issue of information technology security measures that need to be in place and operational. Regardless of the means in which you gather security incident information, your main goal has to be to collect and analyze the information, and use that historical information to manage and reduce your risks. However, never assume that the reports filed will be complete with all relevant facts and information until such time as someone has reviewed the reports and conducted any relevant follow-up as needed.

Security officers or company staff completing the incident reports is one part of the process of documenting incidents. In fact in some cases security officers may not be able to fully complete the report due to time restrictions or access to staff on other shifts. So when you are reviewing your incident reporting process during the assessment, look closely at your processes and see if all of your incident reports contain all relevant information. Much like police officers, security officers work off shifts and may not have the training or time to conduct further investigations into incidents. Police officers will often forward their initial reports to the detective bureau for review and further investigation, yet security officers often do not often have that option. In most cases the report review is conducted by a security supervisor or manager, and in the best case scenario they might assign follow-up to another shift. The reality is that I have found numerous cases where those reports are just filed and no further follow-up is conducted.

When you are reviewing your program you should look closely at all of your processes and what expectations you have of your officers. If you are the person responsible for conducting any further investigation you need to determine if that happens all of the time, or part of the time. The entire process of gathering information post-incident should be reviewed and evaluated to determine if the process is efficient and effective, otherwise it may be just a case of garbage in and garbage out. More so your intent may be to indentify incidents and trends, but the reality is that your information is not comprehensive and complete. As a result you really may have no means in which to properly track the number and types of incidents; therefore you cannot effectively mitigate all of your security threats or risks.

As we will discuss in Chapter 8, the training that you provide your staff is a critical part of your security operations. Training provides for processes to be learned and practiced and can lead to fewer internal department issues as well as overall operational effectiveness.

Security Training

Security training encompasses several distinctive parts of an organization's culture. Generally this is referring to the training not only that the security officers receive, but also that the entire organization's staff receive.

What it comes down to it is that security practitioners often do not define their security training standards unless it is required by statute, and in some cases an organization may be required to follow certain training standards as part of their accreditation or other governing bodies. However, although in some jurisdictions they may not be required to provide any training whatsoever, that is not normally an approach that would be considered "reasonable," and such an approach could work against an organization in the event of civil litigation.

In many cases, the reasonable standard may often defined by a judge or jury during a legal case after the fact. In other words, you may have what you believe is a reasonable training program in place, yet during a trial your program may be compared to industry standards and found to be insufficient or lacking. That is why it is important to know what your training program could be measured against and endeavor to either meet or exceed those benchmarks or standards.

A security practitioner not only must know what the benchmark standards are, but also how to define what they believe is an acceptable standard for training, and how they measure their training program's effectiveness. Since our common goal is to protect our organization's assets, and we often have security staff trained to fulfill this task, we must strive to ensure that they have the proper level of training and that training has been vetted, measured, and at least meets industry-accepted minimum standards.

In the world in which we live, if your organization is not providing some type of security training to staff, you may find that during an emergency your staff may react in a variety of ways. Absent any consistent training or written instruction that requires staff to respond in an approved manner to a security incident, the actual results of their responses cannot be foreseen. In other words, if employees do not know what they are supposed to do, you as a security professional cannot anticipate with any degree of confidence how they will react or respond. Thus, there are general risks your organization faces as a result of insufficient or poorly trained staff.

The risks can be reduced provided there is a trained security presence working at all times, and their numbers are sufficient to address all security incidents independently. However, the reality is that not all organizations have a trained security staff on duty. In addition to that, we as security professionals often view all company employees as an extension of the security department regardless of the number of officers we might have on staff. We often rely on all employees to be our eyes and ears because we as security professionals know we cannot be in all places at all times.

Most large businesses provide security awareness training to all new hires at orientation, and some types of business take it even further by providing annual refresher training of all staff. However, like many other parts of the corporate world, the emphasis on security training is not uniform across the board, and in some cases it is dependent on budgets or corporate cultures. A larger number of businesses will likely have security information of some type included within their "Employee Handbooks" if they provide one, yet there is no means or process in place to ensure that staff actually reads any of that information, and in most cases staff are not evaluated for proficiency with regard to the information.

A successful security program, whether or not you have a security department, must have the commitment of all staff and other users such as tenants, vendors, contractors, students, faculty, and so on depending on your type of facility. A security awareness program is essential and should become a fundamental element of every employer's daily operation and business model. Employees, management, and other personnel that either work or live onsite need to become aware of their roles and responsibilities with regard to security.

Implementing a security awareness program is an important step in reducing liability concerns and identifying security issues at the earliest possible stages, giving you time to make adjustments as a mitigation strategy. So when it comes to assessing the security training of an organization, there are numerous things to consider and evaluate.

STAFF SECURITY AWARENESS TRAINING

There are many different topics and types of security awareness training that your organization can provide to all employees. They range from the basics of how to report a security incident, up to and including to how to respond to an active shooter situation. Unless you have a security staff within your organization, you may require that designated staff know how to handle a few other situations that security would normally respond to, such as how to use a fire extinguisher or how to provide basic first aid or CPR (Cardiopulmonary resuscitation). Let's start by looking at an organization that does not have a security department in place.

When assessing the training program, you should be looking at what training there is, compared to what training could be provided. In other words, what you are doing compared to what other comparable businesses are doing or based on best practices or industry standards? If you are providing no formal ongoing security training, do you at least have security awareness information built into your new hire orientation?

Depending on your organization, and the number of staff or customers that may frequent your property, your risks may range from very low to very high. As an example, if you are a small business that has no storefront and your clientele or the public does not enter your workspaces, your risks may be lower than average. However, there are exceptions to that rule as well. Take for instance—if your staff has a high percentage of females, there may be an elevated risk of domestic violence affecting the workplace, for which you may want to consider having some type of security awareness training in place to address that. Convenience stores have a much higher risk due to the practice that only one or two staff persons are working at a time, and the fact that people are coming and going at all hours. So when you are assessing the security training, you would be wise to consider all possibilities based on the business type, location, clientele, staffing levels, and so on.

Some of the basic security awareness training topics that have been provided to staff in businesses may include the following (this list is not all-inclusive):

- How to report
  - Security incidents
  - Workplace violence
  - Substance abuse issues
  - Threats
  - Bullying
  - Theft
  - Malfunctioning security equipment (i.e., locks, doors, alarms, lights…)
- How to identify workplace violence
- How to respond to aggressive people
- Loss prevention strategies
- Counterfeit currency
- Credit card fraud
- Shoplifting
- Computer security
- Active shooter response
- Fire safety
- Risk management

- Identity theft
- Physical security
- Incident response
- Privacy and legal issues
- Visitor control and physical access to spaces
- Understanding of roles and responsibilities regarding business security

Of course there may be several additional training topics depending on your type of business.

One of the best ways to ensure employees will respond appropriately is to establish company-wide security awareness training initiatives that consist of applicable information being provided via orientation, security awareness Web site(s) or information on your network intranet, classroom-style training sessions, informational training topics of the month or quarter, useful security tips via e-mail, or may be even awareness posters displayed throughout the company or near timeclocks. Some organizations will also bring in security experts annually to provide training to staff. Each of these methods, or others that you may initiate, can ensure that your organization is committed to your employees having a firm understanding of the company security policies, procedures, and best practices, and that your culture is focused on everyone's safety and security.

SECURITY OFFICER TRAINING

Security staff and management should have specific training for their business type. For example, not only should they have basic training in laws of arrest, use of force, patrol procedures, and report writing, they should also have training in school security if they work in an education setting. There are numerous examples of industry-specific security training needs, and in many cases there are new training topics being taught postincident. An example would be that after the each school shooting, training programs are often adjusted to take into consideration new techniques learned from the postincident review.

For those organizations that have a dedicated security staff, whether it is proprietary or contract security officers, they will likely have a much more intensive training program in place for those officers and management. Regardless of whether security is proprietary or contract, it is best to ensure that the security staff receives equal training.

It is not always the case, but in the past when evaluating security programs that use all proprietary staff, all contract officers, or a hybrid approach where they use both, there have been remarkable differences in the amount and types of training that the officers have received. In many cases I have found that proprietary staff receives more training on average, and the contract officers will receive the most basic training. Again, that is not to infer that this is always the case because I have seen just the opposite as well. The point is that many security guard service companies have a different approach to their training programs, and often the amount of training may be dictated by contract or budget restrictions.

In some states, namely California for this example, security training is mandated by state law and all security officers regardless of who they work for must have standardized training before they can work a post. In addition to that, they are required to receive additional training hours within a designated time frame as set by law, and there are also "elective" courses that security guards can take in addition to the minimum standards. According to state law, security guards must receive the 8 hours of training in powers to arrest and weapons of mass destruction prior to working, and then follow up with an additional 32 hours of training within six months of hire. Other states have similar requirements as well. However, there are still states where no licensing or training is required for security officers.

The risks of not training security staff, even if training is not required by statute, can be very high considering that a security program will likely be measured against industry standards or best practices in the event of civil litigation. An attorney may argue that there are no requirements to have a training program, yet there may be an issue of the standard of reasonable measures taken for security training.

Below is a generalized list of security training topics for security officers and supervisors. In those cases where specialized training is required for industry-specific security programs (e.g., healthcare or education), there may be additional training that security staff can participate in. When conducting a security risk assessment where I have been asked to review the security department's training program, I will often use a similar list of topics as a reference.

- Access control
- ADA—working animals
- Alarms
- Arrests, search & seizure
- Batons or ASP
- Blood borne pathogens
- Bomb threats
- Care and handling of evidence
- Chemical agents
- Civil disobedience/disturbances
- Command presence
- Communication and its significance
- Conflict management

- Confronting conflicts constructively
- Courtroom demeanor
- CPR/AED
- Crisis intervention
- Crowd control
- Domestic violence
- Disaster response
- Driver safety
- Elevators
- Emergency/first responders
- Emergency response
- Environmental/hazardous materials
- Electronic use/CCTV
- Ethics & professionalism
- Evacuation procedures
- Evidence handling
- Firearms (handling/storage)
- Fire safety
- First aid
- Gangs
- Handcuffing
- Handling disputes
- Harassment & discrimination
- Helipad safety
- Identifying evidence
- Introduction to diversity
- Introduction to executive protection
- Labor actions, disputes, strikes
- Labor relations
- Law enforcement's role
- Liability/legal aspects
- Loss prevention
- Lost/found articles
- Note taking
- Parking/traffic control
- Patrol techniques
- Post orders
- Powers to arrest
- Preserving the incident scene
- Public relations
- Radio procedures
- Report writing
- Reporting processes

- Role of a security guard
- Safety awareness
- Securing the immediate area
- Self defense
- Stun gun/tasers
- Substance abuse & mental illness
- Supervision
- Terrorism awareness
- Threat assessment
- Trespass laws
- Use of force policy
- Verbal diffusion skills
- VIP protection/privacy
- Weapons of mass destruction (WMD)
- Witness/participant identification
- Workplace violence

When considering what training topics that your program may include, the above-mentioned topics are often used to some extent.

There are two factors that you should consider when assessing your security training program, or that of another organization if you are performing this assessment at their request, and those two factors are the competency of the trainer and how you are measuring the competency of the training received.

When it comes time to identify who will be conducting security training, you should consider the trainer's background, competency, and qualifications to train. In simple terms, if you were to designate a trainer to teach your staff proper handcuffing techniques, is that person qualified and competent to conduct the training? When this often comes into play is in those cases where handcuffs were used and there is an allegation of improper use or injury. In that scenario, the security officer and their employer, as well as the trainer, may all be parties to a litigation claim. If, as a cost-savings measure, you had a security officer conduct the training who has never been formally trained as a trainer, it may become an issue. Some security departments will request and receive training for certain topics from their local police department. If you choose to go that route it might be best to ensure that the police officer who provides the training is a certified instructor. Just keep in mind that whatever trainer you use, whether it is in-house or an outside entity, that trainer may have to prove competency in a litigation case, and if that person's competency or qualifications are questionable, you may have an issue of negligence or liability.

Measuring the competency of the training received is basically referring to how you determine if the officers or staff members have received the training and understand what they were taught. In the past, and to some extent still today, when training is completed the only record of it was a sign-in sheet. That in-and-of-itself is not proof that the officers did anything else except for showing up to sign in. To be able verify that the officers/staff received and understood the training, it is recommended that there be some type of exam that measures their knowledge of the subject matter post-training.

In some specialized training programs, say, for example, training in the use of TASERS, there will be just such an exam. For other training programs, it can be as simple as taking the objectives and key points of the training and developing an exam to measure the effectiveness of the training.

Remember that if you are assessing a security training program, and there is no documentation of the training provided other than the sign-in sheet, you may wish to reconsider the overall intent and goals of the program.

TRAINING DOCUMENTATION

Maintaining the proper files for a security training program is important. As part of your files you should have the training outline, course syllabus, trainer information, sign-in sheets, original exams, and any other related documentation. If your training is regarding existing policy, ensure you include a copy of the policy that was in effect at the time. Later on if you were to be asked to present a copy of the policy, and it has changed over time like many policies do, you will want to have the policy that you trained for at the time, not just the revised one.

When training is conducted online, it should be standard practice to print a copy of the training materials and exams, as well as any certificate, and maintain those items in the training file.

In most cases, records of security training should be documented, kept current, and maintained by the security department or human resources.

FREQUENCY OF TRAINING

How often a security officer is required to be trained or recertified is often mandated by internal policy or statutory requirements. In certain industries there may be standards or guidelines that you can measure to or use as a benchmark as well.

In general terms, after the initial training upon hire, it would be considered reasonable to provide updated training annually. In other words, upon hire, a new security officer may receive 8 hours of training in powers of arrest or use of force, yet annually after that the refresher course for these subjects may be 2–4 hours each. If a security program does not have any annual refresher training, or elects to conduct training only every other year or at longer intervals, you may find that your training program is not up to date with that topic. The training program will be meticulously dissected by lawyers and security experts in the event of litigation derived from security officer's training, or lack thereof. If an employer has provided minimal or no security training, or simply training that was provided upon hire, which was several years ago, you may be facing an uphill battle from the start.

The key to being able to effectively assess a training program is to know what the requirements or standards are for such training. If you are conducting the security risk assessment, and you are not aware of the requirements and standards, how can you provide an accurate assessment and determine compliance or not? If an outside consultant is conducting the security risk assessment, and you have questions about your training program or documentation, now is the time to get those questions addressed so that you can ensure that your program is in line with any applicable standards or statutory requirements. Training is an important part of the security program, both initial and ongoing, and any program, process, or certification that you subscribe to needs to be able to stand up to scrutiny.

PROFESSIONAL CERTIFICATIONS

In many security departments, professional certification is either a condition of employment or a desired qualification of security officers and security management. There are several professional security associations that have certification programs, such as ASIS International, The International Foundation for Protection Officers, and The International Association for Healthcare Security & Safety, to name a few. In the past, some of these certifications were designed so that once you achieved certification you were not required to recertify or complete continuing education to retain the certification. However, for the most part that is no longer the case, and you now have to either retest or provide documentation of continuing education, training, and other forms of competency to maintain that level.

TRAINING RESOURCES

As mentioned earlier in this chapter, there may be a need to bring in outside trainers for your security program. However, in some cases you should also consider using resources from within your own organization as well; a prime example of this would be using someone from legal, human resources, safety, compliance, or risk management departments. When seeking outside assistance, you of course could consider your local law enforcement agency, the fire department, emergency medical services, or security experts. Each one of these groups will bring great resources to the department and help increase the awareness of security, security's skill levels, credibility, and professionalism. Keep in mind that even if you use internal resources, you still need to maintain the appropriate documentation for your files.

Other possible sources for training, which can be completed online and at no cost, include the Department of Homeland Security—Federal Emergency Management Agency online resources for security awareness, active shooter, and several other programs. Each of these programs has an exam and will provide documentation of the training for your records.

You can also look at professional associations as a source for training programs or materials. As mentioned before, many security professionals are members of security associations for their industry type, and being a member, they have access to online resources such as forums where other members share ideas on a variety of subjects. The numbers of resources available to you for training ideas are numerous; all you need to do is know where to look or just consult your peers. Case in point, if you are a member of LinkedIn you can join groups of other professionals in your trade and share ideas or ask questions. The group discussions are going on all the time, and members often share policies, training ideas, and numerous other resources without hesitation. No one person knows everything there is to know about security training, and it is in your best interest to network and learn from others. Remember Aristotle's quote, "The whole is greater than the sum of its parts."

SUMMARY

To summarize the training needs for security, the types of amount of training required or recommended are directly related to the type of business you operate and the services that you require your staff to perform. Specialized industries may have different requirements as a result of statutory requirements or accreditation standards. Even if your organization does not have designated security staff, you will likely still provide some security awareness training to your company's staff. Just remember to know the requirements for your business type, what laws may apply to your state, and what the recommended industry standards are for training. And lastly, remember to document your training and keep good records.

CHAPTER 9

Workplace Violence Risks and Vulnerabilities

Workplace violence is becoming the highest risk for injury or death on the job. Whether it be verbal threats or the extreme of an active shooter, the potential is ever-present in today's world and is a risk factors that you as a security professional must assess for to determine your risks, vulnerabilities, and plan for mitigation and prevention strategies.

So what exactly is workplace violence? It can be threatening behavior, verbal abuse, or a physical assault occurring in the workplace. It can range from threats, intimidation, and harassment to physical violence or assault, up to and including homicide. A workplace can include any location where someone works, which can by definition include a private residence, business, school/college, transportation services (e.g., airline, train, bus, taxi), and numerous other settings. In many cases, violent acts can be random, for example, the recent trend of the "knock-out game," yet in most cases there are warning signs that a violent act is likely or possible to occur. The recent mass shootings in the United States have dominated the news with regard to violence in the workplace the last few years, and all indications point to the fact that such acts are increasing in numbers.

On August 20, 1986, the term "going postal" first entered our lexicon when an employee named Patrick Sherrill shot two supervisors at the Edmond, Oklahoma post office and then continued his shooting rampage by killing 14 coworkers and wounding seven others. The term "going postal" has been used to describe numerous other workplace shootings for many years to follow; however, now the term most often used for mass shootings is an "active shooter." Although news reports will commonly refer to these types of workplace violence incidents as being random and offer no indications of what triggered the event, in many cases it is later learned that there were numerous warning signs that could have been indicators of a high risk for some type of violence in the future. The most challenging obstacle that often gets in the way of preventing such acts or even the most minor acts of violence is the fact that apathy and the feeling that *it cannot happen here* is often the mindset of many people.

Years ago I was attending a security conference where a physician from Oklahoma City was presenting on the Oklahoma City bombing of the Alfred P. Murrah Federal Building in April 1995. During his presentation the doctor spoke about the mindset prior to this tragic event as being *it could never happen in Oklahoma City*. During this conference, the presenters identified the ranking for acts of terrorism for each state based on Bureau of Alcohol, Tobacco, Firearms and Explosives statistics, and the state where the conference was being held ranked in the top 10 in the nation. The mayor of the city that was hosting the conference seemed aloof to the possibility that anything like that could ever happen in her state, let alone her city, yet the facts were undisputable.

There was another example of a medical center in an average-sized city that was surrounded by farms and ranches, and whose residents prided themselves on being a safe community. The medical center had a security department in place, yet the role of security by all accounts was not taken seriously. Then came the night when an upset father of a patient took two security officers hostage inside the hospital and held them at gunpoint for an extended period of time. After a successful round of negotiations with the police, the suspect surrendered and the hostages were released unharmed. In the aftermath, a security risk assessment was completed, and there were a variety of reviews and meetings to discuss what happened, and forever the attitude of the medical center and the community changed.

If any organization or community out there still believes that a violent act of an active shooter or an act of terrorism cannot happen at your business or in your community, I would personally challenge you to reach out to similar communities or businesses that have had actual incidents and ask them about their experiences. Since I started writing this book, there have been over a dozen cases of an active shooter across the United States in workplaces, and if anyone believes that it cannot happen where they work, shop, or go to school, all I can say is I hope you are right.

Workplace violence has occurred in every type of workplace environment from daycare centers to police stations. It affects white-collar and blue-collar workers, and crosses all lines of social and economic demographics. The most common theme among the people who escalate to become violent is a change of status in their personal relationships or employment. By all indications, these attacks do not just happen as if it was a spur of the moment decision, as many are found to be committed by someone that has demonstrated violent tendencies in the past along with questionable behaviors prior to the incidents. Our job as security professionals is to conduct ongoing assessments of our workplace environments in search of warning signs and vulnerabilities, and this cannot be done in a vacuum. We need to ensure that all staff, and specifically management, understands what warning signs to watch for and how to report any concerns in a timely manner. Failure to act at the earliest possible indicators can, and often will, mean the difference of prevention verses reaction to a security incident.

VIOLENCE INDICATORS

There is no definite technique to predict human behavior. There may well be warning signs; however, there is no precise profile of a potentially dangerous person. The best prevention comes from recognizing any problems in the early hours and dealing with them without delay.

In general terms, workplace violence has two different phases, verbal and physical. As noted in Figure 9.1, the progression of violence escalates from verbal actions all the way to homicide in the most egregious cases.

The key to workplace violence prevention is identifying the risks at the earliest possible point, and taking action to eliminate or reduce the likelihood that the act will occur or reach the next level.

There are a number of diverse events in the work environment that can prompt or set off workplace violence incident. It may even be the result of nonwork-related situations like road rage, domestic violence, or a number of other precipitating factors which you have no control over. Many cases of workplace violence begin as a simple disagreement or misunderstanding. Other factors that may result in violence of some degree may include any of the following:

- Downsizing, layoffs, transfers, terminations
- Depression, paranoia
- Evaluations
- Lack of advancement
- Domestic issues
- Bullying, harassment

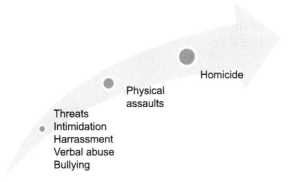

FIGURE 9.1 Escalation of violence.

- Discipline
- Discipline not fairly administrated
- Employee versus employee personal relationships
- Failure to recognize efforts and achievements
- Discrimination (sexual orientation, gender, race, etc.)
- Poor management practices
- Health problems, themselves or loved ones
- Bitter marital disputes
- Loss of job
- Extreme financial hardships
- Environmental or societal influences
- History of violence
- Relationship problems, or lack thereof
- Legal issues
- Known substance abuse problems

However, just because someone may be experiencing one or more of these situations does not mean that they will become violent. It really comes down to the person, and how they deal with stress, changes, and other environmental factors. The key to prevention is recognizing not only the warning signs and risk factors; you must also understand how employees react to each of them.

SUSPECT PROFILING

Workplace violence can be caused by employees, supervisors, managers, customers, patients, visitors, family, or a stranger. Although there is a developing trend to establish a "profile," it should be emphasized that you should not focus on this as being anything more than a historical compilation of numerous suspect profiles. Keep in mind that anyone can be an aggressor. I am aware of elderly women and elementary school aged children who were named as suspects in violent acts in the workplace, so to focus on only those that fit the possible profile could be fatalistic. That being said, if there is such a thing as a profile of someone that will commit an act of violence in the workplace, past history indicates that they may be:

- White male
- Late 20s to mid 40s
- Easily frustrated
- Feels victimized
- Withdrawn or loner
- Tends to blame others for his problems
- Low self esteem
- History of drug/alcohol abuse
- History of aggression

- History of mental illness
- Often chemically dependent (also includes prescription drugs)
- Easily stressed, or may be under constant stress, self induced or otherwise
- Engages in romantic obsessions

There is also a common myth that all cases of workplace violence are directed at the business or employees that work there. In other words, when a severe act of violence is committed at a business or other setting, the suspect is committing the act as revenge against the business or someone that works there. However, many acts of workplace violence are found to have no direct relation to the business. Case in point, there are many active shooter incidents that have been committed in hospitals, movie theaters, and shopping malls that the suspect has no current or former ties to. In fact, in several cases the suspects likely chose their targets randomly or in an effort to have the most potential victims in one place at one time.

It should be clear by now, there is no one specific type of personality characteristic that indicates that an employee or anyone else has the makings for violence in the workplace. There is also no one thing that will trigger a person's violent act. There are many variables and situations that will have different outcomes.

As a security professional, you and your team need to understand what risks your business faces based on historical information, whether it is information from within your organization or from outside sources. What is often found is that there was ample internal information available prior to an incident, and yet no one recognized the value of such information, or they were in denial that the information could actually lead to an attack. So as you are conducting the security risk assessment, you must be aware of all possible sources of information and how to mine that information for future use.

WORKPLACE VIOLENCE RISK ASSESSMENT

When you are reviewing your policies, past incidents, and other sources of internal information sources, you have to consider as well past incidents in your industry. History has proven that copycat acts of violence do occur and because of that we need to consider that even though a violent act occurred on the other side of the country, that act may have given someone else the idea to commit the same act in your community. So as we conduct the assessment, we must base our approach on what vulnerabilities exist as well as any other risk factors as we know them.

For the most part the majority of small businesses do not have a security department yet the employees working in them are clearly prone to be victims of workplace violence. However, unlike their counterparts in much larger businesses, those that work in organizations that meet the criteria of a small business are much less likely to get any type of training in identifying warning signs or responding to workplace violence threats or incidents. In fact, up until a few years ago it was often difficult to prove the value of such training to management, and in some cases the training was offered only after labor groups demanded such. We need to keep in mind that our employees are aware of violent trends and recent news stories, and even though they may not be pushing for training they are watching management's response to such incidents. Our job is to get all staff on board as part of our security team, and to give them the tools and resources with which to recognize threats and warning signs and direct that information to the appropriate department.

One of the easiest ways to get information from staff is to listen to them. Yes, it is that simple, yet in many cases it has been found that staff is talking but no one is paying attention, or in some cases management is not taking the information seriously. There have been numerous times where I was conducting an assessment and I was able to gain very critical information from line staff that management claimed they did not know about. However, upon further interviewing staff, they were able to provide names of management that they told, and even in some cases the dates they told them.

What works best for me is to conduct random staff interviews throughout the assessment listening for key indicators when the staff is talking. Never assume that you know what they are talking about until you ask them follow-up questions. As discussed in Chapter 5, a pre-assessment survey is a great tool, and in many cases staff will answer an online survey anonymously before they will speak on or off the record. Whichever means of information gathering you employ, the important factor to remember is you need to seek out information and understand that it can come from a number of different sources. Your questions will often dictate the responses you receive; basically if your questions are too direct, the employee may answer them pointedly and not give you any more information than what you are asking for. I have found that open-ended questions work best, with some questions that are more direct; really, it depends on what it is you are looking for.

The questions below are a fair representation of the types of questions that can be asked of staff and management:

- Do you know how to report any type of workplace violence?
- Rate how safe you feel from workplace violence at work.
- Do you know of weapons (define weapons) of any kind ever been identified on company property?
- Have you or any other employee ever been assaulted, threatened, yelled at, or verbally abused at work?

- Do you know of any incidents of workplace violence that resulted in serious injury?
- If you have experienced workplace violence while at work, did you formally report the occurrence(s) to management?
- Have you been assaulted by a coworker, customer, or anyone else while at work?
- To your knowledge have incidents of violence ever occurred among your coworkers?
- Have you personally ever observed a situation that could lead to violence in the workplace?
- Have you received any training in recognizing workplace violence threats or how to report them?
- In the event that someone is acting aggressively toward you or someone else within the workplace, do you know what to do?

Again, you can set the questions to be site specific. Your main goal is to gather enough information to ascertain whether or not your program is effective and if staff knows what is expected of them. Since time is of the essence, and people become bored easily when taking surveys, it is best to keep the number of questions manageable so that staff completes them.

DOCUMENTATION REVIEW

There are several sources of information that you can pull from during your assessment. They can include your department files, incident reports, human resource records, Occupational Safety and Health Administration (OSHA) workplace injury reports, and in some cases court records.

Another source that you can rely on is the crime statistics that you have likely already pulled from the local law enforcement agency. From that information you will determine what crimes of violence have occurred outside your buildings that may not have been reported to your security. For example, the public streets, parking areas, parks, or sidewalks around your campus may have a history of violence that you are not aware of, and the police records will give you a better idea of what vulnerabilities or risks surround your property.

In the inner cities you may also want to collaborate with your neighboring properties to determine what risks that they face, and if they will share them with you can ask for their statistics for violence. It is not so much that you want to know the facts of each case, more so since the neighbors may only be 100 ft away from your business you really need to know of any risks that may affect your business. In other words, if they are facing a potential violent attack from a terminated employee, would that not be important information to know to keep your staff safe?

THREAT ASSESSMENT TEAM

In the past most businesses did not have a formal threat assessment team in place to review all threats to the staff or organization and determine the course of action that will be taken to mitigate that threat. The formation of a team is becoming common in many larger organizations as a result of an increased number of threats, and such teams should be considered for all sizes of businesses.

The actual assessment team within the agency can pull together the key personnel that assisted with your onsite security risk assessment, as most of those same management members would normally be on such a team.

A threat, whether it is verbal or written, should be investigated without delay and assessed to determine the level of security risk associated with it. A threat assessment team of several internal personnel, which can include outside resources (e.g., police), should review all threats and respond as appropriate. If the business or staff receives a threat of any type, you should have a reporting system in place and an organized and trained team that will gather the relevant information and meet to go over the facts as you know them. The decision to investigate should be a team decision, or at least two management personnel. Once a full review has been undertaken, the team will dictate a plan of action, which may include calling in the local law enforcement agency for assistance with handling the threat. To ignore any threat, thinking it is "just words," can prove deadly. Never should a business take a threat lightly, as it may be your only opportunity to prevent the actual act of workplace violence from happening.

The following are potential members of such a team as applicable:

- Management representative
- Employee relations
- Human resources
- Risk manager
- Police/security
- Safety officer
- Corporate attorney
- Employee assistance program representative
- Union reps (if applicable)

PREVENTION STRATEGIES

When you are conducting the security risk assessment, you should be looking to see how your department and organization handle the following:

- Do you have a "no tolerance" policy for workplace violence and has all staff reviewed it?
- Does your organization enforce the policy consistently?

- Do you provide training to all members of management and supervisor groups?
- Does the training teach all staff the policy, warning signs, and how to respond?
- Does the organization cultivate a positive workplace environment?
- Do you have a complaint system in place that encourages reporting of potential problems and violent incidents so you can prove that you were taking *reasonable* precautions?
- Do you offer a confidential tip line/hot line to report incidents or potential for incidents?
- Do you have in place prevention measures (i.e., nonviolent response and intervention, conflict resolution, stress management)?
- Do you have an Employee Assistance Program that encourages participation and use it as a means to give employees a resource to use as a preventative measure?
- Do you use an Alternative Dispute Resolution program as a preventative strategy?

Training
Teach everyone:

- The definition of workplace violence at your organization.
- How to recognize the warning signs.
- How to report a concern.

Training needs to take place upon hire, followed with refresher training annually or at a minimum every other year. Management personnel should receive refresher training annually.

Liability Reduction Considerations
- You can be liable for employee's actions that results in violence if you failed to use reasonable care. *The definition of reasonable care will be determined by a judge or jury at trial.*
- Your company hiring practices (i.e., background checks, reference checks, pre-employment screenings) may be called into question.
- Your response to complaints about the employee may be questioned.
- During background issues, the standard is, did you know about past problems, or you reasonably should have known that the employee was going to be a problem? In many cases it will be a review of the adequacy of your pre-employment investigation that will determine this.
- As for "negligent retention" of an employee, if their performance while working for you reasonably should have put you on notice for the

potential of violence, and you did not react reasonably, you may have increased liability.

■ Review your pre-hiring screening process now before a major incident and civil case where a judge or jury will review it for you. You could be held to a reasonable standard yet to be defined.

RISK FORESEEABILITY

Workplace violence is quickly evolving as a substantial risk factor for employers. Even if your business has not had a significant case of workplace violence in the past, that does not mean that you will be exempt from litigation in the future. The General Duty Clause under OSHA generally requires that employers provide their employees with a place of employment that is free of recognized hazards that are causing, or are likely to cause, death or serious injury. So in essence an employer has an obligation to take all reasonable measures necessary to protect the life, safety, and health of their employees, including implementing practices, operations, training, and preventive measures to create and maintain a safe and hazard free workplace.

Foreseeability is defined as—to perceive, know in advance, or should have reasonably anticipated that harm or injury will probably ensue from acts or omissions thereof. It is also referred to as a measurement used to prove alleged negligence with regard to security and is discussed in further detail in Chapter 13. Basically, when we are speaking about how your organization can find itself at risks, it is when you knew or should have reasonably anticipated that an act of workplace violence could occur.

To take it step further, let's say that your organization has documented prior workplace violence incidents that have all occurred in one department and during the same shift, and during your investigations you have come to the conclusion that an employee has the tendency to become easily agitated and has made verbal threats in the past. Yet your organization has not taken any steps to mitigate risks associated with this employee. In another example, let's assume that your business is a financial institution located close to other similar businesses that have all been a victim of armed robberies over the last year, and to date your organization has not taken any steps to reduce your risks of similar acts. In both cases, the organization may be facing a premise liability issue as a result of their inaction, and it may be possible that any future acts could be found to be foreseeable based on prior similar acts.

An employer who becomes conscious of risks, threats, intimidation, or other indicators or vulnerabilities, or has experienced acts of workplace violence in the past, or reasonably should have known that the potential for violence in the workplace exists, would often be considered on notice of the risk of workplace violence. At that point, they should take reasonable steps to implement a workplace violence prevention program in conjunction with organizational changes and environmental controls. As part of their organizational changes they need to consider training for all staff so that they understand the risks and mitigation strategies, and how to report any future incidents.

SUMMARY

To summarize the process of assessing your risks for workplace violence, and how your organization responds to risks and/or vulnerabilities that are identified, it is incumbent on the person that is conducting the security risk assessment to thoroughly review all historical data, current practices, and policies, and to firmly understand what risks or vulnerabilities exist for your type of business. This process mainly entails research of existing records, yet you also have to consider information that may not be documented. Remember that oftentimes staff does not report all security incidents for a variety of reasons, and in some cases security may not be fully aware of human resource information such as pre-employment background findings.

The entire process of assessing your risks and vulnerabilities will cover both internal and external risks/vulnerabilities and determining the potential for workplace violence based on both historical data and threats that may not be defined or known at this time. Although you may only conduct a security risk assessment every 3 years, a workplace violence threat assessment is an ongoing process that has to be updated as often as needed to mitigate any changes or newly identified risks.

Not all offenders who will commit an act of violence in the workplace will show signs in advance, and no one can predict when a person is going to resort to violence. So since you cannot always tell when an act will occur, you should focus on prevention by addressing or stopping small incidents at the first opportunity rather than trying to deal with the incident after the act has occurred.

> It is safer and less costly to prevent an incident then it is to act in response to one.
>
> **John M. White**

CHAPTER 10

Financial Risk Assessment

We will now move into the area of the security risk assessment that may or may not be addressed within your organization's assessment. In other words, whether or not you will complete a financial risk assessment will be totally dependent on your identified needs as well as any predetermined internal issues or requests.

The fact of the matter is that security is often in place to protect the organization's assets, and a number of the largest losses in business have been financial losses at the hands of an employee. The losses have ranged from till taps to major cases of embezzlement that were well in excess of a million dollars. With that in mind, it is best to understand the risks associated with your type of business and work with department heads to manage those risks.

FINANCIAL ASSET MANAGEMENT

Not all security departments will delve into the financial areas of their organization. In fact, the majority of internal security departments will not likely have any responsibilities for the majority of internal financial management practices. There are a number of reasons why this might be the case, but what it really comes down to is in most cases there are internal controls in place for financial assets that are outside the scope of security. However, there may be still several areas in which security will have responsibility to some degree over financial risk management.

In almost all businesses, there are cash funds that are vulnerable to theft or misappropriation. The most common source of such risks is the "petty cash" fund. I often hear from clients that there are no such funds within their organization, yet when I am conducting the assessment, they are located in many areas of the company. So why the discrepancy? Simply put, senior management never asked or they assumed there were no such funds.

During one security risk assessment several years ago, it was discovered that an organization had over two dozen such funds throughout their operations, and the amounts of cash in each fund ranged from a few dollars to well over $500.

In all cases, it was discovered that there was zero accountability for any of the funds, and in fact there were several departments that were found to have never audited their expenditures and income sources. In over 50 percent of the funds reviewed, it was also discovered that there had been numerous issues of unexplained losses, and in the majority of those cases department management had cause to believe that there was a staff member misappropriating the funds.

Also discovered during the assessment was that the vast majority of the funds were not properly secured, and in many cases the funds were left in an envelope in an unlocked desk. The majority of the funds were used for coffee, newspapers, vending machine reimbursements, and similar other reasons. The main concern with these types of funds is the fact that when improperly managed they often provide for the opportunity of misappropriation.

When I mentioned these funds to the administrative team of the organization, the chief financial officer (CFO) became very interested in the findings. In fact, he started firing off questions as to the source and use of these funds. His concerns, and those of the administrative team, were that the organization may have an issue with the Sarbanes–Oxley Act of 2002. This act protects shareholders and the general public from accounting errors and fraudulent practices of businesses. According to the CFO, the organization must account for all funds in their possession and report them as required. Again, in most cases security may not have part in the financial management practices of the organization, yet they are responsible for identifying security risks, and unmanaged cash funds are vulnerable to theft and misappropriation, both of which are security risks.

CASH HANDLING

When a business deals with cash (e.g., retail, parking, and food services), there need to be additional security measures in place to manage the proper handling, storage, and transporting of the company's funds. Absent reasonable security measures and proper staff training, the chances that there will be misappropriation or losses of the funds are significantly greater. If your organization has any type of cash handling, you should include those areas in your assessment.

The things that you should be looking for are signs of mishandling of the cash receipts, which will include till tapping, maintaining too much cash in the registers, unsafe transportation, and many other factors. If you are not familiar with the many ways that cash can be at risk, it would be a good idea to do some research prior to conducting the assessment. Whether you know it or not, there may be numerous warning signs right in front of you, but if you do not know what to look for, you will probably never see them.

When conducting assessments for clients, I am looking for both the obvious and not so obvious signs. When I see an issue it does not mean that there is theft occurring, it only means that I need to look closer and determine what the risks are, if any.

For example, one of the warning signs that have been around for many years is that of coins lying out on top of or near the cash register. To most people, including most management that oversees cashiers, this is not a concern. On the other hand, some of you may recognize this as being a high risk indicator for theft by the cashier. Either way there is no legitimate reason to have coins outside of the register.

The placing of coins on or near the register is one of many ways in which a cashier can keep track of how much extra money is in the register at any given time. At this point if you are asking yourself why would there be extra money in the cash register and why would the cashier be tracking it with coins, the answer is simply that they are shortchanging or overcharging the customer and they are planning on diverting those excess funds for their personal use. So let us explore how this practice works, and how you can eliminate the risks.

The ways in which a cashier can overcharge a customer range from not properly using the register to taking advantage of someone that does not understand our currency system. Not using the register properly is often found where a cashier keeps the drawer open at all times and the businesses' inventory is not individually priced. How this process works is that the cashier knows that items presented for purchase are not priced on each item, and in many cases the cashier may know the actual price from memory. In these cases, they might just tell the customer what they owe without ringing up the sale. In some cases, they may inflate the actual costs of the items when they verbally give the sale amount, and if the customer is not paying attention, they may overpay for their purchase. Or the cashier could just give back the wrong amount of change for a sale they rang up properly (e.g., giving back change for a $10 bill when the customer gave them a $20 bill). After doing so, they will keep track of how much extra should be in the register by using coins.

To further explain the process of using coins to track excess funds is rather simple. Each value of the coin represents a dollar amount. For example, one cent represents $1; a nickel represents $5; a dime is $10; and a quarter is $25. So if you were to find one-quarter, a dime, and two pennies in change on the register, that *may* indicate that there is $37.00 in the cash drawer that is not accounted for. The reason why a cashier leaves the money in the register is because the customer may realize the mistake and return for their money. Also, employees know that someone may be watching, so they will not remove funds and place it in their pockets several times during their shift, rather they wait until the end of their shift and then move the money only one time.

Management should know how to watch for this potential risk and how to counter it. A simple way to identify if in fact an employee is stealing from the customers or registers is to conduct unannounced visits to the registers to look for the warning signs. If management observes any coins lying out, they should immediately without notice pick up the coins and run a subtotal tape. Once this is done, management should conduct an immediate cash count of the drawer to see if it coincides with the subtotal tape. If the cash in the drawer is in excess of the register tape, and it closely matches the amount of coins as explained above, you likely may have identified an employee that is stealing. I often ask management how often they conduct surprise drawer audits, and the responses range from whenever they suspect a problem to never.

When it comes to someone not understanding our currency system, this is normally in businesses that cater to foreign tourists who in many cases may not speak English. During a security risk assessment at a popular tourist destination, I observed numerous times where the customers did not understand how much money they owed so they just handed over large sums of money for the cashier to take what they needed; there were even two cases where people handed over their wallets to the cashiers. When this happens, your organization must have a plan in place to address this, otherwise you may be placing your customers and staff at high risk. In the cases where I observed this happening, the employees took only the amount that was due, but the risk of mishandling the funds was very high. Employees can also be accused of stealing when in fact they did not take more than what is required for the sale.

There are several operational processes that should be in place to reduce your risks, such as:

- Position security cameras over each point of sale and record all transactions
- Consider installing a point-of-sale software system that is integrated with the security cameras that tracks every sale
- Conduct unannounced cash drawer audits
- Require that cash drawers be closed after each transaction
- Do not allow for any coins, or anything else that could be used for counting, to be on or near the registers
- Do not allow employees to handle customers' wallets

PAID PARKING

When conducting a security risk assessment at a parking garage that charged for parking, it was discovered that the parking service accepted cash only. Although this is not uncommon, it did present a risk due to the fact that this operation was not using any type of cash register or formal accounting. There was absolutely no accounting system in use to properly manage the cash flow.

This property had also been a victim of a strong-armed robbery in the past, and yet they had no security system in place other than some cameras in the structure that may or may not have been monitored at any given time.

Worse yet, their only way to track their cash flow was by using a piece of paper and a pencil, tracking how many customers paid by recording marks for each car that exited. There was no safe to store the money in, and as I mentioned there was no cash register, only a drawer (with no lock) used to hold the money. To put things into perspective, this parking operation had gross revenues of close to $1 million annually. I think it is obvious what risks were present and how they could reduce their risks.

If your business has paid parking, what are your security systems or cash handling processes in place to properly manage your risks? Whenever you have a system in place that has minimal cash controls, or that is not tied to a parking management control system, the risks of theft or robbery are higher. However, even if your parking management system (i.e., entrance and exits gates) is tied to your cashier equipment, there are still ways in which the system can be circumvented and theft can occur. Case in point—at an airport parking operation it was found that cashiers were manipulating the system so that transactions were not showing up as paid and the employees were pocketing the parking fees. This practice was likely going on for many years, but once the issue was identified and proper auditing was put into place, their risks of theft or embezzlement was greatly reduced or eliminated.

LOST AND FOUND

In businesses that have security departments, you will often find that security is responsible for the handling of all lost-and-found items. That being the case, the majority of the time there are very few issues identified with the proper handling and storage of such items. However, like many things in life, there are exceptions to the rule. Therefore, in this section I will try and help you identify security risks associated with lost and found whether it is managed by your security department or some other department within your organization.

When it comes to the security risk assessment the most often identified issue with the lost and found is that of the proper handling and storage of such items. The one item that seems to cause the most concern is cash. So let us look at both the handling and storage of lost and found and, more importantly, at the processes in place for receiving cash or other high value items.

Most security programs do an exceptional job at managing lost-and-found items, and they have no real risks associated with such. However, if your program is not managed well, and if processes are not in place to properly control the items in inventory, you may fall into the trap that some security programs have found themselves.

Many times I have had security managers complain about having to handle the lost and found, but let's face it, historically speaking this service almost always falls under security's scope. That being said, you must ensure that you have a system in place that accounts for all items. The intent of your program should be to get the items that are turned into your office back in the hands of the rightful owners, not just to store and dispose of the items after a period of time. If a program is not well managed, do not be surprised if items like cash and jewelry come up missing. Again, this is the exception to the rule, but it does happen more often than most managers want to talk about.

Here are a couple of examples of poorly managed operations that I have come across when reviewing lost-and-found programs.

■ Example 1

When reviewing the lost-and-found storage area, a small fireproof lockbox was located. When the security manager was asked what is in the box, he stated that they stored found cash in the lockbox. He was asked how much cash was in the box, but he could not provide an answer. We then inspected the contents of the box only to find it empty. So next, I asked him if he had a record somewhere of how much money was found, and he advised that they did not have any such record. So I asked him how much cash is turned in during an average month, and he advised between $5 and $40 per month. Next, I inquired as to what the process was when no one claims the cash, and he stated that he used it for pizzas or going to the movies—yes, you read that right, pizzas and movies for the manager and officers. The reality was that they had no accounting system in place and there was no cash in the box, even though there apparently should have been money in it per the manager. In the end, there was a potential loss of hundreds of dollars annually that the security management was apparently using as personal funds.

■ Example 2

As part of an organization-wide security risk assessment, I was asked to review the security department operations and management practices. In the department, the lost and found was found to be a concern due to past thefts and workplace violence issues. The program was managed in a way that if no one claimed an item, whoever originally found the item became the owner by default. Seeing how that does work in some law enforcement and security departments, you might be wondering what the issues were with this program. Well, the issue was that security had removed valuable items in the past and when the staff that found the item and came to claim it after 90 days, there were fist fights between the officer that took the item and the employee that originally found it.

Looking at this program further, I found that found money was treated in the same way. There were also past issues where friends of security officers were allowed to review the lost-and-found log to see what was turned in, and then come in later and claim items as if they were theirs. It should be obvious by now that this security department had a serious credibility issues within the organization.   ■

Therefore, when reviewing your lost-and-found program, you need to look at all the processes and determine whether or not you are at risk for misappropriation of funds or property. More than once I have seen where security management had good intentions and policies in place, yet the security staff had not bought into them.

If you find that your program is at risk, you may want to change the way that you receive, handle, store, and dispose of lost-and-found property. In some states the disposal of such property is regulated by state law, and any high value items or cash must be turned over to the state government. If you are not required to turn over valuables to the state, you should consider either donating the items to a charity or selling them and using the proceeds for an employee assistance program. It is never a good idea to allow security staff to convert the property to their personal use, as this can cause a trust issue within your department and/or organization.

TRANSPORTATION OF MONEY

When conducting the security risk assessment you need to ascertain how your organization is transporting cash internally or to a financial institution. Granted, not all businesses move money around, but if yours does, you need to evaluate the handling practices and identify any risks.

A few years back I was conducting an assessment at a large corporation when I noticed several times each day that a female staff person was walking around campus with large bank bags, the type that armored car services use. In some cases she was being escorted by a security officer, but at other times she was alone. In an effort to determine what she was transporting I contacted the business office. During my review it was determined that when she was under escort internally, she was moving large sums of money to and from several departments. However, when she was alone with the bags, they were either empty or they contained cash and she was taking them to her car to make a deposit at the bank. Another manager told me that when the employee was alone the bags were empty—like that makes it okay for her to do that! After a brief moment of "are you kidding me?" I responded that no one else knows the bags are empty.

When we discussed the employee going to other sites to get their deposits and then taking them all to the bank, they soon realized that the staff person was transporting thousands of dollars in her personal car without any security escort. That employee's risks were very high, as you might imagine, and it was recommended that they reduce their risks by using an armored car service to move their funds.

If you use a security officer to make bank deposits, you should consider the fact that security officers have been robbed at gunpoint when performing such duties. Although some security officers are armed, they are still at risk when moving money off campus. Remember, the bags might only have a few hundred dollars in them, but as far as anyone else knows that bag may contain tens of thousands of dollars. Is the risk worth the savings your organization might realize by using security instead of an armored car service?

FIDUCIARY RESPONSIBILITY

Years ago when I was speaking with a chief operations officer–executive vice president of an organization I asked him why staff in management roles over the organization's finances did not seek outside audits of their files, or why when someone was promoted they did not get an updated background check. He advised that there was no need to do either, as the employees are long-term employees and they are trusted without reservation. Several years after that COO had left the company it was discovered that a senior member of the finance department had been embezzling funds from the company for many years. This person had access to all of the organization's books and files and was entrusted to authorize disbursements and receive cash payments upon request. All of the warning signs were present for many years, yet no one took notice until a new chief financial officer (CFO) was hired and requested an outside audit. At first, the suspect in this case insisted that she could perform the audit and save the organization money by not hiring an outside auditor, but the CFO made the right decision and the audit was performed and the embezzlement was exposed.

What are the warning signs that embezzlement may be occurring in your company? (Note: Most of these indicators are for employees that work with the company's financial assets.)

- Accounts receivable and payable do not balance
- An employee who wants to take work home
- An employee works late, on the weekends, and refuses to take vacations
- An employee's standard of living changes to a degree that is inexplicable based on their salary
- An employee who is resistant to change
- An employee who is overly protective of their duties
- Bank deposits delayed or do not match your accounting records

- Bank reconciliations have too many outstanding checks
- Duplicate payments are being made to individuals with the same name or address
- Financial documents are missing or only accessible to one person
- Staff in positions such as bookkeeping or finance will not permit anyone else to review the books
- There are unexplained changes in your accounting records
- There are unusually large or numerous credits to a particular customer

Security Professional's Tips for Embezzlement Prevention

- Educate yourself regarding your company's financial systems
- Speak with administration and human resources regarding background checks for potential employees and promotion for existing staff in fiduciary management positions
- Speak with administration and human resources regarding the separation of duties of staff in fiduciary management positions
- Learn and identify current systems at risk including petty cash funds, office supplies, product inventory, accounts payable and receivable, and all other assets

The examples within this chapter are just a few of the ways in which an organization can be at risk for loss of their financial assets. Although there are several other possible security risks based on an organization's business type and management practices, the main point is to review your practices and *think outside the box*. Do not take anything for granted when it comes to identifying risk potential, because your operations may be placing your staff or organization at risk needlessly or unintentionally. Work with the management of all departments that may handle cash or other valuables and learn their systems. Remember, they are not the security expert within your company, you are, and you need to know what risks exist and how to mitigate them.

CHAPTER 11

Security Technology Assessment

A major part of any security risk assessment is the review of existing security technology equipment in use to ascertain the operational effectiveness of such equipment. In doing so, it is also common to evaluate the need to move, remove, replace, or install new equipment if it is determined that either the existing equipment is no longer effective, improperly utilized, or if there is a justifiable need to add equipment.

For security practitioners who set out to conduct a security risk assessment, this may be an area where there might be a concern with impartiality. For example, if they have installed security systems under their watch but now realize that the equipment is either not properly utilized or is in fact not needed, there may be a tendency to not disclose that information. Think of it this way: if 5 years ago you pushed through a capital budget request for tens of thousands of dollars for security equipment upgrades or new installs, but now you realize it was the wrong equipment or in the wrong location, how likely is it that you would document that fact within a report that will be read by administration? Now, on the other hand, if you had identified an issue in the past after operational changes that administration was aware of and you were forthright with that information at the time, you will likely not have an issue including that finding in your report and it may not raise any red flags.

The key to properly assessing the technology and documenting your findings and recommendations is to do so in an unbiased approach. So does "impartial" and "unbiased" mean that you cannot identify errors in past upgrades or replacements? No. You should document all of your findings and recommendations to mitigate any present and potential future issues, and do so in a way that is detached and neutral.

You can do this by identifying the concern and explain what has changed over the years that made it an issue at this point, and more importantly document your planned remediation of the issue. However, before making any recommendations, it is best to conduct proper research to determine how exactly to correct the problem and how those changes will affect the budget. You should not fear disclosure of a problem that may cause some unwanted attention; if

135

that information comes to light in another setting and you have not previously disclosed it, your credibility or integrity may be called into question. Remember too that a consultant will identify all of the issues regardless of any past history, and they do so to get the change process started.

When security consultants are asked to conduct assessments, they normally do so in a constructive manner and base their review on industry standards. That is not to say that some consultants do not come in and overly scrutinize a program to the point where their reports read like a smack-down. However, those are exceptions to the rule. The majority of professional security consultants fully understand the intent of the assessment and are there to give expert advice to improve an existing program. If they find concerns with the security technology, they will often document that concern and viable solutions based on proven methods. Whoever conducts the assessment needs to fully understand both the original intent of the technology and its current effectiveness, and provide solutions and recommendations to mitigate any deficiencies or excesses.

When attempting to determine the original intent of existing technology, security management may have that information available in their files. However, in those cases where the management is new to the organization, they may find that the information no longer exists. If that is the case at your organization, you will not likely devote a lot of time in determining the intent, but rather focus more on the effectiveness.

The effectiveness of any security technology is often measured by what it is preventing or protecting, as well as if the technology is still performing as intended. During your physical assessment, if you locate a camera that is directed toward a wall because at one time there was a door located there, then that camera is not effective and will likely be removed and relocated as part of your findings. The same holds true for panic or burglar alarms, card access control devices, and others. If they are not needed or are not being used effectively, then you should document that finding and recommendation for corrective action.

Another important consideration as part of the technology assessment it to determine whether or not there is any testing or preventative maintenance plan for the equipment. Often, technology is purchased and installed, then most people forget about it. The reality is that if an employee activates a panic alarm they assume it will work, but that is not always the case. If your security program is not conducting monthly tests of all alarms, you need to consider doing so and documenting your findings.

The following sections will address common security technology that is found in most businesses. For businesses that have additional security technology systems in use, you should be able to formulate an assessment plan for that equipment based on the identified concepts within this chapter.

LOCKS AND KEYS

The use of locks and keys are still the most common form of security measures used today. However, in most cases, they are the weakest link in many security plans because keys can be duplicated and locks can be picked. Whenever I have mentioned this during an assessment, I almost always get a response such as, "Our keys have *Do Not Duplicate* stamped on them." That may be true, but unless they are a certain type of high-security key (e.g., Primus or Best), a person can often get keys duplicated if he or she knows how to convince an employee at a retail store that it is okay to make a copy. Anyone can stamp Do Not Duplicate on any key and claim it is for their small business or personal use; because of that, how can a locksmith or hardware store employee know any different? If you have never tried getting a key made that was stamped Do Not Duplicate, you might be surprised to find that those three words will not prevent copies from being made.

As mentioned, certain key systems offer a much higher level of security, and they also require that only authorized locksmiths make copies with the proper authorization forms. These types of keys have security features built into them that require special, strictly controlled key blanks. Often, these keys will have more than one key cut on them and use special core locks. If you are only going to use locks and keys to secure your facilities, you should probably look at these types of key systems for security-sensitive areas because they offer the highest security measures available with regards to locks and keys. Regardless of which lock-and-key system you use, you will want to evaluate the security and integrity of your access control system.

Access control that includes locks and keys is a substantial part of all security programs; as such, it will require an above-average time commitment as part of your assessment. Therefore, locks and keys, as well as electronic access controls, are discussed more in depth in Chapter 12.

SECURITY CAMERAS

Security cameras are very common in today's world, and the chances of you being filmed with or without your consent dozens of times each day is a reality. Security cameras are used to record activities, so the likelihood that someone is actually watching the video streams live is low. For the purposes of the security risk assessment, we will look mainly at active monitoring.

Active monitoring of security cameras is found in very few industries such as casinos, airports, government buildings, and very large operations such as universities, medical centers, and amusement parks or sports venues. Staffing a surveillance room with personnel who are actively watching cameras can be very costly. The benefit is that security can certainly cover more areas with cameras, and an officer can be dispatched more efficiently once an incident is identified. Also, if a security concern is reported, the dispatch/monitoring station staff can get eyes on the area within seconds and either dispatch the appropriate response or verify that the report is unfounded.

When assessing the security camera control center, you need to ask yourself what the intended purpose of the service is; in other words, is the center just used for surveillance or is the staff performing other services such as switchboard, cashier, receptionist, and so on? This is important to know. Often, the staff is multitasking by performing several different duties, so the amount of actual time monitoring cameras can be quite minuscule. Another factor to consider is the relationship between surveillance and security. For example, in casinos, the surveillance department is not a part of security, mainly because surveillance is watching everyone, including security.

It is also important that the actual physical controls for such a service are also evaluated, including the layout of the room, how many monitors there are, at what angles the monitors are placed in relation to the staff's position, and how easy it is to use the equipment. If the monitors are placed too high or if they are located behind the staff, the chances of staff checking them often will be diminished to some extent. Distractions within the center also need to be evaluated. If security officers or anyone else tend to socialize in this room, surveillance staff will not likely notice all potential security incidents due to the conversations or other activities.

To assess these departments, start with the program's intent and ascertain if it is being met. Look at the types and locations of the equipment and ensure that it is easy to use. The overall security of such a space is also important to reduce the number of unauthorized staff or visitors that might enter this area.

Video quality is often the main issue with security surveillance. The older a system is, the more likely it is that the quality will be substandard. If the system is still using VHS recorders, an upgrade should be considered. In addition, until that time comes, you need to look at the recorders to determine if they are cleaned and serviced on a regular basis as well as how often the tapes are replaced.

While conducting an assessment at one large campus, I toured the dispatch center where all security cameras were monitored; overall, more than 200 cameras were monitored in this center. However, more than 50 percent of the cameras were either not working or of such poor quality that they were basically nonoperational. There were also old black-and-white monitors in use and the video picture was very substandard, making them more of an annoyance than anything else. The intent was to actively monitor the security cameras, yet the staff's actual abilities were far less and the overall effectiveness of their system was more of a liability then an asset. Systems that are not properly working can be a liability. People may rely on security watching them at night, expecting that if they get into trouble, someone will be observing the situation and come to their aid.

You should also look at the record rate for the video system. If it is too slow, you will likely miss seconds of video when you record; the playback may not show someone walking in front of the camera due to the low record rate. When working with clients to recover from a serious incident, it is often found that the important parts of the incident were not recorded correctly because the record rate was set too low. Often, the reason why record rates were slowed was to save storage space on the recording device. However, with newer digital video recorders (DVRs) or network platforms, you can adjust your systems to increase the record rate during important events, such as an alarm.

If you are not recording in real time in security-sensitive areas, or at least have your system designed to increase the record rate when there is activity in the view of the camera or an alarm is activated, you need to evaluate the video systems and consider making changes. Integrating cameras and alarms on to one platform has become very common, and in many ways will increase the effectiveness in your security technology. By doing so, you can get real-time intelligence if you are actively monitoring your systems; when you are reviewing archived video footage, you may be able to save time.

When determining the period of time for which video should be archived, there are some recommended industry standards that many organizations follow. First, it depends on the type of system that you are using. For example, if you are using a VHS recording system (Video Home System), your archives will be directly affected by the record rates and storage capacity for the tapes. The quality of such recordings will be subject to the number of times each tape is re-used. Some businesses still use one tape per day, and then reuse those tapes each week. The reality is that the tapes will not last very long. Another pitfall of such a protocol is that tapes are often recorded over before you realized that something has happened. Because of that, many organizations have gone to a 30-day archive of recordings and have switched to a DVR or network-based platform.

The DVR has come a long way in recent years. It is often only limited by the capacity of its hard drive. Larger drives have more storage capacity; with more storage capacity, the odds are better that you will have the video you need in the event that there is an incident. DVRs can also be tied to the alarm systems and integrated with card access control systems and other security technology, all through the corporate network.

The security of video archives is another factor to consider, especially if a system is moved onto the company's network. If no policy is in place about the downloading and sharing of video, it is highly recommended that such a policy be considered as soon as possible. The risk of not having such a policy, and safeguards to go along with it, is that an organization's video may be passed around social networking sites on the internet.

Many security clients have at one time been asked by other members of the organization or by the police for a copy of video recordings. When the request comes from within the organization, it is often related to a personnel issue, such as when did an employee arrive at work or when did they leave. Law enforcement will often ask for video for a criminal case they are working. In one case, a police department asked for all video tapes from a medical center as part of an investigation. In fact, they threatened the security officers working the overnight shift with arrest if they did not release the tapes immediately. The security director was called at home; he advised the supervising police official that they would fully cooperate with the investigation, but they would not release all tapes without a subpoena. He was also able to advise the police that if they do release the video tapes, the police would not be able to view them without the proper equipment. There was also a very valid concern regarding privacy issues under the Health Insurance Portability and Accountability Act regulations that had to be resolved as well. In the end, the police determined that there was no crime and they did not need the tapes. However, in this case, the security department had a very firm policy in place. Because of it, the security officers knew exactly what to do and how to do it. Without such a policy and protocol, you could lose control of your video recordings.

With the proper policies in place, it would be in your best interest to not allow anyone to download video to any external device without a supervisor's approval, and then only after you have discussed such actions with the legal or risk management departments. The more staff that has the ability to download video, the more likely it is that your recordings may be compromised. It is not uncommon for security video to find its way onto the internet or into the hands of reporters without the consent of senior management. For the most part, this breach of protocol is a result of nonmanagement personnel having too much access; this includes security officers.

Although there have been several security officers who have argued the point over the years, there is no reason why they need access to video archives and the ability to download footage. There are numerous liability and privacy concerns with security recordings. Unless you have taken firm measures to ensure that officers or other staff cannot make copies of videos, do not be surprised if this becomes a legal case or public relations embarrassment due to a breach of privacy.

For example, after a university installed high-quality cameras in their parking areas due to several incidents of vandalism and car burglaries, another serious issue became apparent. At the time of the installation, the security director was not knowledgeable regarding the equipment, and therefore was not thinking ahead as to what problems may result with this new technology. Shortly thereafter, a new security director with extensive experienced was hired on and immediately performed a security risk assessment of the campus, which included the security technology. Upon reviewing the security cameras, the new director found that the quality of cameras was above average, and that the security officers had been using the camera inappropriately for some time. In this case, the officers had been using the pan-tilt-zoom feature to view into private residences adjacent to the university campus or into the dorm windows. After identifying the risk these cameras presented, it was a quick fix to digitally block the camera's view into any residential or dorm windows, and therefore the privacy concerns became a moot point. However, anyone conducting a security risk assessment needs to understand the video systems and their potential risks, ensuring that they are reviewing your technology for all possible vulnerabilities, risks, and privacy concerns. You not only need a policy that addresses the use, maintenance, and training required for your systems, you must also take measures to ensure that you have identified and mitigated all known issues.

Other considerations for security cameras include the intended view and location of the cameras. First, it has long been debated whether cameras should be watching who comes into the building or who exits. In some industries, it is recommended to position the cameras to ensure that you get a full face view of anyone who is leaving an area or building. The reason being is that you will often know when a security incident occurred, and from that point forward you want to determine who left that area. There are recommendations to get face shots of all people who enter an area or building as well. However, it comes down to knowing the proper recommendations for your type of business or industry.

One of the often-stated cases for directing the video cameras to the inside, and therefore recording who is leaving a building, is due to the backlighting issues that you will almost always find during the daylight hours. On sunny days, the reflection of the sun off of the glass windows, sidewalks, and other reflective materials outside can often be so intense that the light will cause the camera's iris to close; as a result, the video quality will often be distorted.

SECURITY ALARMS

When it comes time to assess the security alarms within your organization, you must consider all existing alarms as well as any planned installs as a result of remodeling or identified risks. For the existing alarms, you will need to conduct a test of each—not only of the functionality of the alarm, but also the response to each alarm. Your benchmark should be the alarm policy and all related protocols and training. So, in essence, you are evaluating the entire system from the proper location, ease of use, response, effectiveness, and operational effectiveness. Alarm systems will often include a hybrid of sorts, where there are internal security alarms as well as ones that are managed by an outside vendor.

Many security programs have monthly testing of the alarms built into their operations, that document their findings, failures, and mitigation processes. If your program does not conduct such tests of your system, you are missing an important opportunity to be proactive and know whether the alarms are properly functioning or not. When someone pushes the panic button or enters a restricted area after-hours, security needs to be notified as quickly as possible because any delay in notification could result in a potential loss of life or property.

When conducting one assessment, I found that a maternity unit of a large hospital had never conducted any tests of their security alarms. When we started an operational test of their system, it was not a surprise to find that more than half of the door alarms were not working. Worse yet, the security systems that were supposed to lock the doors in the event that an infant was near any exit were not working either. It was later determined that the system had been offline for months and no one knew it. If you have never tested your alarms, this type of security lapse could happen at your organization.

Monthly testing should be conducted of all security alarms, regardless of your industry. Due to a variety of reasons, alarms, like other electronic systems, do stop working on occasion. Testing often requires two staff members—one who activates each alarm and one who monitors and resets each alarm at the alarm panel. All alarm testing needs to be documented, and those reports should be maintained with all other security logs and reports.

If you find that an alarm is not properly functioning when conducting the alarm tests, you should note that information on the report and make the proper notifications to whoever repairs your systems so that the issue is resolved as soon as possible. While you await the repair, it would be prudent to have in place a plan that compensates for the security risks due to that alarm not working. In other words, if the alarm is not working, you may decide to increase security patrols in an area; in a high-security area, you may elect to place a security officer in that space full-time until the alarm is properly functioning. Once the alarm has been repaired or replaced, another test needs to be conducted of that alarm; the results should be noted on the monthly report. Therefore, you are testing the systems, identifying discrepancies, making repairs, and then retesting.

In almost every security risk assessment that I conducted in the last several years, staff shared the same concern: the availability of alarms is poor at best. Many times, staff has identified a need for a security panic alarm. In the majority of cases, the security department will concur with that necessity. However, it almost always comes down to money as being the main reason why alarms are not installed.

Another concern that is often expressed once all parties agree to the requirement for an alarm is that the labor and materials needed to install such alarms is often cost-prohibitive. In many cases, there may be great distances to run wires, or the legacy alarm system may be at capacity. However, due to recent advances in technology, many of these concerns have become moot points.

For example, network-based alarms systems can turn every network computer into an alarm point. These newer systems can integrate existing systems, whether they are cameras, alarms, access control, or other security technology. They can also be used for mass notification in the event of serious security incidents. The days of running wires and cables to each alarm point or camera is fast becoming a thing of the past, and the information flow is becoming much more cost-effective and easier to install and maintain.

The most important aspect when you are assessing your alarm systems (other than if they are working) will be whether the alarm points are in the proper locations based on known security risks or vulnerabilities. If they are not, it is recommended that any proposed changes address this disparity.

MASS NOTIFICATION SYSTEMS

Some organizations have an automated system that notifies all or selected staff in the event of an emergency. Many school systems, universities, and large businesses have installed such technology due to the threat of an active shooter. They have determined the need to make instant notifications to all parts of their campus or facilities with very little effort, all in an effort to ensure that proper notification is made in a timely manner.

Of course, not all organizations have gone to an automated system; in fact, it is probably safe to say that the majority of businesses do not have such a system in place. However, in many cases, they may have a basic emergency action plan established that will include a telephone call list and evacuation plan. Because almost everyone carries a cell phone these days, many businesses may use text messaging or social media to get the word out to affected parties in the event of an emergency.

During an active shooter incident at a university, the campus police used Twitter to notify faculty and staff and gave them instructions regarding what they should do to be safe. Whatever system that your organization is using, you should review the process and plan to ensure that it is up to date. If there is no system or protocol in use, it is probably a good time to include the recommendation in your report to research and evaluate your options. The possibilities for such a service range from inexpensive social media services, all the way up to electronic systems that can send text messages and/or make phone calls as predetermined by your organization.

The often-stated reason why that organizations do not install a mass notification system is cost. However, the technology has improved and the prices have come down in recent years.

SECURITY OFFICER EQUIPMENT

The equipment that the officers carry and use as part of their jobs also needs to be evaluated during your assessment. You will want to determine if they have the tools needed to perform their duties as assigned and if those tools are appropriate and functioning as intended.

Radios

Because communication is a very critical part of security officers' duties, they will often have two-way radios with them at all times. When you are looking at this equipment, there are several factors to consider:

- Do they work?
- Do the batteries last for the entire shift?
- Is there radio coverage in all areas that the security officers might enter as part of their job?
- Does the officer know how to use the radio?
- Do you record your radio traffic?

During a past assessment, I noticed that the security officers were carrying radio batteries in their pockets. I asked an officer why he was carrying a battery; he replied that the batteries only last about half of shift, so they always carry a spare. During another assessment, the security officers coming off shift were observed passing the radios to the oncoming officers; it was determined that the department only had four radios, which meant that there were just enough radios for each officer working. In both cases, it was obvious that the quality and quantity of the equipment were not sufficient to address the needs of the department.

When it comes to the number of radios or flashlights that should be available to the officers, it is best to consider the fact that there may be times when you will staff up due to special events or emergencies. To ensure that you have a sufficient number of radios, flashlights, keys, or other equipment, plan to have at least one piece of each equipment for each officer on staff; that way, if you have to increase staffing, you have enough equipment. This also helps when equipment fails or is lost or stolen, because the working staff will have spare equipment as needed and will not have to go without. Building up your supply of equipment does not need to happen at once; often, it can be accumulated over time as budgets allow.

Weapons

Weapons are another thing to consider when you are addressing the tools and equipment that the officers may carry. If so, ask the following questions:

- Does the equipment belong to the company or the officers?
- Is the equipment inspected on a regular basis and are those inspections documented?
- Are the officers trained in the use of the equipment by a certified trainer?
- Have you reviewed your policies as a part of this assessment?
- Are the policies up to date and are they being followed?

Each of these questions may factor into your liability risks in the event that the equipment is used and there is a litigation case filed against your organization. Training the officers on how to use a weapon is just the beginning of managing the risks associated with weapons.

Keep in mind that you may not authorize officers to carry weapons as part of their duties, but they may in fact be doing so right now. As mentioned in Chapter 5, I always request certain policies from the security department prior to my site visit. My intention is to know as much about the department as I can before I am onsite. When a policy states that the officers are not authorized to carry weapons, it is my normal protocol to verify that during the onsite assessment. Several times, it was discovered that officers will admit to carrying a variety of weapons, up to and including firearms. Therefore, you may not authorize weapons, but they may be out there. When you are conducting your assessment, it is advised to determine compliance with all of your existing policies.

SPECIALIZED SECURITY EQUIPMENT

Depending on your security department, you may be using additional security technology as part of your program. The technology may include security phones in parking lots and garages, wireless duress alarms, computerized panic alarms, guard tour systems, emergency lockdown procedures, or a number of other equipment or services. Each and every service, program, or piece of equipment needs to be evaluated as part of the assessment.

Often, when an organization has numerous parking lots or garages, they will install security telephones throughout their parking areas and in other locations on the campus. If you have these phones, it would be prudent to test each phone as part of your assessment if they are not tested monthly. If they are tested each month, then a review of the documentation and a test of a sampling of the phones would likely be sufficient during your assessment.

Many organizations use guard tour systems to ensure that the officers are making rounds as assigned. If you use such a program, you will want to review the reports to ensure that it is in compliance with your policy. Some of the questions to be answered would include; Are the predetermined locations for each tour based on risks and vulnerabilities? Are officers required to conduct a preset tour at least three times during each shift? Are two of those tours scheduled to be conducted within the first and last hour of each shift so that the officers know the condition of their post at the beginning and end of each shift? If an officer fails to make the required tours, what is your process to address this?

Metal Detectors

One of the often-stated concerns addressed at an assessment kickoff meeting is that the organization needs to install metal detectors. There are a variety of reasons why staff may feel the need for such equipment, but it usually comes down to not feeling safe and the fear of an active shooter. When this topic comes up, there is often a period of discussion by management that revolves around the demand by staff for such equipment, yet there is almost always a pushback from management to be resistant to change their systems and install such equipment.

If that question is identified during your assessment, you will need to examine the issues thoroughly and with an open mind. Some security directors will jump at the chance of installing metal detectors, and others will proceed very cautiously and may even reject the notion that they are needed. There are several serious discussions that need to take place if there is a move to install detectors, and they range from perception, staffing, budgeting, training, and the substantial culture change that may result from installing this equipment.

The perception issue will be that the place is not safe anymore. In some cases, this perception will be on the minds of staff, and eventually it may be the perception of your customers and others. If you are seriously considering the installation of metal detectors, it would be a good idea to speak with senior management and your public relations staff. Even though you may not put out a press release about the new equipment, that does not mean that the media will not find out and make a story about it.

Another thing to consider is the secondary screening that often is a result of the need to conduct a more thorough search of someone due to an alarm on the walk-through device. Depending on your type of business, this may cause a public relation concern when a child or elderly person is physically searched in front of others. For example, the Transportation Security Administration has received much publicity about this issue, and there are many videos online as a result. There are also numerous complaints lodged about inappropriate physical contact. Any or all of these concerns may happen if you decide to install the equipment. These examples are only intended to get the conversations going as part of your needs assessment.

Staffing for such equipment will often require three staff members at each location at all times. Therefore, if you have one location and this entrance is always open (24 hours, 7 days per week), you will need upwards of 12.6 full-time employees, not counting management. This can be an expensive operation due to the equipment costs and installation, as well as the required staffing.

During the needs assessment and planning stage for such equipment, you will likely be faced with the reality that, due to the equipment and staffing costs, you will limit your installation to one location. As a result, you may be faced with making an operational change that requires all staff and customers to enter through one entrance, versus the many that you may presently use.

As far as your security risk assessment is concerned, you will more than likely be reviewing your policies, training, staffing levels, equipment calibration, and testing of any equipment that you have in place. You may also find that your needs have changed over time, and you may consider adding new screening areas or even removing existing equipment. In fact, in 2013, the University of Southern California Medical Center in Los Angeles did just that after 20 years of using stationary metal detectors. Their reasons for removing the equipment were to make their facility more welcoming to patients; they stated that the metal detectors gave the impression that the county facilities were dangerous.

SUMMARY

Your security risk assessment is all about identifying your organization's risks and vulnerabilities, then coming up with strategies to either eliminate or minimize them based on proven methods, not hunches. If you are installing security technology without an end goal in mind, then you may be just throwing money away. For example, if you are installing a camera in a hallway just for the sake of having one there, yet another location within your facility has a higher risk for theft or violence, would it not make sense to place the camera where the risk is greater? Each and every installation of security technology should go through a needs and strategic planning phase that is based on the findings of your security risk assessments.

When it comes time to evaluate your existing security technology, your focus should be on whether or not the technology is being used properly, if it is functioning, and if your organization has a preventive maintenance plan in place.

One type of security technology that was not fully addressed in this chapter is that of access control. Chapter 12 goes into detail on electronic card access control systems.

Access Control

A substantial part of your assessment will review access control measures throughout your properties. This will include everything from vehicular and pedestrian traffic flows to the process for making keys, changing locks, supply storage, inventory controls, master keys, electronic access controls, and many other factors. If any of your systems are managed by outside entities (e.g., locksmith services), you should also look at their processes to ensure that they align with your program's intent. At each step of this process, you have to determine your risks and vulnerabilities, as well as the available strategies to either eliminate or minimize the risks based on proven methods.

When it comes time to evaluate your existing security access control technology (electronic or mechanical), your focus should be on whether the measures are being used properly and are functional, as well as whether your organization has a preventive maintenance plan in place.

LOCK AND KEY CONTROL

When you look at your processes for key controls, be certain to evaluate the important but often overlooked points, such as how many keys are in circulation, who has them, and who can authorize a new key to be issued.

One of the common questions asked during a security risk assessment is how many keys are issued to staff; however, the majority of the time, respondents cannot answer that question with anything more than "many" or "a lot." Key control in many organizations is not comprehensive; innumerable times, it is found to be out of control. Take, for example, one organization where I conducted an assessment in the 1990s. This organization had a master key that they referred to as the "69" master. When I asked how many of these keys were issued and who has them, the reply from security was, "Who doesn't have one?" I later found out that even vendors and delivery services had the master key—and that key controlled more than 75 percent of the locks on a very large campus of multiple buildings. That organization had untold risks and vulnerabilities due to lax key control, and the only absolute way to correct this problem was to rekey many of the buildings. However, the organization elected not to spend the money to rekey; therefore, their risks and vulnerabilities likely went on for many years.

Lock and key controls encompass numerous different facets of the security program, from the storage of the lock and key supplies all the way to collecting keys when someone leaves your employment. When it comes time to determine what kind of security will be on a door, you basically have four common choices: no locks, key lock, cipher lock, or an electronic access control device (e.g., card reader, key fobs, biometrics).

Your review of the lock and key system should include the following:

- Are there any signs of pry marks or tampering?
- Regarding key control processes, who gets keys and who authorizes the issuance?
- Master keys
  - How many master keys are issued and to whom?
  - Are there any grand masters in circulation? If so, who has them and why do they have them?
- Are locks changed when keys are lost or stolen? Are lost master keys treated any differently?
- Who controls the key blanks?
- Who does locksmith services?
- Does security authorize all new keys?
- Do all keys get returned when someone leaves employment?
- Do any vendors have keys? If so, why?

Without a doubt, the most often identified risk or vulnerability discovered in an access control program is the mismanagement of keys and all the processes related to them. Take, for example, the authorization of keys. In many cases, security may not have any control over who gets a key. Although it is recommended in numerous published materials that security should have control over the lock and key management, maintenance/facilities often manage this process.

There often is a control issue regarding locks, and I have witnessed some fairly intense arguments over the controls of locks and keys. In one such situation, the maintenance department stated they would control all locks and keys; if they had to give the locks and keys to security, they would also give security the job of repairing all door hardware, which they viewed as also related to building security. At another facility where I performed an assessment, I found that security did in fact change door hardware (including crash bars, handles, and hinges); security officers were often spending more than 80 percent of their shifts working on doors. What it comes down to is this: everyone needs to understand their roles and work together to secure a facility. It is my recommendation that security authorize all lock changes and key issuances, regardless of who does the actual work of changing locks or cutting keys.

Over the years, it has been proven that outsourcing locksmith services may save an organization money. However, some companies use a hybrid approach, with facilities doing some of the work and a locksmith doing everything else. Whatever approach your organization uses, you must ensure that your oversight of such services is comprehensive and that you conduct audits of any outside vendors.

When you are dealing with authorizations for keys and the management of key blanks, both of these parts of the program should fall under security's control. As a security professional, you need to ensure that the number of keys, especially master and grand master keys, are managed properly. There should be a process in place to get keys returned by staff who no longer needs those keys or who have terminated employment. Your program should also have a process for handling lost or stolen keys. Some organizations will rekey any lock that is controlled by a master key that has been missing for more than 1 hour. They consider the key to be compromised at that point, and they need to eliminate the risk associated with that key.

When it comes time to do a rekey, especially for a master key that controls numerous locks, it can become very expensive. However, security will often charge the department that lost the key for all labor and materials needed to bring security back to an acceptable level, regardless of the costs. There is a risk associated with such a policy: a department may not disclose to security that a key or set of keys is missing. This was the case with two past clients; in one case an entire set of master keys, which controlled over 10 buildings, was found to be missing for 2 days. Management of the department knew they would be charged for the rekey and it would amount to more than $5000, so they made the decision to not say anything. They knew that an employee took the keys home by mistake and that employee would bring them back. The employee did in fact return the keys, but no one can be sure that copies were not made.

In the other case, I was asked to complete an assessment for a large facility. During the assessment, it was found that the security director, who was recently terminated, had taken a complete set of keys with him on his last day. Although he did return the keys 2 weeks later upon demand by administration, there was no means to determine if any copies were made of the keys. In this case, it was recommended that all locks be changed to mitigate any risks or vulnerabilities associated with the prolonged loss of the keys.

CIPHER LOCKS

The use of this type of locking device is fairly common in some types of businesses. These locks are easy to use, as well as abuse. In some of the brands available, there is a keyway in the door handle; however, in most cases, keys are not used to unlock these devices. Cipher locks (shown in Figure 12.1) are used to unlock a door by entering a three- to five-digit code on a keypad. This type of lock is actually less secure than a standard key lock because you do not need to physically have a key to unlock this device. All one needs is the code, which in many cases never changes and can be known by everyone in a matter of minutes.

These types of locks come from the factory with a master code programmed into them. Manufacturers' master codes may be different, but in many cases they use the same or similar codes. The risk with these locks is that many times the end-users never change or remove the factory-installed master code. Therefore, if you know the factory-set code for a brand, you will likely be able to unlock these types of locks wherever you find them. A few years ago during an assessment, I asked the security manager if all factory master codes were removed and he confidently replied that they were. At that point when we approached the next cipher lock, I entered the factory master code. Much to his surprise, the door unlocked.

As mentioned, the main security concern with these types of locking devices is that the access codes are not changed on a regular basis, if at all. In a few cases,

FIGURE 12.1 Example of one of the many cipher locks being used in businesses.

I have found that the numbers on the keypads were worn off due to many years of use, so it would not be hard to determine the code by just looking at the keypad.

When you conduct your assessment of these locks, look around the door frame and on any signs, posters, or bulletin boards near them for the code. Often, you can find the code written down on or near the door frame, especially if the codes are changed often. If you watch staff close enough, you may even see the door codes on their company ID badges. It really comes down to the fact that staff wants the codes to be simple; if you change them often, they will have a tendency to write the codes down near the door or on the back of their ID badges.

When it comes time to change an access code for these locks, it would be prudent to ensure that the codes are not too easy. For example, do not use codes such as 1234, 1111, 911, and similar variations. What might be an easy-to-remember code for staff may also be a security risk. It is just like passwords for computers: the easier you make them, the easier it is for someone to figure them out.

Over time, many businesses have transitioned away from cipher locks and keys due to the vulnerabilities and risks associated with lost keys or compromised codes. In doing so, they transitioned to an access control system that uses an employee's ID badge as their "electronic key."

ELECTRONIC CARD ACCESS CONTROL

Although not all businesses can afford to install a card access control system, there has been a trend to go in this direction whenever possible. These systems can offer a higher level of security because the access control cards can be individually programmed based on the staff person's access rights. The important thing to remember about these systems is that they have to be well managed in both the initial setup and the ongoing management.

The first phase is to develop an operational plan that addresses who will manage the program setup, who will assign access rights, how the ongoing monitoring of the system will be conducted, and how the organization will measure the outcomes of the system.

When assisting one organization in a program setup, I sat in on a training session being provided to the client's security management by a nationally known security technology company. Much to my surprise, the vendor was advising their client to make things as simple as possible, with no more than a few levels of access. Their thought process was that everyone should have the same level of access rights at all times, even though most of the buildings were closed and not staffed at night and on weekends. As the trainer stated, "Why go to all the hassle of making different categories and access levels when you can just keep it simple?" Although the system being installed was very robust, the vendor obviously did not understand operational security. They believed that a cookie-cutter approach was better than putting thought into setting up a system that protected the company's assets.

In another case, a vendor advised security management to turn off all door alarms within the access control system, as they were "Nothing more than a nuisance, and unless you are watching the doors in real-time, there is no reason to use the alarm feature." Really? If someone is trying to get access into an area that they should not be in, would that not be cause for concern?

The key point in both of these examples is that vendors who install systems often do not fully understand operational security. It is your responsibility as the security practitioner to ensure that your access control system is set up and managed properly. In the end, you and your department will be held accountable for the protection of assets, so security management has to understand the system inside and out and take ownership of the access rights of all staff.

When overseeing the setup of another access control system, I was asked by several members of a company's administration about who will decide what access each employee or management person receives. The answer was simple: security. At first, there seemed to be a moment of disbelief. I went on to explain that security management should make all decisions in the end, but they will take direction from other management on a department level. Basically, security will allow for a department's management to authorize access rights within their department as needed, but they cannot authorize access for other departments or areas.

It has been my experience that if security allows managers of other departments to authorize access rights in general, they will often authorize the highest levels of access possible. Generally speaking, managers do not want to tell one employee yes and others no, so they will often go with the path of least resistance and give everyone the same access. Therefore, security management needs to ensure that only those who need the access get the access.

When you are assessing your access control system as part of your security risk assessment, you need to ask the following questions:

- Do you have an access control policy?
- How was the access control program setup?
- Who authorizes access?
- Who has what access levels?
- Does anyone have full access? If so, why?
- Do vendors have cards with access?

- If so, what levels?
- Do their badges have an expiration date if not used?
- Is their access set so that they cannot enter the property after-hours?
- Are they required to turn them in daily or at the end of a project?
- Are all cards turned off the same day that an employee terminates employment?
- Do you get all cards back from employees who terminate employment?
- What is your process for managing lost or stolen access cards?
- How often do you audit your access control system?
- Do you review all alarms daily?
- Do you follow up on all unauthorized access attempts to security sensitive areas?
- Does security have oversight and management of all access control systems in use?
- Who all has the ability to change the program's access rights?
- Who has administrative rights to the software?
- Can you manage this system from remote locations through the network in case you cannot get into the security office?
- What is the default setting for the access control systems in the event of a power failure?

As basic as many of the above questions are, you might be surprised to find out that no one may bother to audit the software or program rights after a system is installed. I have seen cases where system installers have given themselves full access to all areas regardless of the client's restrictions. Other times, vendors were found to have access rights 24/7, even though the business was only open during normal business hours. In another case, it was found that a business had their access control system set to default to unlock in the event of power failures; therefore, at night when the business was closed and the power went out, the exterior doors automatically unlocked. So, when auditing your system, it is recommended that you fully investigate all aspects of the system, including the software, hardware, management, policy, and any other related equipment or processes.

DOOR HARDWARE

Other types of locking devices include what most people refer to as "crash bars" or "panic bars." However, these devices do not always work properly. In many cases, these devices require that someone physically lock and unlock the doors at a scheduled time; if that person is unavailable or forgets, the door may not be locked after-hours. There is also the possibility that anyone with an Allen wrench can lock or unlock the door from the inside for their convenience.

Not all doors have to be physically locked or unlocked by security. In some cases, the doors are always locked so that no access is permitted from the outside but you can still exit the door from the inside. These doors often have automatic closures on them that pull the door shut, which in turns activates the lock. However, these closures do not always work properly and often need maintenance and adjustments. Dirt, debris, snow, and internal air pressure can all have adverse effects on any external door; if these doors are not checked regularly, you might have an unsecured portal for hours or days.

When you conduct your assessment rounds, look closely at all doors for proper closing and locking. Give external doors with closures affixed to them extra scrutiny. One of the easiest ways to check these doors is to push on the doors from the inside, not using the crash bars, and see if the doors are locked when closed. If you are outside, pull on the door and see if it will open.

VISITOR MANAGEMENT

The management of visitors, which can include vendors, contractors, patients, family members, delivery personnel, and many other groups of people, can be a very important part of your security program. If you do not manage their access to your business, you cannot predict with any certainty where they will go and what they will do on your property.

Take, for example, schools that have made substantial changes to their visitor controls in recent years. I can recall being able to enter my son's schools without doing anything more than opening an exterior door, walking inside, and eventually entering their classrooms—all without anyone asking me the purpose for my visit. Try that these days and you will likely find that schools are on constant lockdown. In some cases, you will have to give up your driver's license in order to enter the building. Is this unrealistic? Have the schools gone too far? Not at all. They have adjusted to the threats, risks, and vulnerabilities that confront our society today, and they have taken prudent and reasonable measures based on the historical events and threat assessments.

Other businesses have made similar changes, such as in hospitals. In years past, it was likely that you would find most exterior doors unlocked during the normal visiting hours. Anyone could enter the building and have unrestricted access to the patient floors. Not all hospitals have changed this practice, but it is becoming more common that the number of exterior doors that are unlocked has declined. In many hospitals, you have to register with security as a visitor prior to being allowed past the lobby area. In general, businesses are adjusting to the risks that they have identified. In some cases, this may result in restricting access to some extent.

If your business has little or no visitor controls in place, is it because there are no identified risks, or is it because the corporate culture is to be open and inviting? Being open and inviting has long been the culture that many businesses have worked within, but times are changing. Workplace violence issues are on the rise; with the increasing numbers of violent acts in the workplace, that "open culture" is undergoing change. As mentioned, almost all schools have changed their culture, as well as some other businesses. Airports, courthouses, government facilities, and numerous other types of industries have also made the change to better manage visitor controls.

As you set out to complete your assessment, you need to understand your existing risks and vulnerabilities, as well as the threats that your industry is facing in today's world. The often-stated reason for failing to accept recommendations to change the existing open access is the corporate culture and how management will resist change. However, just like any other type of facility that has gone through this process in the past, changes will be easier to implement once a serious event occurs. However, why wait to make meaningful changes until an adverse event occurs? As our country changes, so too should your security awareness.

CRIME PREVENTION THROUGH ENVIRONMENTAL DESIGN (CPTED)

Controls of your perimeter will often include physical measures such as fencing, landscaping, walls, berms, and other stationary objects. The overall intent of many perimeter controls is often related to a concept called crime prevention through environmental design (CPTED). CPTED is a concept in the security industry, basically meaning that you may be able to reduce criminal acts from occurring with the proper design and planning of an environment. In theory, you can make changes to the physical environment that allow for better physical and operational controls of the property; as a result, it can further your crime prevention strategies.

According to ASIS International, over the last 40 years,

> The term Crime Prevention Through Environmental Design has become the preferred way to describe the following security concept: The proper design and effective use of the built environment can lead to a reduction in the opportunity, fear, and incidence of predatory stranger-to-stranger type crime, as well as result in an improvement of the quality of life. CPTED is the design or redesign of a venue to reduce crime opportunity and fear of crime through natural, mechanical, and procedural means.[1]

---

[1]Protection of Assets-Physical Security-Copyright 2012 by ASIS International.

Once you have identified a risk or vulnerability in your assessment, you can often use the CPTED concept to mitigate risk (or make recommendations to mitigate risk) based on this concept. Raising a counter or installing a physical barrier to separate staff from aggressive people, controlling unchallenged access past reception desks by use of doors, and repairing and/or upgrading lighting levels in parking and pedestrian areas are some examples of the use of CPTED principals. Most architects understand this concept, and I venture to say that most business owners will as well. They may not know the term CPTED, but they likely will know the basic concept as they encounter it almost every day in society.

For example, in many residential areas, you will find fencing or even a row of hedges that create a natural barrier to redirect people from walking a certain route. Even a screen door can be considered a barrier, as most people will not just open the door and walk into a house; however, if that door is not there, there is nothing to deter a person from doing so.

There are likely many examples of the CPTED principle being used at your properties already; you just may not realize it. It is recommended that you fully understand this concept and how it can be applied to your security program as well as any future remodels or additions. There are numerous books available that go into great detail how this concept should be applied. The following books are good references that I include in my professional library.

- *Protection of Assets: Physical Security*, published by ASIS International
- *Crime Prevention Through Environmental Design*, by Timothy D. Crowe and Lawrence Fennelly, published by Butterworth–Heinemann.

By using the CPTED concepts, you may be able to reduce your risks, vulnerabilities, and ongoing operating costs. For example, if you only have one exterior door open for visitors, you may be able to reduce the number of reception desks that are staffed. However, you need to keep in mind that this concept may work better for new construction and remodels than for existing buildings. Suppose you were to recommend as part of your assessment report that several existing exterior doors be secured at all times, but your parking lots are near those doors that will be locked going forward. Staff and customers would need to walk long distances to get to the only open entrance, so you would likely face monumental push-back from staff, management, and customers. That being said, I am not suggesting that changes to that extent are not justified in some cases. You just have to be able to qualify your recommendations based on known risks or vulnerabilities. Also, you should be able to document the facts as you know them to ensure that the recommendations are based on sound and proven practices and standards.

An open and inviting facility can be a very strong obstacle to overcome no matter how noble your recommendations might be. During your assessment and the report phase of the project, try to focus on the most critical changes needed based on your organization's operations. To do so, you must determine the needs based on historical information, the existing design, and potential reduction in risks or losses. If you can qualify and quantify significant reductions in risks, or if you can address past liability cases where there was a loss and then make recommendations based on proven methods, the chances for positive changes may be easier to obtain.

GEOGRAPHIC CONSIDERATIONS

Because every location is unique in some way, being that businesses could be located in the inner-city or in a rural community, you will have to take into consideration the geographical location of each site when you are conducting the assessment and making recommendations for access control improvements. You would be hard-pressed to make recommendations for drastic changes to security if your business is located in a small community that is relatively void of most crimes or serious security threats. If you were to recommend installing metal detectors at a school or hospital in that small community with no history of criminal activity or loss due to security lapses, you would likely be ignored.

On the other hand, if your business is in the inner-city and the neighborhood around your site is a high-crime area, it is more likely that you would make recommendations for changes, unless your facility already had above-average security measures in place and the risks and vulnerabilities had all been addressed in the past. Each and every business type and location has its unique challenges. You must consider them all based on your location, risks, threat levels, vulnerabilities, and several other factors.

BIOMETRICS

Biometrics is best described as a personal identity verification system, meaning that your personal identity is verified by using individual and unique physical characteristics such as your fingerprints, hand geometry, speech, eyes, handwriting, or facial recognition.

Although this type of system is not often used in most businesses, biometrics has been around for some time; it is more likely to be found in operations where there is a higher level of security in place, such as research and development departments, military control centers, and buildings or departments that house top-secret operations. However, some businesses have biometrics in their operations but are not high-security operations. These systems are often used in conjunction with other access control systems, such as an access card or personal identification number, so that there is more than one means required to gain access into a secure area. They have also been used as part of a time and attendance system—in a sense, a biometric time clock.

If your organization uses biometrics, you need to include a review of the equipment, processes, and operational effectiveness of the system within your assessment. These systems have been known to fail to the extent that they may authorize access when that person does not have clearance, or they can deny access even though the employee requesting access has the proper authorization levels. Each time a failure occurs, security should document that failure and any remediation steps that they took.

CHAPTER 13

Legal Considerations and Prevention Strategies

LITIGATION AVOIDANCE

Even those organizations with security operations that are considered exceptional can be vulnerable to litigation because there is no absolute way to avoid it. The fact of the matter is that anyone can sue another party for a number of reasons, and it is costly to litigate even the obviously flawed civil suits.

Organizations can and often do make themselves vulnerable to litigation as a result of not addressing their risks and vulnerabilities. More times than I can count, organizations have conducted security risk assessments and then failed to act on even the most serious findings. In addition to that, even organizations that take corrective actions find that they remain vulnerable to civil litigation because they fail to document their corrective actions. The fact of the matter is, your best defense is to conduct a security risk assessment and thoroughly review the findings in a timely manner, implement appropriate changes, and document all changes as well as your reason for not following any recommendations. This will not absolve your company of all liability, but it may reduce your exposure.

There are a number of theories that a party can bring civil litigation against a company, and they include but are not limited to security negligence, excessive force, and negligent hiring or retention. Several litigation cases that I have been asked to provide an opinion on were related to security training, policies, or negligence.

In the case of security training, the most common vulnerability is with regard to the amount, quality, documentation, and trainers' qualifications. In some cases, state laws or accreditation standards may require a certain level of training, and yet there are organizations that fail to meet the requirements. This may be a result of the person responsible for security not knowing the laws or standards, or for whatever reason they merely fail to comply. In addition to that, there are security programs that have industry standards that their programs may be measured against, even if they do not subscribe to the associations or groups that published the materials.

Security policies will almost always be a part of any litigation case, and the lawyers and security experts will review them. If your policies have not been updated, or at least reviewed on a regular basis (e.g., every three years), or if your policies are not being followed and that fact is being mentioned throughout the discovery process or trial preparation, you may find your organization on the defensive throughout the entire legal process.

One of the common comments that I have heard during the review of policies with security managers is that the policies are current *but officers have discretion when it comes to following them, or we know the policy states one thing and the officers do something different, but we are okay with that.* If you allow officers to use discretion in following or enforcing policies, why not include a statement to that effect within the policy? To not do so, you may give the plaintiff's counsel an avenue to attack your program and credibility. Your claim that staff has "discretion" may be construed by a judge or jury as merely your excuse to defend negligence.

The review and updating of policies has to be an ongoing process because most operations change over time or as you identify new vulnerabilities, threats, or your facilities change. Once you publish a policy, post order, or standard operating procedure, it is subject to review in the event of a legal action, and it is difficult to defend a document that is obviously flawed or outdated.

Post orders generally refers to a procedure used for security assignments. They can be specific to a facility or be more precise and be specific to an identified location within a facility. Post orders must be detailed to the extent that even a new security officer could understand them and carry them out with little or no training. They are often intended to ensure that security officers perform their duties in a prescribed manner and yet do not go beyond the instructions of management. When you have officers that do not follow the orders or if you have no written orders to follow, your liability may be limitless.

And finally, "foreseeability" in general terms is the measurement used to prove alleged negligence or premises liability with regard to security. The most common way to prove that an act was foreseeable is the prior similar test, meaning were there prior similar incidents where an organization or person knew in advance, or could reasonably anticipate that an event would likely ensue due to an act or failure to act? This is why it is important to conduct your security risk assessments and review your security incidents ongoing. This also includes gathering crime information from outside sources (e.g., law enforcement), because as we discussed in Chapter 5, not all crimes are reported to property owners. Just because you are not aware of similar acts being committed on your property, or adjacent to your property, this does not mean that you can use the defense that you did not know. Property owners are required to take reasonable steps to protect the people that use their property from foreseeable harm.

Remember, it is not possible to completely prevent a negligent security lawsuit from being filed against your organization. However, you can reduce the potential for claims and place your organization in a much stronger position to defend against litigation if your security program is designed to reduce your liability exposure and it meets or exceeds industry standards.

CRIME PREVENTION

Crime prevention is defined as the anticipation, identification, and assessment of the risk of crime as well as the initiation of procedures to eliminate or diminish it. There are numerous crime prevention strategies in use today that use proven methods to foresee, identify, assess, and focus on crime and/or the causative factors of crime. Crime prevention measures may be focused at different levels and applied differently depending on several distinctive factors. For example, the types or locations of businesses may dictate different strategies.

Crime prevention is often focused on the preclusion of crime, that is, preventing a crime from occurring. Often the strategy is to make proactive changes to infrastructure, operational processes, or a corporate culture to reduce the likelihood of a criminal act from occurring. In the example in Figure 13.1, there are three elements in relation to a crime, and they are identified as desire, ability, and opportunity. If a person has the desire to commit a crime, and the ability and opportunity are also present, the risk for such a crime is extremely high. However, if you take any one of the three parts out of the equation, you will likely reduce or eliminate an incident from occurring. Keep in mind that you may not be able to change a person's desire, but you can take steps to eliminate the ability or opportunity.

When developing your crime prevention strategies, you need to look at both internal and external influences. Internally it should be an organization-wide effort to prevent crimes from occurring anywhere on your property. It is important to get all of your organization's staff involved in this effort, and one of the most effective means in which to accomplish this it to develop a security

FIGURE 13.1
Crime prevention elements.

awareness program. Employees need to understand that they are a crucial part of your security team and that security and risk management needs them to report all suspicious activity. All staff should be encouraged to be observant and know what action to take when they identify a potential risk. Policies and protocols must also be put in place so that staff know what to do if they see suspicious activity. It would also be prudent to look outside of your organization for additional assistance.

Your crime prevention measures need to extend past the property lines of your facility and include the areas and influences in close proximity to your business. Working with your business neighbors to discuss ongoing security issues is a must.

Your organization should have a security representative meet with any neighborhood groups and law enforcement agencies to discuss crime prevention measures that impact your geographic area. Just because your business does not own and manage the other properties in the area, you will still be affected by their presence, as will the other businesses, schools, or residential developments be affected by the presence of your facility. Working with neighbors to discuss security concerns that they are having, and any issues that you may be experiencing, can offer each other another layer of security. If the neighborhood stores/businesses know that you are experiencing car burglaries, they too can be extra eyes and ears for your organization, and in return, you may find out about an issue that they are experiencing that you have not yet discovered on your property. Although such a relationship will take time to develop, the long-term results can have a positive impact on your organization and may save your organization, an employee, visitor, or vendor from being a victim of crime. In essence, you are developing a neighborhood watch of sorts for the area in which your business is located.

Security needs to have open and ongoing conversations with the law enforcement agencies that provide services to all of your properties, and during these conversations you will want to identify what crimes are occurring in the area of your properties and what concerns you should be on alert for. Ongoing dialog with law enforcement is crucial, and if a representative with a law enforcement agency is not met with at least quarterly, preferably monthly, you may never know about crimes that may affect your campus unless they make the news.

Another part of a crime prevention program will include the principles of Crime Prevention Through Environmental Design (CPTED). As we discussed in Chapter 12, CPTED is a concept that should be utilized in existing environments, or in new construction or remodeling. It can include a whole range of features, such as visibility/surveillance, traffic controls, street and pathway design, lighting (exterior and interior), and target hardening.

Target hardening effectively makes targets more challenging to strike. A target can be anything that a criminal would desire to take or damage. It can be an item, person, or property. Examples of target hardening include, but are not limited to:

- Quality window and door locks
- Alarms
- Security cameras
- Fencing
- Barriers (natural and man-made)
- Access control (electronic or environmental)
- Removing a person from a high risk environment

Your goal has to be the removal of vulnerable property when possible or the protection of such if it cannot be removed from its environment. In simple terms, this means ensuring that any item that has the potential to be stolen or damaged should not be visible or accessible. An easy way to explain this would be the often-stated crime prevention method regarding items of value in your car—out of sight, out of mind.

Other examples of this include:

- Removing high value items from store windows or display cases at night
- Moving small vulnerable items nearer to cash registers
- Make sure that items that are capable of being used in the commission of a crime are not accessible

Anything that deters or requires more time or effort for an offender to commit a criminal act, or increases the possibility of detection of such, is an effective method of prevention. Criminals may be less likely to engage in criminal activity if they perceive an increased risk of apprehension or detection.

Your crime prevention strategies should have an end goal to reduce the potential of a criminal act to the lowest possible probability. The number of steps that your organization can take to accomplish this goal are endless, but your first step is to identify your vulnerabilities and risks. Your second step would be to identify proven mitigation measures, and your final step would be to implement those measures. Keep in mind that your crime prevention measures will need to be adjusted over time, and there should be ongoing monitoring of your processes to ensure that they continue to be effective.

LOSS PREVENTION STRATEGIES

A part of any security program involves loss prevention, namely security measures are in place to prevent theft or other losses. Even though the often-stated belief is that loss prevention is all about shoplifting, it actually entails a much broader part of the overall security and risk management programs.

Loss prevention programs are generally implemented by companies to minimize the potential and prevent losses. In essence, a business may implement a workplace safety program in conjunction with security as well as a workplace violence prevention plan. Other examples of loss prevention strategies can include companies installing GPS systems to their fleet vehicles, installing alarm systems, and control access to their properties by erecting fences or barriers that direct all traffic through designated entry points, all in an effort to control losses. A good example of this can be found at many hi-tech manufacturing facilities where you will often find that employees must enter and exit through designated portals, and when they do, their persons, purses, briefcase, lunchboxes and other similar items are searched.

According to the 2012 National Retail Security Survey, retail losses were $35.4 billion (U.S.) in 2011 due to employee theft, shoplifting, paperwork errors, or supplier fraud.[1] Also according to the same report, the majority of loss was due to employee theft. Employees were responsible for a total loss of $16.2 billion (U.S.), which is 43.7 percent of the total losses, and shoplifters were responsible for $12.2 billion (U.S.), or 32.6 percent. By far, most businesses put their time and financial resources into shoplifting prevention strategies, and they place far too much trust in employees, and because of that shoplifters are much more likely to be caught and prosecuted than an employee would, and the employees know it.

Many employers who have discovered an internal theft often will not prosecute and instead opt to allow the employee to resign rather than terminate them for cause. The normal reason giving for this action is that they do not want the "bad press." However, this mainly results in the problem just being kicked down the road to the next employer, and again, employees know this.

With that being said, when you are conducting your security risk assessment you have to consider that your loss prevention strategies may not be focused at the highest risk factor. In other words, you may be more focused on threats from the outside rather than internally, and because of that your true losses may be misreported.

Whether your losses are inventory, supplies, information, finances, or lost production, it would be in your best interest to conduct a comprehensive evaluation of your loss prevention intent as well as the outcomes of the program.

Another aspect of the loss prevention program is that of reducing the likelihood of losses or litigation. We all know that we live in a litigious world these days, yet there are steps that all organizations can take to reduce the likelihood of being sued. For example, being proactive in loss prevention, risk management, and security can all reduce the opportunity for losses if properly managed.

---

[1]www.nrf.com.

Security officers are often a critical part of being proactive because they are trained to be observant and report their findings. A well-trained security department will note unsafe conditions or other situations that could lead to a loss, and at that point security and/or risk management has to ensure that corrective actions are taken to mitigate the risk.

Loss prevention is certainly more than just preventing theft or fraud by your customers and employees. To develop a successful loss prevention program, you should assess your internal and external theft issue, supplier fraud, system errors, preventive maintenance of facilities and grounds, security rounds, fire safety, and any other concern that can negatively impact your business. A well-implemented and managed loss prevention program will aid you in identifying most problems at an early stage, as well as assist you in determining why they are occurring and how to rectify or eradicate them.

SECURITY VULNERABILITY ANALYSIS

A security vulnerability assessment (SVA) is a process that characterizes, identifies, and classifies the security vulnerabilities (weaknesses) and the potential for criminal activity as it relates to a security system and/or program. It analyzes risks, determines the threat level, and identifies industry-proven countermeasures. The SVA will ascertain the highest-level vulnerabilities, how an antagonist could take advantage of the vulnerabilities, and what the impact of such a security breach could mean to an organization. At the conclusion of the SVA, an organization will then use the findings to determine what asset protection measures can be implemented or changed to reduce or eliminate any associated risks.

In many cases the vulnerability analysis may be a part of a comprehensive security risk assessment, and together they will often forecast the effectiveness of proposed remediation efforts as identified. In addition to that, the final report should give you an idea of the expected results once the recommendations are implemented.

If security vulnerabilities are discovered as a result of security risk assessment, a detailed plan of action that addresses the steps to be taken, changes to be made, and the expected outcomes of those recommendations need to be identified and documented. Depending on the classification of the vulnerability and the probability that an incident may occur, you will likely assign a threat level ranking to each finding.

In most cases the risks identified and associated with the SVA will fall into two categories: acceptable and unacceptable. Acceptable risks will be those that present no tangible loss potential for an organization, and they may be recorded in your final remediation report as no further action needed. Those that are unacceptable will always require some type of action, and recommendations must be provided as a means to remedy the problem. These types of risks can further be separated into different levels of criticality, and therefore classified in the order of importance based on the severity of the risk.

Those vulnerabilities that are classified as "high-level threat" should be given top priority and immediately addressed, and all other lesser levels of vulnerabilities may be given a defined amount of time (i.e., 30–90 days) to correct the issue depending on the risk level assigned. The timeline for vulnerabilities is different from the majority of recommendations that are identified as a result of the security risk assessment. Depending on the vulnerability risk level, they may require immediate remediation. However, in general terms, many of the recommendations that come from the assessment may involve a much longer implementation process due to budgets and planning, and in many cases they may not be critical to the organization's risk management program. In simple terms, they may be operating efficiencies and process improvements, but if an organization does not implement them, it may not result in an elevated risk, loss, or litigation.

A security vulnerability assessment is a baseline of sorts for all protection strategies. Properly conducted, the intended purpose of the assessment is to document all findings and plan a response to prevent, deter, and mitigate the risk.

A successful vulnerability assessment will often encompass policies, operational systems, and protocols. For example, if you your organization had a policy that regulated the access into a restricted area, and required that all visitors be under escort at all times, you may elect to test this requirement to determine if someone could in fact enter the area without an escort. What many businesses have found is that although they have policies, operational protocols, and security systems in place, vulnerabilities still exist to some extent. Case in point—during an assessment a few years ago, I walked into a highly restricted plant operations space of a large facility unchallenged, and had I wanted to, I could have shut down their entire electrical system and other utilities. Their policies clearly stated that the space would be secured at all times, and they have several security layers in place, yet anyone could have entered this space without being noticed or confronted.

Consider the fact that the fundamental objective of a security program is to reduce risk. If your security program only identifies vulnerabilities once they have come to light as a result of an incident, then your program is operating in a reactive fashion and the overall effectiveness of the program will be very limited.

The corrective action processes for identified vulnerabilities need to not only identify and correct the deficiency, but also the process that caused the vulnerability in the first place. A related process is often referred to as the root cause analysis.

A root cause is the fundamental malfunction or failure of a process that, when identified and corrected, will prevent a similar recurrence. A root cause analysis is a process that is used to focus on a problem or nonconformity, so as to determine the root cause of the problem. When properly utilized, the outcome of such actions can correct or eliminate the cause and preclude the problem from reoccurring in the future provided mitigation steps are implemented and effective.

THREAT IDENTIFICATION

Threats are based on several factors and may often be different at facilities of the same industry yet different geographic locations. For example, known threats at an oil refinery in Western Asia may have no direct or indirect threat to similar facilities in North America. In simple terms, although the industry is exactly the same, the threats do not correspond across the board.

The same holds true for just about any industry or service. When you are assessing your threat level, vulnerabilities, or risks, you would be wise to consider what other similar facilities are facing, even those in other geographic locations, yet you cannot assume that your facility has the same threats without extensive research and investigation. In order to properly evaluate, address, and mitigate a threat, you must gather enough credible information to properly define what the threat is and how it impacts your operation. Once you have completed the research and fact-finding, you will want to start your process of identifying the steps needed to counter the threat and formulate a plan for mitigation.

During this process of research and response, you will likely be working with internal departments and outside organizations (i.e., law enforcement), as the more serious the threat is the higher the likelihood that your security department will need assistance from external entities.

Largely depending on your type of business, your threats may come from the inside or outside of the business. That is not to say that you may not experience threats from both sources because that is entirely possible, as well when an insider works in collaboration with an outsider. During your assessment, you should be looking at all possible sources for threats, real or perceived, and it would be advisable to not downplay or diminish the credibility of any threat until such time that an extensive evaluation has been completed.

Threats to your organization can fall under one or more of these groups:

- Crime of opportunity—internal theft (e.g., embezzlement, shoplifting, trade secrets)
- Criminal acts—robbery, information theft, technology breach
- Disgruntled employee, former employee, customer
- Terrorist activity (domestic or international)

Threats that your organization may encounter often come from people that are very calculated in their actions and planning.

Conducting a threat assessment is the process of gathering and assessing information about an individual or group of individuals who may have the fascination, intent, capacity, and motive for mounting an attack against an organization. Determining the potential threat to and the vulnerability of a targeted organization is fundamental to preventing an act of terror.

It is advisable for every business, and for that matter every person, to understand how to assess a threat. Due to the high number of random mass shootings that have occurred, or other random acts of violence that we hear about in the news every day, there are not too many places that I go where I do not conduct a threat assessment for my personal safety. The chances are pretty good that you and your family may not realize that you also conduct similar assessments daily. For example, if you are walking the streets of a major city at night, you are probably making mental notes of the people around you, lighting conditions, and indicators for violence such as robbery or sexual assault, and you are doing so subconsciously. If you are not making observations such as these, you may be placing yourself in a vulnerable position unnecessarily.

SUMMARY

Businesses are often subject to civil litigation as a result of real or perceived negligence, failure to take corrective actions to correct security risks or vulnerabilities, and many other factors. It is not possible to be completely void of all litigation risks, yet there are numerous prevention techniques available that have been proven to be effective. In order to reduce your organization's liability exposure, you must understand your risks, vulnerabilities, and threats that have been identified as a result of your security risk assessment, and you must act in a reasonable manner to address those findings. Failure to do so may only increase your exposure to litigation.

CHAPTER 14

Contracted Services

Many organizations have contracted out services as a result of not knowing how to manage a service in-house, or for budgetary reasons. In some cases, they contract specialized services that will be short-term services, for example, an employee shuttle service during a major construction project that will severely impact parking. Whatever the case, it is important that the organization's management has thoroughly vetted the vendor and has taken into consideration some basic oversight measures.

For each of the services mentioned in this chapter, there are some basic considerations that you should address when conducting the security risk assessment project, provided that the contracted service is the responsibility of the security department. They are as follows:

- Are the maintenance/service agreements reasonable? Are the terms competitive?
- Is the vendor meeting the terms of the contract? Basically, are you getting what you are paying for?
- Were competitive bids sought?
- How do you measure the service agreements to determine return on investment (ROI)?

POLICE SERVICES AND CONTRACTED STAFFING

In selected types of businesses, you may find that the organization has contracted with a law enforcement agency to provide some level of police protection, often in the form of security services. For example, healthcare organizations may contract with an agency to provide a police officer in their emergency room either 24/7 or just during peak times when the chances of violence are greater. These types of service can vary depending on the state or local jurisdiction, and by that, I am referring to how law enforcement agencies will handle such requests by private businesses.

It has been my experience that some law enforcement agencies will not allow their officers to work off-duty jobs under any conditions, or they may restrict

171

them to do so only if they do not wear their police uniform while performing security services for a private entity. One of the often-stated concerns is that a police officer is really never off duty, and therefore they still have police powers to make an arrest. Local and state governments have found themselves in the middle of civil litigation cases as a result of off-duty police officers working private jobs, and in some cases they may even require that the company that hires a police officer to work part time sign a release of liability. What it comes down to is if you utilize police officers in your business, you need to know what risks this might present to your organization, and it needs to be clearly stated what your expectations are of the officer.

Regardless of the system in place to manage the police officers working for a private company, there have to be some grounds rules established that all parties agree on. By this, I am referring to schedules and duties. The question as to whether the police officer will be wearing their police uniform or a security uniform also needs to be determined, as well as the issue of weapons.

During a security assessment with one client, it was discovered that they had several off-duty police officers working as security officers. The company policy was no weapons, yet it was found that at least one of the police/security officers was carrying a weapon. When asked why, he simply stated something to the effect of, "I may be in a security uniform, but most people know I am a police officer and I will not be unarmed." However, the private company where he was working as an employee at the time had no idea he was armed.

Another concern with employing police officers as security officers is what is your expectation of them in the event of an emergency? In other words, do you expect that they will not perform any police duties, or have you identified upfront any exceptions to that? I have found a few organizations where they did not determine these standards upfront and when push came to shove, the security officer acted as a police officer. In one case, the police/security officer even left the site to respond as backup to another police officer several blocks away on a call not related to his security job.

If you contract police services, and the officers wear their police uniform, when it comes time to evaluate that service as part of the assessment, you need to look at several different factors such as:

- Do they have training based on your organization's policies?
- Who supervises them onsite?
- What are their duties?
- Are you getting the services that you have contracted for?
- Who handles their scheduling?
- Have you evaluated your ROI?
- Do the police officers comply with any security-related accreditation or regulatory requirements?

These are just a few of the examples of the questions that need to be addressed, and you will likely have additional questions. Each of the above and any additional questions that may be unique to your type of business needs to be evaluated and answered. This process will often require coordination with the law enforcement agency as well.

ELECTRONIC SECURITY CONTRACTORS: INSTALLS AND MAINTENANCE

Depending on the number of electronic security systems that you might have in place, you may elect to retain the services of a security vendor/contractor to handle all installs, repairs, upgrades, and changes. It is very common for such arrangements, and they are almost always set up under a formal written agreement (contract) that addresses all the terms, costs, indemnity, service calls, and scheduling.

In most cases, the need to contract out such services is due to an organization not having qualified staff in-house to perform such services. Although large organizations may have personnel from their information technology or security department perform these duties, most medium- to small-sized companies cannot afford to have dedicated staff because the amount of work does not often justify the expense of an employee on staff.

If your organization has contracted these services to an outside vendor, there are a few key considerations to evaluate with each agreement:

- Are they providing the number of hours as contracted? This applies if your contract has designated a set number of hours per month that the contractor will be onsite.
- Was the contract established as a result of competitive bids?
- Does the contractor's work comply with the building codes? (e.g., permits)
- Do they meet the required time frame for repairs once a problem is reported? If there is no predetermined time frame set in the contract, you should consider such as part of your contract renewal.
- Are they ensuring that fire codes are being met with regard to wall penetrations?
- Do you open up the bidding process each time an existing contract expires, or do you automatically renew a contract?

Other considerations that an end user needs to take into consideration when seeking out bids or prior to signing a contract for new technology or service agreements may include:

- Are state-specific licensing requirements being met by security integrators, service providers, or value-added resellers? It is important for the end users to validate compliance because in most states legal action against contractors could be hindered or restricted without performing due diligence prior to signing a contract.

- An organization should give serious consideration to not purchasing technology that does not comply with the current "open" standards. You should validate that any new product clearly meets open industry standards specific to the type of technology being considered.

- Geographically exclusive vendors may limit your opportunity to seek competitive service providers. However, in some cases you may not have a choice if the product manufacture will only allow designated resellers or installers to work with their product.

- It is recommended that all new technology be "IP enabled" (Internet Protocol) out of the box. This includes all new "wired" and "wireless" technology. Coax and multipair copper cable systems are no longer being considered for new projects or construction. It is also reported that even the Federal Communication Commission is promoting this modification. Existing fiber, coax, and standard copper cabling can be converted to IP (Internet Protocol) network compatible using special data switches and converters when construction or the cost to replace exceeds budget projections.

- Many new installs are now using power over ethernet to a centrally located power device as a means to reduce costs, rather than using individual power sources for each new piece of equipment. However, regardless of the way you or your contractor sets this up, you need to verify that the increased heat load to the data switches and closets they are located in is acceptable because the increased heat can more than quadruple the existing ambient temperature. Verify with your information technology department what the heat restrictions are for each location.

Because many security systems are being transitioned from a standalone system to the company network, this can result in a considerable risk to both the end user and the contractor. It is your responsibility to ensure that your organization and your contractor completely comprehend encryption and the potential security risks.

One final point is to ensure that the hardware, software, and technology being installed are current models. By that, I am referring to current industry-accepted models and not something that has become outdated. In simple terms, some technology companies or integrators may try to off-load old products that they have in stock. An example of this happening is where a large-scale construction project was in the final stages when the client was notified that their new access control software was not comprehensive enough to handle all of the card readers in the project. The integrator then asked for an additional $25,000 to upgrade the software for the client, and the client at that point had no other choice but to pay. Upon further investigation, it was found that the integrator had performed this same bait-and-switch tactic with past clients as a means to low bid a project and then require upgrades. As with any contracts or service agreements, it is the end user's responsibility to conduct their due diligence to ensure that the products being purchased are current.

BACKGROUND INVESTIGATION FIRMS

Whether or not your security department conducts the preemployment background checks or ongoing background investigations for employees that are internally promoted to a fiduciary position, you need to consider just how reliable and diligent your background firm is. That being said, let me assure you that this may be easier said than done.

Not all security departments conduct the background checks for new hires; in fact, it is probably safe to say that the majority of organizations will either conduct this function within the human resource department or contract it out to an independent firm. Unless you have been living under a rock for the last year, you likely know how a government contractor, namely Eric Snowden, was able to pass a background check without any problem. The same thing happened with Aaron Alexis, the lone shooter at the Washington Navy Yard in Washington, DC, who ended up killing 12 people and wounding three others. Although he had a questionable past, his background was cleared and he was given access to the facility.

Inadequate background checks are not new. In fact, in the 1980s there were dozens of cases where police applicants were hired even though their background included serious criminal incidents. One must also take into consideration that trying to get information from past employers is not easy because most employers will only provide a former employee's title, dates of employment, and salary when they were employed. Other than that, many employers will not give anything more, and more often than not, they refuse to do so because they do not want to be sued by the applicant.

Those employers that hire a large number of employees often retain the services of a background investigation firm that promises to verify all past employers, references, criminal background checks, and education. However, there are limitations regarding what information they can access as well. Most of their resources are online databases, yet not all court records are online. Therefore, in those cases they will often hire a subcontractor to physically go to a courthouse and conduct a records check, or at least they are supposed to. It may be a difficult task to verify the quality of their services, especially if they are located in another state. However, if this service falls under security's oversight, it is incumbent on the person conducting the assessment to perform their due diligence, which likely includes an audit at some level. The quality of preemployment background checks is often questioned after it is discovered that the system failed to uncover unfavorable information, but many times it comes down to the fact that the missed information was caused by a data entry failure.

The errors that can happen while doing online checks can include such things as inserting the wrong name, date of birth, or social security number; thus *garbage in, garbage out*. Data entry errors could be as simple as typing in the same information incorrectly or missing it altogether. Look at it this way, law enforcement agencies do some of the most detailed background checks on prospective police officers and they even send investigators across the country to conduct in-person reference checks, and at times they still miss crucial information. The federal government has proven that mistakes can be made and those mistakes can be costly. So the best advice I can give you is to review your processes and those of any contractors used for this service.

PARKING MANAGEMENT FIRMS

Let us face it—most security practitioners despise parking and would outsource this service if they could. Parking is often the one service that security departments provide that causes them the most issues. Everyone wants free or convenient parking, and most would prefer a reserved spot if you would give them one. However, parking is a necessity and someone has to manage it, and that someone is often security.

For the most part when you are assessing your risks in parking lots and garages you are looking for risks or vulnerabilities as they relate to the vehicles and the people that are in the parking areas. Parking areas can be a magnet for criminal activity due to the large number of cars and the valuables that are often in those cars. It is often easy for someone to blend into a parking lot and go unnoticed by most people. A suspect about to commit a crime will have numerous places to conceal themselves, one of which may include their own vehicle. If you have contracted out the parking services to an outside vendor, it is important that they understand the risks and how to report all security concerns in a timely manner.

Parking companies are not often in the security business, and may in fact only provide the revenue collection service. If that is the case with your organization, there are still numerous security considerations that you must investigate in addition to the inherent risks as mentioned above.

First, the process of revenue security and management is often the highest risk associated with fee-based parking. This can include everything from cash handling, ticket auditing, to bookkeeping. Although you may have outsourced this service, you as a security manager should understand the entire system or you may have no idea if funds are being diverted.

The amount of cash that changes hands in fee-based parking can be substantial. The larger facilities where I have reviewed parking services have had annual revenues between $500,000 and $2.5 million. For the most part this was all cash, and diversion of funds in operations such as this can be fairly easily accomplished and not easy to catch unless you fully understand all of the processes and equipment.

Unfortunately, there are numerous ways to circumvent the accounting systems by the cashiers or management, and during your assessment you have to look for the signs. If your collection process is not using an electronic revenue selection system that is integrated with the parking gates and ticket dispensers, you may be at a higher risk for theft by staff. In the past, I was reviewing a large parking operation where I found a revenue collection system that was nothing more than a piece of paper and a pencil. Cashiers would make entries on the paper for anyone that paid, yet there was no means or system in place to correlate those notations with the actual number of cars that paid for parking. In simple terms, the cashier could collect funds and not make an entry and no one would know anything different.

If you have a contracted service or an internal department that manages a fee-based parking system, the following are some of the factors that you need to consider when assessing the risks associated with the fee collections and the staff that handle the revenue:

- Do staff make frequent drops of money into locked safes?
- Does someone other than the cashiers audit all deposits, cash register tapes, shift reports, and ticket validation systems?
- Are the cashier booths secure?
- Do the cashier booths have panic/holdup alarms, and are they tested at least monthly?
- Do you use a computerized point of sale revenue management system?
- Do you conduct random cash register audits?
- How do you handle complaints from customers regarding improper change?
- How is the revenue moved from the cashier booths to the cash counting office?
- Has staff been trained regarding counterfeit money, robbery prevention, security awareness, dispute resolution, and any other security measures?
- Are staff required to maintain minimal amounts of cash in their registers?

There are numerous other questions that may come up during the assessment, but suffice it to say that the person assessing the parking operations and management firm needs to know what risks are associated with such services. They also need to watch for signs of embezzlement or diversion of funds throughout the entire process, from the point where a car enters the parking facility to when the revenue is deposited in the bank. At any point along the way, there are real risks and vulnerabilities related to parking and the fees collected.

DOCUMENT SHREDDING SERVICES

Locked confidential bins are often found in different types of businesses that handle sensitive documents. A primary example of this can be found in medical offices or healthcare facilities. These bins are often placed in numerous areas and allow for staff to discard sensitive documents into a locked container for shredding and disposal by an outside contractor. Although conducting this service in-house does happen, the majority of businesses utilize an independent contractor.

The risks associated with such a service are often the security of the bins and the documents within them. One of the most important considerations for these bins is access management, and this will almost always involve keys.

Key control for these containers is often the weakest link in the security system, as it is commonly found that there are several keys available or even unaccounted for. For the most part the intent of these bins is that whatever goes into them is confidential and needs to be secured. However, the reality is that in many cases staff can get access to the contents. So as part of the assessment not only do you need to review the use of the bins but you also need to look at the key control and under what conditions the bins can be opened, as well as the firm that your organization contracts with to collect and shred the documents.

Vendors that provide pickup and disposal of confidential materials should also be evaluated as part of the overall assessment. The review of their operations should follow industry standards and guidelines, and this will often include compliance with ISO/IEC 27001:2005—information security management standards. Another source for research material on this service may include the National Association for Information Destruction (NAID), as well as the Certified Secure Destruction Specialist Accreditation and NAID AAA Certification Program.

Somewhere in your assessment process should be a review of their operations, whether they are mobile operations or at an off-site facility. This inspection can be performed by a person from your organization that deals directly with the contractor, or it can be completed by a person on the assessment team. Either way your goal is to ensure that your documents are handled as per existing industry standards, and that your information is secure at all points in the chain of custody. Keep in mind that just because your organization has outsourced this service to another firm, your documents are still your responsibility throughout their life cycle, and if your confidential materials are compromised, you may still face liability.

CONTRACT SECURITY SERVICES

The debate whether to use contract security officers or proprietary officers is an ongoing one that often comes down to preference or costs. However, for the sake of this chapter we will only look at reviewing a contract security operation as part of the assessment.

Whether your organization utilizes all contract security, or has a hybrid department where you have proprietary and contract officers, your approach to conducting the review of the vendors' program is basically the same.

First, start by reviewing the contract that establishes the business relationship. Your focus should be on the terms of the contract, whether or not they are being met to your satisfaction. It is often surprising to find that long-term relationships may result in an automatic renewal of contracts versus a competitive bidding process. Although it may not happen a lot, there have been times when it was found that the contract was not being met, basically meaning that the vendor was not providing the quality or quantity of services that were set in the original contract. What is more interesting is the fact that the longer the term of the contract, or if they have been automatically renewed several times, the details and terms of such agreements are often forgotten by the client. When that happens one can assume that the client cannot possibly measure the ROI of the service, and therefore may not understand how they may be losing money.

There are contracts in use today that have established the number of hours to be staffed, at what locations, during what hours, and yet they have no measurement standards built in so that the client or contractor can measure the effectiveness of the services or outcomes. These are favorable to the contractor in most cases, and the client often measures the program's effectiveness based solely on complaints, meaning if they receive no complaints, it must be working just fine.

The most often reported complaint with contracted security services is the issue of turnover. This problem is present in contract security services at a rate that is often higher than proprietary departments. The most common stated cause of this is the low wages paid by many contract security firms or the insecurity of hours worked versus promised. The main concern that your organization needs to look at regarding this is the fact that your security officers may not be experienced enough to maintain the level of security that you would otherwise require. More than once I have come across security officers that were pulled off other sites to work at facility that required a higher level of experience, yet their experience was minimal at best.

One guard service I reviewed wrote it into their contract that they would only provide site-specific training to their officers if they worked more than 60 days at a site. In other words, they were saying that they were under no obligation to train their officers for your site unless that officer actually worked at your site for 60 days. It was never proven, but in reality, they could staff your site with untrained officers provided they rotated them out every 60 days. In most cases, the property owner may not realize that the security staff was not trained.

The key to assessing this potential at your facility is to ask the management of the guard company for their turnover rate information and how they handle the concern of undertrained staff working at sites that they are not familiar with. In the end you need to determine whether or not the level of services provided meets your expectations. Depending on your type of business, you may want to consider requiring within your contract that all contract officers be trained for your site prior to working. Remember, you as the client should establish your requirements upfront and require that your guard service contractor meets your terms.

Other considerations that you should review include the following:

- Patrol procedures
- Security policies and post orders
- Security officer's appearance
- People skills
- Communication skills
- Knowledge of duties
- Incident reporting
- Report writing and documentation skills
- Department and company emergency procedures
- Officer training—initial and ongoing
- Compliance with state laws
- Compliance with accreditation standards
- Safety-awareness training
- Security officer's qualifications

Keep in mind that many of the above points will also be addressed with proprietary security departments as well, however, the difference is that contract security companies often have their own requirements and/or staff expectations, and it would be advised to review them to ensure that they are not in conflict with the client's requirements.

More than once I have heard a client state that they do not review the internal operations of a contract security company in order to avoid the co-employer concern. However, in several of the conversations that I have had, the real issue was that the client did not understand their rights or how a contract security firm operated, and therefore they used the co-employment defense as an excuse.

Co-employment is commonly defined as an association between two or more employers in which each has tangible or probable legal rights and obligations with regard to the same employee. Co-employment is intrinsic in the contract security firm and client connection, since they equally have contact with an assigned officer and they both may give those officers directions. By and large, in this type of affiliation the contract security firm is viewed as the principal employer and assumes the majority of the liability for the officer. However, although I have been advised by some clients over the years that they have no liability for a contract security firm's actions, I assure you that this is not always the case and anyone that believes that they bear no liability because they have contracted out the security services needs to consult their legal counsel for advice.

Other considerations to address when reviewing a contract security service often will include details with the contract. For example, is the contract flexible enough to meet the client's needs, and does the client have the right to replace an officer if they are not performing to your satisfaction?

Since most end users do not understand the industry standards with regard to contract security services, or how to measure their effectiveness, they often will consult with independent experts that can provide for an unbiased review and assessment. There have been cases where another contract security firm has been asked to review a contract and related services, but let us be frank, does anyone truly believe that a competitor will be unbiased? Your best option is to have a firm that is independent, meaning they do not provide similar security staffing services, to perform a security risk assessment to determine how well the contract agency is performing. When doing so, the client should always have oversight on the assessment, not the contract security company.

SUMMARY

Your end goal in evaluating your contracted services is to ensure that your contracted program or services meet the terms of the contract as well as industry standards, best practices, all applicable statutes and regulatory standards, and that your vulnerabilities and risks are properly identified, managed, and mitigated. If you do not know the level of compliance or competency of your contracted services, or how to measure their performance or effectiveness, it is probably time to bring in an independent security expert to conduct a full assessment and program review.

CHAPTER 15

The Security Risk Assessment Report

At this point, you have planned and executed your security risk assessment. In doing so, you have collected reports and an extensive list of notes of identified security vulnerabilities, risks, and/or areas of concern. With that information, it is now time to generate a comprehensive written report of the findings and detail your recommendations for improvements.

In this chapter, each part of the report will be discussed in an effort to assist you in assembling your report. The sections discussed in this chapter are not all inclusive; your report may not use all of these categories, and may in fact include others that are specific to your project. Depending on your industry or the industry that you are serving, there may be additional sections in your final report. For example, in the healthcare field, you will likely have separate sections for security-sensitive areas, such as the emergency room, maternity unit, and pharmacy. To ensure that the report flows well and does not provide the end users with too much information, it is best to use separate sections.

Whatever means you use to generate your report, you document not only your findings, but also the methodology you used to conduct the assessment, all industry standards and best practices used as measurements or guidelines, and many other factors. In most cases, the best manner by which to document the report is by following the outline as noted in this chapter, and adding or removing sections as appropriate. The addition of methodologies, best practices, industry standards, and other foundation materials brings measurable credibility to your findings and ensures that your report is factual and based on reliable information.

REPORT WRITING

Software versus Paper

As mentioned in several parts of this book, some security practitioners will use software programs to conduct their assessments. However, keep in mind that the programs I have reviewed are not comprehensive enough in my opinion to address all industries with anything more than the basic needs of security. To ensure that your report has addressed all security issues and provides enough detailed information to explain the deficiencies to your administration or legal departments, you will likely still need to document the majority of your findings in a separate written report, even if you use one of those programs.

Opinion versus Facts

As you set out to write the report, remember to stick to the facts and leave personal opinions out of it. There is a difference between personal opinions and opinions based on factual information.

COMPONENTS OF THE ASSESSMENT REPORT

Table of Contents

To ensure that readers can find the information they need without reading the entire report, it is always best to include a table of contents that lists each section, subsection, and page number.

Executive Summary

Depending on what books you have read, you may be confused on whether to include an executive summary for your report. In many cases, the senior executives or board members may not have the time to read the report in its entirety. Therefore, an executive summary is often used as an abridged version of the report, which identifies the most relevant findings and their factual bases.

This summary is often a high-level snapshot of the report's contents and recommendations. It may be provided to your administrative team if they choose not to read the report in its entirety. It is recommended that only the most important findings be addressed within this section.

Below is a sample of an executive summary:

> On July 10–15, 2013, an onsite security assessment was conducted at the Widget USA facility, at the request of James Johnson, President/CEO. The purpose of the assessment was to identify and evaluate security-related risks and the protection of the staff, guests, facilities, resources, services, and other assets from the real or perceived threats of external or internal security incidents.
>
> As part of this assessment, interviews were conducted with administrative personnel, security staff, department managers, and numerous other staff members. The emphasis of the interviews was the safety and security of the

organization. As staff was interviewed, we found a variety of opinions about security, both the security staff and operations in general. We also found that some of the opinions were very critical, and yet others were complimentary in nature. As part of this assessment, we take into consideration personal biases, look for factual information within the comments, and take from the statements what is most important and could be verified in some manner.

In addition to interviews, a variety of department-specific policies were requested prior to the site visit that addressed security and the protection of the organization's assets. In order to conduct a full and comprehensive assessment, we needed to know what security processes and policies are in place, how they compare to the industry standards and best practices, and if they are being followed by staff. (For a complete list of requested and received documents, please review this report.)

In this assessment, it was found that there are substantial training issues within the security department. The security staff is not prepared to deal with the complexities of such a culturally diverse operation. Although the staff believe that they have received ample training, there was little or no documentation provided to indicate what training they have received, or if their competency was evaluated upon completion of such. With that stated, we find that there appears to be no department-specific training being conducted within security. Due to the perceived lack of training, it appears that security has not kept up with standardized training to take on a more active role in protecting the personnel and assets of the organization. The reoccurring comments heard from staff during several interviews were that security is not ready. All of these issues can be resolved, and they will be further explained within this report along with recommendations on how to mitigate the current concerns.

Some of the major areas of concerns noted during this assessment that require immediate management attention are as follows:

- *The security department is not in compliance with the Ohio Revised Code Chapter 109–Security Guards.*
- *Security officers are carrying weapons in direct violation of company and/or department policies.*
- *Many of the Widget USA buildings are not secure, with numerous interior door locks being altered or bypassed and unable to be locked due to staff manipulation of the locks.*
- *Security officers do not understand their role in protecting the organization's assets and how to properly make rounds looking for security risks or vulnerabilities.*
- *Security staff uses paper forms for reporting incidents, and because of that management cannot track trends or identity adverse security concerns.*

Project Foundation

In this section, you will want to identify the reason for the assessment and who (if anyone) requested or authorized it. An example of the project foundation section is as follows:

> This security risk assessment and report were authorized by Mr James Johnson, Chief Executive Officer, Widget USA, Grand Union, Ohio.
>
> The primary purpose of this assessment was to identify and evaluate security-related risks and the protection of the corporation, as well as security department operations and management. This project is in response to a security incident on July 10, 2013, in which a former employee entered the executive offices and made threatening comments and actions regarding shooting members of management.
>
> Widget USA is a manufacturer of security widgets with global sales. The corporate offices and manufacturing facilities total approximately 1,000,000 square feet of building spaces located on 23 acres in the city of Grand Union, Ohio.

As you can see from this example, you are laying the foundation for the project and identifying the facility location and other unique identifiers.

Project Methodology

Many different methodologies for conducting security risk assessments are commonly used. These include the methods published by the Department of Homeland Security, ASIS International, IAPSC, as well as the CARVER and RAM methodologies.

In this section, you will identify the methodology used for your project, as well as any industry measurement standards, best practices, regulatory standards, and laws. This is where you will also include the steps in which information was gathered, such as document reviews, individual or group interviews, or online surveys. Physical inspections also need to be noted so that the reader will fully understand how you went about collecting information. Basically, document the method used so it is clear how the project was defined and carried out.

Project Scope

Before you started this project, you defined the project's scope—what it was you were planning to accomplish. Provided you documented the scope, you can merely insert that information into this section. Remember that everything you set out to accomplish within your project's scope will be addressed in the various sections of your final report.

Below is an example of a *project scope* for a hospitality client:

1. *This security program assessment will be conducted at the Angels City Resort site located at 12895 Mission Avenue, Los Angeles, CA. The project includes all buildings, parking lots/structures, utility equipment, public spaces, and grounds of the site.*
2. *This assessment will result in a comprehensive review of the current facilities security measures, which will include: card access, video surveillance (CCTV), lock and keys systems, automated building locked down system, building intrusion detection alarm systems, security policies, security staffing levels, security training, workplace violence prevention, entry/egress access control measures, interior/exterior security patrol operations, visitor/employee notification program, and security report/documentation.*
3. *A full and comprehensive review of the security department will include operations, management, training, staff competency, program effectiveness, program professionalism, and security policies/procedure reviews. This will also include department group or individual meetings of staff to ascertain their concerns, as well as interviews with management from within this department and other service lines as needed.*
4. *Assess exterior lighting levels, parking lots, and site landscaping to determine potential security concerns/issues.*
5. *Review past security incidents and crime statistics to identify trends and opportunities to make operational changes to the security patrols and services.*
6. *Identify ways for the resort to help prevent crimes from occurring, especially those affecting guests/visitors and staff on this site.*

There is no limit to the items that you place in your scope, but remember to be precise with your scope. Ensure that all parts of the project's scope have been addressed at the completion of the project. For example, if your project is a result of violent incident, you will want to include information regarding assessing the workplace violence policies, training, investigations, and threat assessments as well as your findings for such in the final report.

Policies and Documents Requested and Reviewed

This section may look different depending on whether or not this assessment is being conducted internally or if the organization is retaining the services of a consultant. For example, if you are conducting the assessment using internal staff, you may change the section title to "Policies and Documents Reviewed." In general terms, both internal and external project managers should list the items reviewed. Again, this relates to the completeness and credibility of the project. If you have not reviewed the security policies, for example, how did you determine the program's intent or effectiveness?

In some cases, I have requested documents and policies for a client's project but they were not provided. I know that the items existed, yet the client failed to produce them. If that were to happen as part of your assessment for a client, you will certainly want to document that information. If that happens during my projects, I will still list the documents that I requested as well as any items that I did receive. If I was not able to fully assess the security policies or incident statistics, I will state that fact within the final report.

Assessment Findings

Now that you have laid the foundation for the report as well as identified the methodology, main body of the report documents your findings as related to each part of the assessment. This is where you will address all parts of the project's scope in detail. When appropriate, you should include photographs and examples to clearly explain your findings.

An example of the how to use photographs in your report, which can be very beneficial to the reader, can be seen in Figure 15.1. As you will note, the photograph clearly demonstrates what the finding was so that the reader has a clear understanding. Included with any photographs should be the location where it was taken, such as a building name and room number if available.

FIGURE 15.1 Unrestricted roof access.
This ladder should be enclosed to restrict the ability to use it.

Access Control

Access controls can include lock and key systems, electronic access control systems, security doors, visitor management processes, and any other process or system used to control access in or out of the buildings and properties. This section can address organization-wide findings; more precise information can be used in the building-specific section of the report. Generally speaking, this section will be an overview of the access control systems and processes. Exact examples may be documented elsewhere within the report.

Building-Specific Security

Depending on the project, multiple buildings or structures may be assessed; if so, they need to be documented separately within this section. The best approach is to list each building; under each building's section, list any internal department-specific information. By separating the buildings and internal departments, you are providing the reader with a breakdown of information that is much easier to read and comprehend compared with an all-encompassing section that merges all information into a catch-all section. This can also be helpful if the project manager assigns subcommittees to address each building; in that way, they can provide the subcommittees with site-specific information and not the entire report.

In this section of the report, you will also reference information that you have documented in other sections. For example, you may have documented your findings regarding an access control issue in the Access Control section, but you may also list that information within the building-specific section. Keep in mind that you do not need to restate your findings word-for-word in all sections; you only need to reference information so that the reader understands that there are not multiple findings but rather the same findings being cross-referenced.

Grounds

In this section, the property grounds will be addressed. For example, you may document findings on signs of criminal activity, such as gang tagging, graffiti, abandoned cars, and so on in this section. You may also insert findings on vulnerabilities associated with the property being too open and accessible to everyone, or concerns about the flow of the vehicular and pedestrians on or through the site. Again, photographs can be very helpful, as well as a very descriptive location of each area of concern noted.

Landscaping

The landscaping of a property can be either an incitement or deterrent to criminal activity. If the vegetation on the property is overgrown and offers concealment for criminal acts, it needs to be explained in this section.

Look for bushes and shrubs that offer concealment near walkways, windows, doors, and parking areas. Trees close to a building that offer an easy path to the second story or roof are also considered security vulnerabilities. Another landscaping issue that is often missed during assessments is those areas of overgrowth that offer cover for homeless encampments. Numerous times during projects, I have located homeless camps on clients' properties that they had no idea existed. These camps present a security risk as well as a fire safety risk, so they need to be identified and documented.

The trimming of trees and bushes is one of the easiest ways to increase visibility and line of sight, as well as increase the feeling of a safe and secure property, yet it is often overlooked.

Lighting Summary

As we discussed in chapter 6 of this book, lighting is a key element in the safety and security of a property. Without proper lighting, your risks and vulnerabilities will likely be higher than normal, as will the potential for criminal acts or accidents.

In this section, you will document the findings of the lighting evaluation and insert the standards and measurements that were used.

Parking

The parking areas of a property can be the most substantial risks that staff, customers, or others will face while on your property. Many crimes committed in parking lots or structures are crimes of opportunity and are often the most difficult to prevent. In most cases, a property owner has no control over whether or not vehicles are locked, or if valuables in the vehicles are secured or placed out of sight. They may also not have any control on who comes and goes in vehicles or on foot. Because of the adherent risks and vulnerabilities associated with parking areas, a security practitioner needs to pay special attention to these areas.

When conducting a security risk assessment of parking facilities, you have to look at all aspects of the parking, including the lighting, fencing, access control, landscaping, pedestrian routes, geographic area, crime statistics, signage, revenue management, and many other factors.

Every risk, vulnerability, or other security-related concern has to be addressed in this section, even if it has been identified in the past. In some cases, a business may not have off-street parking; however, they still need to assess the security of whatever parking their staff or clients use. Even though parking may be owned by a government agency such as a city or shared with a business neighbor, most businesses may still be liable, depending on established written or verbal agreements or based on past security incidents or criminal acts.

Security Operations

When the department operations are being assessed, the findings may be extensive. In some cases, the findings may not be easy for existing management to read because outside sources may be conducting the assessment and may be very critical of the security program. That is not to say that there will be only negative findings, because that is not always the case. The key here is to be impartial and professional and to document the findings based on industry accepted standards, not personal preferences.

If you are conducting this assessment using internal staff, this would be the area where you address the parts of your program that need to be changed or updated based on best practices or standards. In a sense, this is your opportunity to identify needed changes, explaining why they are needed and how they will benefit both the department and organization.

Also in this section, the department operations will likely be broken down into subsections and compared to industry standards or best practices. An example of this may include information on scheduling, staffing levels, security officer duties, and assignments, among other things.

Security Department Management

Assuming that this project is being conducted by an outside security consultant and they have been asked to review a security department's management at the request of administration, this section is where the findings may reside. Although the findings may have relevancy, if there is one section of a consultant's report that can instantly diminish the author's credibility, this is that section.

It is important that the findings for this section are based on facts. For every finding, there needs to be corroborating information to establish your observations. Simply put, if you include a finding that the department's management is deficient, you must include supporting information based on industry standards and/ or best practices. Failure to do so may result in the entire report being discredited.

Although not all consultants will do so, positive findings (those that are complimentary in nature) toward the department leadership should also be included in this section.

Security Department Job Descriptions

How comprehensively documented this section should be will be based on who is conducting the overall assessment. An internal project manager will have access to department personnel files that an outside consultant will not.

As part of the assessment, you would have reviewed the job descriptions for each position within the security department and evaluated them to ensure that the existing staff meets the minimum requirements. Job descriptions may also include job-specific duties required of staff. You also can measure and compare those written requirements against what the staff is actually doing.

Another important inclusion in this section is documentation of any proposed changes to the job descriptions. In some cases, you might propose a complete overhaul, or just minor changes.

Security Equipment and Uniforms

Regardless of who conducts the assessment, there is always a review of the tools and equipment that the officers carry or use as part of their duties. This may include items such as flashlights, radios, handcuffs, batons, chemical agents (e.g., mace, pepper spray), ballistic/stab vests, stun guns, and metal detectors. Each tool that the officers are assigned, or may use as part of their jobs, needs to be reviewed for things such as maintenance, upkeep, availability, warranty, and training.

In this section, there may be findings that the equipment is not properly working or has never been tested. For example, I have seen ballistic vests that were so old that the manufacture would not certify them to stop any projectile or stabbing instrument. In order to identify any potential concerns, the person assessing the equipment has to look at each item and understand the shelf life of equipment such as chemical agents and vests. In cases where the officer supply their own protective equipment, there needs to be a determination if that equipment meets the standards for the organization and if it is maintained properly. Even though staff may supply their own protective equipment, you as an employer may still have liability to some extent if that equipment fails to perform.

The uniform that the officers wear are not always reviewed. However, if there seems to be an issue with the professionalism of the security staff or their appearance, a review may be in order. When a department is suffering from a lack of professionalism or credibility, one of the easiest changes that can be made, in addition to the operational deficiencies that caused them, is the changing of the officer's appearance (i.e., uniforms). Several departments that I have reviewed have exhibited serious morale issues that revolved around the uniforms to some degree. Once the uniforms were changed, there was a remarkable improvement in morale and the entire organization's staff changed their perception of the officers as well.

If you are going to make recommendations on the equipment or uniforms, do so in manner that explains the issues and solutions and why they are needed. If you just write that the officers need stun guns without justification for such, your recommendations will likely go nowhere.

Security Operations Verification

The security operations verification primarily relates to guard tours systems. Many organizations use some type of electronic system, or in the rare cases the antique clock and key system. In this section, any findings regarding the operations, design, management, effectiveness, and use need to be documented.

More than once, I have found guard tour systems that were either not properly setup or not being used at all (even though the system was in place). When reviewing such a system, look at the system's design, where the buttons or barcodes are located (are they located in those areas that are the highest risk?), and how often rounds are made. Review the reports to ensure that the rounds are being made properly and within the established protocol.

If there is no existing system in use and you can demonstrate and justify the need for one to reduce incidents by requiring security rounds in critical areas, now is the time to explain the need and write the justification for one. Many times, such a justification can be supported by incident trending and calls for service logs. Managers cannot be in all places at all times to ensure that the officers are making the appropriate rounds, but an electronic guard tour system can provide verification that policies and protocols are being followed if it is set up correctly.

Security Records and Policies

Security records often refer to the reports of security incidents, daily activity logs of the officers, alarm reports, reports about unsecured areas, and numerous other reports or logs that your department is generating daily. A thorough review of the incident trending and mitigation measures should also be untaken.

Policies are never the same from one organization to another, or even sometimes within the same company but at different locations, so a comprehensive review of the policies is always warranted. If the assessment is being conducted in-house, there might be a tendency to skip this part or not give this process the proper attention that it deserves. On the other hand, if a consultant is reviewing your program and asks for the policies, which is very common, it is in your best interest to provide them. Either way, in an effort to properly review your security program, there has to be a review of the documents that establish the program and from which the officers carry out their duties. Remember, in the event of a civil litigation case, your policies will be subject to subpoena. If they are called into question, you want to ensure that they are current and meet the industry standards and/or guidelines at a minimum—or better yet, that they follow best practices.

If you discover issues with the policies or documentation, you will likely insert that information into this section of your report. In the event that you are going to address a specific policy or statistical information, it would be a good idea to include a copy of that information in the report's appendices section so that the reader can easily reference your comments or recommendations as needed.

Security Surveillance and Technology

This section will address all security technology that is not covered in any other section. Not all businesses use security cameras, or for that matter any type of technology. In those cases, there still may be recommendations to install such equipment as a means to reduce security risks or to mitigate a new or previously identified issue.

For organizations that are currently using security technology, this section would be used to document the findings if there are any issues with the equipment. Some of the findings may be related to the location, equipment type, proper functioning, monthly testing, staff knowledge (both security and end users), and many other possible concerns or issues. For example, if a security camera was needed in an area due to a significant number of security incidents, you would want to include both the need, justification, and the projected benefits of such a camera. The same is true for any other type of new security technology, as well as any existing equipment that needs to be moved, repaired, or replaced.

In many cases, the person doing the assessment may also identify new equipment or software as part of the assessment findings and recommendations. However, in the case of independent security consultants, they may only give you the type of technology as a recommendation versus an actual brand name. Their motivation for not being brand-specific is an effort to remain independent and unbiased. Independent consultants are familiar with most of the security technology equipment and systems on the market, yet many of them will steer clear of recommending one brand over the other.

Regardless of who conducts the actual assessment, when it comes time to make recommendations on new technology, there is often an extensive research phase required in order to conduct a fair and balanced evaluation of all possible solutions.

Security Training

This is another section that can be quite different depending on who is writing the report. There are numerous opinions on what kind, how much, and how often training has to be conducted. However, if you are using the industry standards, guidelines, or best practices as a guide to measure the existing training program, you should be fine.

The training review will include the training topics, curriculum, trainer's qualifications, classroom time as well as practical exercises, and how often the training is conducted. The training records for the security staff will be reviewed to ensure that everyone has the training and the training received is current, meaning the material is up to date. For example, I was asked to give an expert opinion on a security use-of-force litigation case. The case focused around the amount of force used to control another person, and the security department involved trained their officers using a program that taught them how to respond to an aggressive person. While these programs are very common in security and law enforcement, the program training material used at this organization was more than 15 years old. So much has changed over the years with this type of training, so in this case, their tactics were seriously outdated.

Keep in mind that several states mandate minimum training standards for security officers, and some industries do as well. It is important that the person conducting the assessment knows what those requirements or standards are, and then measures the program against those statutory requirements or industries standards.

Threat Assessment

Threat assessment refers to how your organization responds to threats. For example, existing policies or protocols should be reviewed in this section. Threat definitions may also be reviewed and recommendations made to what the organization should consider a threat.

In this section, you would include information on any current threats that were not already addressed in other parts of your report. It would also be common to find information under this heading as to what threat assessment programs are in place, and what if any recommendations there are to improve such a program.

Next Steps

This is the one section that many reports fail to include. For whatever reason, many reports identify the problems and recommendations, but there is no mention of what an organization needs to do in response. In a sense, it is like a cliff hanger that leaves the reader with questions about what happens next.

As we will discuss in the next section, recommendations are often plentiful and in most cases meaningful and warranted. Executives who have read various assessment reports in the past often comment that the information is impressive; however, they also ask questions about what are they supposed to do with this information. Security professionals know what all this information means and what we need to do to take corrective action. However, the high-level decision makers in most organizations are not the security directors. Therefore, when you write these reports, ensure that you not only document the findings and recommendations, but also what to do with the findings and how to do it.

It may seem as if the findings and recommendations should stand on their own. However, if you want an executive to read the report and approve the changes, it is best to give them the most comprehensive information possible. When you include a section on what the next steps will be, you are in effect giving them the most important piece of the puzzle so that they will know what needs to happen next and what the expected outcome is.

When it comes to the expected outcome, you must comprehend and be able to qualify and quantify what your recommendations and next steps will mean for your organization, as well as how you will measure those changes. If you cannot do so, how do you expect anyone else to buy into your recommendations or finance them?

Recommendations

Recommendations must be specific to an identified finding that is documented in the report. In other words, if you are recommending that the organization install an electronic card access control system and there is no justification for such a system within the report, your chances of getting approval are likely nil.

Your recommendations also should be listed in order of priority, and that priority level should be commensurate with the level of risk or vulnerability. The recommended changes that are most critical should be addressed first, as they will likely give your organization the greatest risk mitigation opportunities.

Because there may be several high-priority recommendations, it is my practice to break the recommendations into categories, and within those categories list the recommendations based on priority. In essence, I will list my recommendations in sections such as Access Control, Security Training, and Security Technology (to name a few) under each one of those sections, I will list in order of importance the recommendations. It has been my experience that the client appreciates this setup as it allows them to better plan their response and action plans, and they can assign out sections of recommendations to specific departments such as information technology, engineering, risk management, and so on.

Appendices or Attachments

Under this section, the report writer will attach any supporting documents, security standards, applicable laws or regulations, accreditation requirements, or other information that has either been mentioned within the report or recommendations. Each item should be listed separately with the source of the document/information, so that anyone reading the report will know the location and agency that the information came from.

CHAPTER 16

Conclusion

We have come a long way from the early stages of determining what a security risk assessment is all the way to completing the final report of the findings and recommendations. Now that we have completed this process and know where we need to be in the future, how do we know if we did it correctly? How do we implement the findings and recommendations or track and measure our progress?

Whether this was your first or 500th assessment project, you still need to know what to do with the findings, how to implement the changes, and how to determine if the changes resulted in a reduction of vulnerabilities and risks. In reality, once you have written the report, you are really only at the midpoint of the project.

If you retained a security consultant to conduct the assessment, he or she has likely sent you a very detailed report of the findings, with supporting documents for your review and consideration. At that point, their portion of the project is basically over. In most cases, they will answer any questions that you have regarding their findings. However, unless you have retained them to assist with the implementation of the recommendations, their services have likely been met in full and your contract with them has concluded.

So, now that you have the report, the implementation phase belongs to your organization. Therefore, regardless of who completed the actual assessment, it is now up to you to plan, oversee, implement, and measure your progress as you act on the assessment findings.

IMPLEMENTATION PROJECT MANAGEMENT

Like any other project, as well as the actual assessment project that you just completed, the organization has to assign a competent staff person to manage the next phase, which will entail some or all of the following:

- Budget management
- Information technology (IT) liaison/integration
- Policy development/changes

197

- Procurement
- Project management
- Training
- Vendor management
- Project planning
- Product/services review and selection
- System design
- Technology product selection/installation
- Vendor review and selection
- System testing

There are additional duties or oversight responsibilities that the project manager will encounter along the way. In many cases, there will likely be a team of staff that meets regularly to plan, implement, and monitor the change process. Also as you move forward, there will be challenges to improving the security systems and processes. Both the project manager and team need to flexible and ready to make adjustments over time.

PROJECT TEAM

A project team may be comprised of personnel from several different departments, which may include security, facilities, risk management, administration, information technology, finance, quality, legal, human resources, and any other services that may be affected. However, as with any good team, there needs to be one project manager.

As controversial as this may seem, the project manager does not need to fully understand all aspects of the technology and services. In other words, trying to find someone within an organization that fully comprehends all service lines that are a part of this project may be impossible. However, the project manager has to take responsibility and ownership for the entire project.

In one of my projects, the security director was the project manager; however, whenever there was an issue with equipment or services other than security, he would hold someone else responsible and not take any ownership. The problem with this kind of leadership is that the project manager becomes ineffective. The project will often fail to maintain a schedule and will often go over budget due to delays, change orders, and many other miscalculations.

To avoid overwhelming one person (depending on the size and scope of the project), an organization may also have subcommittees in place to manage specialized services, such as information technology. I have seen at least one case where the actual project manager for the entire project was from the IT department and not security because the majority of changes were to the technology services. In that case, it made sense to set up the team in that manner; security was not able to comprehend the network and technology side of the organization, and would have likely just slowed the project down. In the end, the most desirable approach is to have one project manager overseeing the project team.

CHALLENGES

There will be numerous challenges along the way for most organizations—generally, the same types of challenges that any large-scale project will encounter. Some of the challenges may include vendor selection, requests for proposals (RFPs), product review and selection, budgeting, scheduling, change orders, contracts, building/fire codes, construction, and so on. In reality, the list of possible challenges has no limits. The best approach is to continuously look ahead in an attempt to be proactive. The key to being successful is to be ready to deal with any problem that arises and get the right people working on it at the earliest possible stages.

The types of challenges that you might encounter include the following:

- *Budgets*: When planning a budget, you have to consider potential price increases, product availability, contractor costs, and any other factor that could translate into potential expenses. If your budget is planned based on known expenses (e.g., you have firm orders not to exceed quotes), you still must consider changing orders or latent conditions and ensure that you have a contingency budget in place.
- *Changes to the project scope*: "Scope creep" is a well-known term to describe when project management permits the scope to extend beyond its original intent. Eliminating scope creep completely is not always possible. However, you must recognize it when you see it and determine if the project scope needs to be changed. There are times when someone will request a new service or equipment that was not in the original scope. If that change is a result of new information coming to light, then your contingency budget may cover the expense and your project schedule may be adjusted. The project manager has to decide whether the change to the scope is warranted and how it will impact the budget and schedule.
- *Communication failures or deficiencies*: A lack of communication or slow responses to questions is a challenge that many project teams encounter. There are a number of reasons why this happens—most of which are not legitimate reasons but cause delays nonetheless. In the early planning stages of your project, you will need to identify the means of communicating (e.g., email, memo, person-to-person) lines of communications and the team's expectations of response times. When failures or deficiencies are identified, the project manager has to take immediate corrective actions in order to keep the project on schedule and within budget.

- *Failure to manage risk*: All projects have some risks; the project manager has to have the skills and ability to identify and deal with those risks. In the planning stages or after the project is underway, once you have identified the risks, you will need to determine your tolerance of such, then determine what mitigations steps are needed or if that defined risk is acceptable and will not cause harm.

- *Failure to set or define goals*: The goals for the project are often determined upfront and included within the project scope. Further defining the goals will occur when the team determines how best to meet the original intent. As a result, each phase of your project may have supplemental goals. However, the underlying reason why many projects have issues is a result of goals that are not clearly defined from the outset. To ensure that your goals are clear and concise, your team should spend an appropriate amount of time developing them. The team should be flexible as time goes on because projects can change for a number of reasons; as a result, the goals will need to be adjusted as well.

- *Unrealistic deadlines*: Assigning deadlines to a project, staff person, or vendor that are impossible to meet is only asking for failure. Tight deadlines have often resulted in numerous delays, a decline in morale among team members, and in some cases sabotage of the project. Keep in mind that everyone works under numerous deadlines as part of their primary job duties, and assigning tasks for the project may not be a high priority for them. That is not to imply that they do not care about this project; it is only suggesting that their priorities may require their attention for other duties. The project manager needs to discuss assignments and deadlines with each participant. One of the most common problems is that of a project schedule that either is unrealistic or does not plan for the unexpected. For example, weather or supply issues often cause delays; if a project schedule is too tightly planned, any delays will derail it. Many projects may experience schedule slippage when the original schedule was not planned out well or did not allow for the unknown to some extent.

- *Inadequate skills*: As mentioned before regarding the skill level for the project manager, the members of your team have to have the ability to perform their parts of the project. You have to assign team members based on their overall abilities, knowledge, and availability. As project manager, it is your job to determine the qualifications of your team members and those of vendors, consultants, or outside services. Just because someone sells security services does not mean that they are an expert in those services, so you will need to vet each and every team member for their qualifications and ability to perform.

- *Outside factors (vendors/suppliers)*: When you are in the early planning stages of your project, you will likely have an idea of what equipment or services will be needed to reach your goals. A challenge that often presents itself is the fact that your project may not be a high priority to a supplier or integrator. Another issue may be that the vendor or supplier has undisclosed inventory or supply issues, which may not come to light until late in the game. In either case, if you have planned for unexpected contingencies, this may only result in a slight delay while you work with your vendors or search out other vendors/suppliers.

- *Resource competition*: Like any other project, yours will be competing for resources whether they be internal or external, such as competing for funds, services, personnel, scheduling, and so on. With proper preplanning, this may not be an issue if you have received administrative support from the beginning, unless the organization's priorities and goals have changed for undisclosed reasons.
- *Team members/end users not engaged*: When you have a team member, end user, or vendor that is not engaged, your project will likely fail, either partially or completely. In an effort to avoid this problem, the project manager has to engage each stakeholder, ensure that all participants are kept informed, and ensure that the communication process is open and two-way.
- *Unreliable accountability*: As with the security director who failed to take responsibility for issues that came up in a project, a failure to hold team members accountable can bring a project to a grinding halt. The project manager has to ensure that each team member takes responsibility for their actions or lack thereof. If it is determined that a team member is not taking responsibility for their assigned tasks, the project manager has to determine if this can be corrected or if they need to find a new person to complete the assignments. Until the issue is resolved, the project is in danger of failing.
- *Vague contingency plans*: Although you cannot plan for every possible issue that may arise during a project, it is crucial for a project manager to recognize unerringly what path to take in advance for unforeseen developments. If they have not been proactive in their planning, they may find that one issue can stop a project in its tracks.

Any one of these challenges can derail the best-laid plans and may cause the project to fail, or at least exceed the projected schedule and/or budgets. All of these possibilities need to be addressed early in the project planning stage so that, when or if they were to come to fruition, your team is prepared to respond in an appropriate and timely manner.

IMPLEMENTATION PHASE

With your assessment report in hand, team assembled, and a project plan in place, it is now time to get the project underway. Provided you have a schedule and project map established, your team is now tasked with several steps that will include, but may not be limited to, the following:

- *Administrative functions*: Take steps such as obtaining proposals, quotes, permits, plans, and other required documents not already in hand.
- *Development (e.g., policies and training)*: If your project involves policy or training development, this function can commence at any time. However, if the training is related to new technology, you will only be able to set the training curriculum at this point, or possibly send someone from your team to a train-the-trainer course. In some cases, integrators or technology companies can bring working technology or equipment to your site for user training, so check with your vendors to determine if this is possible. With regards to policy development, it may be advantageous to seek out technical information from the vendors in advance so that the information can be included in the policy development stages. I also suggest that you reach out to your peers or professional associations that may also have policy templates available to their members. This will save you time and money if you only have to tweak an existing policy, rather than write one from scratch.
- *End-user training*: As mentioned, training for end users can occur at any time, and it is advisable to have the training completed as soon as possible to avoid any delays once the equipment or software is installed. Most manufacturers of software products can provide a working copy of the software so that your team can set it up in advance with user profiles and company information. If the systems being installed will require numerous staff persons to be trained in the use of it, you will need ample time scheduled for this training to take into consideration personnel schedules, meeting rooms, and equipment setup.
- *Installation*: With the previous phases completed, the process of installing software, hardware, or technology will be addressed during this part of the project. In many cases, this may be where your project is most vulnerable to delays.
- *Product/service evaluation*: This is where you may be seeking RFPs, requests for information (RFIs), or requests for qualifications (RFQs) from vendors, consultants, and integrators, as well as reviewing services and product specifications and cut sheets.
- *Selection (e.g., vendors and products)*: This phase is where you will review documents or information from vendors or manufacturers and determine their ability to fulfill your requirements.
- *Staff training*: This refers to the staff that will be working with the new technology or equipment the majority of the time. For example, if you are installing card access control software, your security department management and staff will need to learn the software before it goes live.

If your project is to implement the carrying of stun guns or pepper spray (also known as oleoresin capsicum (OC) spray), you will likely need to designate staff to become trainers (which may require that they become certified trainers).

- *Testing of technology and services*: Once everything is installed, there will be a requirement to test the systems thoroughly in advance of going live. You want to ensure that all systems are working and security is ready to roll out the new technology or service. This phase may require a number of staff that will be available on-call in case there is a failure or to address any technical issues that may present. For example, if you are installing card readers that will be replacing a legacy system or taking the place of locks and keys, you will want someone at each door that is being tested, as well as someone at the computer that is controlling those doors. Having someone available from IT and facilities is also a good idea to handle any network issues or door hardware conflicts. Most importantly, do not go live with new technology until it is thoroughly tested; if you do and the system fails, you may cause long-term damage to your credibility. In some cases, I have seen administrators stop a project and revert back to the legacy system to calm the uproar. Everything that you and your team did behind the scenes throughout your project will mean nothing if the system fails in the end due to inadequate testing. You want the rollout of the changes to be seamless and a nonissue to staff and management.

Each one of the above steps may take an extended period of time to complete. Also, they need to be scheduled in the correct order to ensure that the projected schedule flows properly. A few of them are critical to the success of the others, so ensure that they get the proper amount of time and resources the first time around.

TRACKING CHANGE

The process of tracking your changes can be as simple as a spreadsheet or Word document. For example, when I conduct an assessment, I provide my clients with an easy-to-use tracking form that identifies six key points, as follows:

- *Recommendations*: Recommendation basically refers to the suggestions or recommendations to resolve an identified vulnerability or risk. This spells out the steps, processes, or implementation processes that the organization should consider.
- *Person(s) responsible*: The responsible party refers to the person(s) in the organization responsible for handling this recommendation. This assignment is normally made by the organization's project manager,

and there may be more than one person assigned. However, for accountability reasons, it is best to have one person that has overall responsibility for each assignment to avoid any confusion or finger pointing.

- *Schedule*: Schedule refers to a timeline or schedule for key steps and completion. Depending on the assignment, the schedule may require a few days or months, and it may be adjusted from time to time due to factors not in your control. For example, weather or supply issues may cause delays in the project; as a result, the schedule may need to be adjusted.

- *Actions*: An action refers to what steps or measures need to be taken next at any given point in the process. For example, if you are assigning someone to seek RFPs for a security camera system, you may record the action as *Develop and publish an RFP*.

- *Status*: Status is the current state of the assignment. Using the example above, the current status may read as follows: *RFP developed and currently under review with Legal and Purchasing*. This section will often change depending on the current status. There will also come a time that this assignment has been completed and will reflect that within the tracking report.

- *Outcome*: Outcome is referring to whether or not the project assignment is ongoing, what steps may be next, and any other pertinent information that the project team may deem to be important for tracking.

The nice thing about the tracking tool that I offer my clients is that it is fully customizable to suit their needs and it is not complicated to use. Such a tool takes all of the guesswork out of who is doing what, when will it be done, and where your team is at with that assignment. It is often used as a summary of the project actions and current status. It can be used as a quick review tool by administrators who do not have time to attend project meetings or receive verbal reports on status or outcomes.

MEASURING OUTCOMES

Why measure outcomes? Outcome measurement should be a critical part of your project because you will want to know if the changes that you are making are resulting in the reduction of risks or liability that you had planned for. Outcome measurement is often considered to be a methodical technique to evaluate the extent that a program or change has achieved its projected results.

There are compelling reasons to measure outcomes, such as measuring the effectiveness. How do you know if a change was effective? If the change that your organization made was not effective, you would want to know as soon as possible so that it could be adjusted and improved. Most businesses do not make changes without an end goal or desired outcome in mind. You should have determined what the expectations were upfront and then determine at the earliest possible point if the desired results are being achieved. With the information you accumulate, you can ascertain which changes to continue and build upon. Some changes might be modified and replicated for other parts of your security programs or initiatives based on your results.

So how do you measures the outcomes of your changes? In order to determine measurements, you need to start with a baseline standard. For example, say that your organization has had 32 confirmed incidents of theft in the shipping and receiving department over the last 6 months. This department has no security cameras or electronic access control systems in the area. Access to the department is open from 0800 to 1600 hours daily; after hours, the only security system in place is locks on the doors. With this information, you have established your existing measures and the baseline measurement of 32 incidents in a 6-month period (or approximately five to six incidents per month).

Now say that, as part of your assessment, your team or a consultant has determined that security cameras were needed in this area. In addition, the organization needed to change the access rights for this area to better control who can get in and during what times they are allowed access. In order to do this, your team is looking at installing an electronic access control system, security cameras, and changing all door locks and keys. During your planning, you have determined that the changes desired will cost $75,000 for equipment, software, installation, and training. Now, there are several ways to approach your next steps: you can allocate the funds and start the process of vendor and product selection, or may be you want to test other steps first and determine their outcomes.

Because you have no idea when the thefts are occurring, except that they average more than five per month, you might want to implement your changes in a more conservative manner and measure the outcomes of those changes. In order to do so, the team may change the locks and keys first to determine if the incidents are occurring because the keys have been compromised. The projected cost to change the locks and make new keys is about $500, a fraction of the total projected costs.

With that plan in mind, the team authorizes the project and it is completed. Upon completion, the team also determines that the space needs to be secured 24/7 and not open during the day hours as before. They surmise that department staff can use their keys to gain access, and the facilities department needs to install a window for company staff to use to speak with staff or handle any transactions. The add-on of the window costs $700. Now, the changes have cost a total of $1200 and resulted in a process change for staff. At this point, the team decides to meet weekly to determine if the changes have had any effect on the theft problem or if it still persists.

Three weeks into the evaluation, it has been determined that the number of theft incidents has dropped to zero; so in effect, the outcome has been achieved. Of course, they will want to continue to monitor for potential future problems, and they may elect at some time down the road to upgrade the security systems of this area to include cameras and access control. However, at this point, they not only met their intended goal but they also saved over $73,000 in projected spending.

This example is only intended to demonstrate how your implementation and outcome measurements processes can work. There have been numerous projects in the past where hundreds of thousands of dollars have been allocated and spent to improve security measures, yet they never achieved the outcomes they were seeking. The main point is to look at your options once you have established your baseline measurement standard, then determine a measured approach to resolving your security issues. Throwing money at a problem does not mean that it will cease to exist in all cases, so make sure that you have a way to measure the outcomes of your changes. If they have not achieved your goals, you will likely need to take it to the next level.

Remember too that in some cases outcomes can take years to materialize, depending on the complexity of the underlying problem. Organizations must still apply critical thinking skills throughout the change process and ensure that their risks and vulnerabilities are not ignored or minimized while they gather information and analyze their findings.

LET'S DO IT AGAIN

Now that the assessment is completed, the changes that your organization chose to implement have been completed, the equipment has been installed, and the training has been done, it would not be prudent to just put your program on cruise control and relax. On the contrary, the threats, risks, and liability exposure that many companies face each day never completely disappear. New risks or threats can develop at any point and may not be within your control. Security risk assessments are an ongoing process and require continual mitigation strategies.

More than a few times, I have heard the expression that the security risk assessment report is a "living document," meaning that it is not a one-time report that is destined to collect dust on the shelf in your office. In fact, the report's findings and recommendations as well as the outcomes to the changes that you have implemented need to be reviewed on an ongoing basis. It is likely that you will continue to use the report findings for several years, and as part of your next assessment.

When it comes to how often an assessment needs to be conducted, the industry-accepted recommendation is every 3 years. However, there may be a need for more frequent assessments, full or partial, if conditions and threat levels or risks change. In some cases, the frequency of the assessments may be mandated by statutory regulations or accreditation standards, so you have to be familiar with them and keep current. In addition to that, in the event that your organization experiences a serious security incident, you may be facing civil litigation as a result. If that happens, more than likely your organization will want to conduct an internal investigation into the incident and require that an updated assessment be conducted to ascertain the level of risks present.

Index

Note: Page numbers followed by f indicate figures; t, tables; b, boxes.

Edwards Brothers Malloy
Ann Arbor MI. USA
July 8, 2015